DATE DUE			

A series of student texts in

CONTEMPORARY BIOLOGY

General Editors:

Professor E. J. W. Barrington, F.R.S.
Professor Arthur J. Willis

The Physiology of Flowering Plants: Their Growth and Development

Second Edition

H. E. Street

D.Sc., F.I.Biol.

Professor of Botany
University of Leicester

and

Helgi Öpik

Ph.D.

Senior Lecturer in Plant Physiology
University College of Swansea

CARL A. RUDISILL LIBRARY
LENOIR RHYNE COLLEGE

ELSEVIER
NEW YORK

First published 1970
by Edward Arnold (Publishers) Ltd.,
25 Hill Street, London W1X 8LL

Reprinted 1971, 1973
2nd Edition 1976

Boards edition ISBN: 0 7131 2528 4
Paper edition ISBN: 0 7131 2529 2

Printed in Great Britain by
William Clowes & Sons, Limited, London, Beccles and Colchester

Preface to the First Edition

The present volume is an introduction to the many problems posed by the growth and development of flowering plants. We hope that such an introduction will meet the needs especially of first and second year University students of biology and those concerned with the teaching of biology in our schools.

Chapters dealing with the water relations, solute movement, nutrition and energy balances of the developing plant lead on to those describing growth, growth movements and morphogenesis. Such an approach inevitably omits consideration of major aspects of plant metabolism, more appropriately treated in an introduction to cellular physiology and biochemistry. This restriction of the scope of the present volume has been imposed, not only by considerations of space, but because we feel it corresponds to a widely-adopted pattern in modern university teaching.

Text figures and plates are particularly valuable to the teaching of our subject matter and we are deeply appreciative to authors and publishers for permission to reproduce many of our illustrations.

Throughout the writing and particularly in the final stages of preparing the manuscript, we have benefited from the expert and painstaking help of our editor, Professor A. J. Willis.

Leicester and Swansea   H.E.S.
1970   H.Ö.

Preface to the Second Edition

The revisions introduced for this new edition have, we hope, appropriately updated but not altered the standard and general theme of our 1970 text. Those aspects of plant physiology which feature prominently in current researches have needed most extensive revision; these include the metabolic aspect of germination (Chapter 1), phloem and hormone transport (Chapter 6), growth movements (Chapter 10) and many facets of developmental physiology (Chapters 11 and 12 replacing our original Chapter 11). The treatment of the water relations of plant cells has been rewritten in water potential terminology (Chapter 4). This introduction of new material (with appropriate text figures) has been achieved without substantial increase in size of the volume by deleting (somewhat regretfully) certain sections which seemed less central to our main themes.

We have again benefited from the expert help of our editor, Professor A. J. Willis.

Leicester and Swansea   H.E.S.
1975   H.Ö.

Table of Contents

I

Introduction

*'For this appointment preference will
be given to a whole plant physiologist'*

The quotation at the head of this chapter, taken from an advertisement for a University post, is meant to attract a particular kind of plant physiologist, one interested in the physiology of the whole organism rather than a student of cellular physiology! The distinction implied is sometimes reflected in the University teaching of plant physiology in separate courses, one termed 'metabolism' or 'cellular physiology', and a second termed 'growth and development' or 'whole plant physiology'. The present book attempts to give an account of the physiology of flowering plants from the viewpoint of the whole plant, with particular emphasis on processes of growth and development.

When plant physiology teaching is so divided into two complementary courses, the distinction between them is not only one of subject matter but of emphasis. The course in metabolism, by having the cell as its primary territory, emphasizes the basic similarity of metabolic patterns in different organisms and develops the theme of the unity of living organisms rather than that of their diversity. Indeed many of the experimental data come from work with unicellular organisms, because of their suitability as experimental material. The subject matter of the second course, though also concerned with basic phenomena, must to a far greater extent be concerned with diversity. In the development of a discussion of photoperiodism (see Chapter 12), the differences in response of different species are an essential part of the story. Similarly in considering the initiation of leaves, buds and roots it is essential to emphasize that different species react in different ways to experimental treatment with growth active substances.

The same broad topic may be treated in both courses, but with a different emphasis. Thus the mechanism of water uptake by individual plant cells may be treated in the first course and water uptake by the growing root, water transport to the shoot, and water loss by transpiration in the second course. Similarly such processes as respiration and photosynthesis may be treated as metabolic pathways in one course and as aspects of the overall energy economy in another. The account of photosynthesis developed in a course on metabolism draws upon work with unicellular algae such as *Chlorella* as well as upon work with higher plants and its emphasis is upon the mechanisms of conversion of radiant energy into utilizable chemical energy and with the biochemical pathways of carbon assimilation. It is in the second course that attention may however be directed to such aspects as the intercellular diffusion pathway of gases in multicellular plants, the regulating activity of stomata and the movement of metabolites into and away from the photosynthetic cells. Lectures on salt accumulation at the cellular level in the first course may be complemented by lectures on mineral nutrition in the second.

There are as many ways of teaching plant physiology as there are teachers of this subject. Even when a broad distinction is drawn between 'metabolism' and 'growth and development' or between 'cellular physiology' and the 'physiology of the whole organism' the exact scope of the two aspects will reflect the individual judgements of the teacher concerned. The scope of the present book represents such an individual judgement by the authors. Although we have placed our emphasis on the physiology of the whole organism, various aspects of cell structure and physiology are discussed in so far as they seemed essential to the proper consideration of the major aspects of growth and development which form the subject matter of the Chapters 2, 8, 9, 10, 11 and 12. Within these chapters consideration is not confined to the growth and development of the plant and its separate organs, but extends to include the processes of cell division, cell enlargement and cell differentiation, cellular processes involved in the initiation of organs, in organ growth and in overall plant development. Similarly a brief account of the water relations of plant cells was felt to be necessary before the water relations of the whole plant could be considered.

The development of the text can be briefly summarized as follows: a chapter on germination (Chapter 2) introduces a number of fundamental processes which are then treated in more detail in the immediately following chapters (Chapters 3 to 6). The background of general physiology thereby established forms a basis for the chapters relating to growth and development and to the influence on these processes of the natural environment.

The chapters follow a logical sequence and should normally be read in that order. Nevertheless it is recognized that a different, though equally defensible, order of presentation may be followed in the student's course at his/her University, College or School. With this in mind we have endeavoured, even to the extent of introducing a very limited element of repetition, to make each chapter as self-contained as possible and therefore readable on its own. Further each chapter is linked to other relevant parts of the book by cross references.

It is always possible to criticize a work of this kind on the grounds that it states what is known without indicating in sufficient detail how that knowledge has been obtained by observation and experiment, and further, that it favours this or that hypothesis or interpretation of the experimental data without a really critical evaluation of the theoretical and technical considerations involved. Shortcomings of this kind are inevitable when a large body of knowledge is surveyed in a book of limited size and when it is regarded as important that basic concepts and inter-relationships should not be obscured by excessive facts, figures and references. With this in mind we have, at the conclusion of each chapter, referred the student and teacher not only to *Further Reading* but to *Selected References*. The latter are particularly important to those seeking the 'nature of the evidence' and details of important techniques. For advanced students each of our chapters can thus be regarded as the essential background to contact with primary data through the discussion of these and other research publications in tutorials and seminars.

We need not emphasize that the student reader should pursue a parallel course of practical work. The challenge of the study of plant physiology can be appreciated only by handling the research material, using techniques of measurement and interpreting one's own experimental data. The organization of such a course is, however, the province of the teacher working with the particular laboratory facilities available. Our text will, we hope, be of assistance to those concerned with developing such practical courses in so far as, at many points, it indicates useful plants for experimentation and outlines experimental approaches to the study of particular problems. Rigorous control of the physical and nutritional environment is the essential basis for the experimental study of many of the physiological problems raised in this book. Growth rooms represent, in this context, an important technical facility for which many of the design problems have now been satisfactorily solved. Growth room construction and details of other physical techniques applicable to the study of plant physiology are discussed in *Physics in Botany* by J. A. Richardson (Pitman and Sons, London, 1964). It will also become clear, particularly in Chapters 9, 11 and 12, that our understanding of a number of aspects of plant physiology has, in recent years, been advanced by using the techniques of organ, tissue and cell culture. Certain of these techniques are valuable in developing an interesting practical course on plant growth and development. Comprehensive accounts of the techniques and their application to the study of a wide range of problems will be found in *Cells and Tissues in Culture* Vol. 3 (ed. E. N. Willmer, Academic Press, New York, 1966) and *Plant Tissue and Cell Culture* (ed. H. E. Street, Blackwell Scientific Publications, Oxford, 1973).

COMPLEMENTARY READING TO THIS VOLUME

CUTTER, E. G. *Plant Anatomy. Part 1, Experiment and Interpretation* (1969); *Part 2, Cells and Tissues* (1971). Contemporary Biology Series, Edward Arnold, London.

ROBARDS, A. W. (1970). *Electron Microscopy and Plant Ultrastructure.* McGraw-Hill, London.

STREET, H. E. and COCKBURN, W. (1972). *Plant Metabolism*, 2nd edition. Pergamon Press, Oxford.

TROUGHTON, J. and DONALDSON, L. A. (1972). *Probing Plant Structure.* Chapman and Hall, London.

2

Germination

SEED STRUCTURE, CHEMICAL COMPOSITION AND META-BOLISM

The life of a flowering plant normally begins with a double fertilization within the embryo sac of the female parent. The egg nucleus fuses with one of the male nuclei contributed by the germinating pollen grain to form the zygote, while the two polar nuclei of the embryo sac and the second male nucleus fuse to give the triploid endosperm nucleus. Sometimes this sexual fusion is by-passed (apomixis) and an embryo develops from a diploid cell of the ovule. In either case, the embryo usually passes rapidly and without interruption through its early embryology (see Chapter 12). Then growth stops, water content falls and metabolic activity slows down prior to seed dispersal.

The degree of development of the embryo when the seed is shed varies; in the orchids (Orchidaceae) the embryo consists only of a small group of undifferentiated cells; in the grasses (Gramineae) several internodes with leaves and several embryonic roots are already distinguishable within the grain. Usually at least a radicle and plumule, each with an apical meristem, are differentiated, and one or two first leaves, the cotyledons. The triploid endosperm nucleus gives rise to the endosperm which may be a transient nutritive tissue or persist; the nucellus may also persist as perisperm, but more usually it disappears. The seed coat or testa is derived from the integument(s) of the ovule; sometimes, as in cereal grains, the testa and the ovary wall (pericarp) fuse to form the protective coat. Seeds present an immense variety of size, shape and structure, largely associated with modes of dispersal and with the conditions encountered in the natural habitat of the species. Some examples of seed

structure are given in Fig. 2.1. The mature seed when released from the
parent plant nearly always contains the embryo in a metabolically inactive,
dormant state, capable of withstanding adverse environmental conditions.
The success of the flowering plants is in a great measure due to the
effectiveness of the seed as a perennating and dispersal organ.

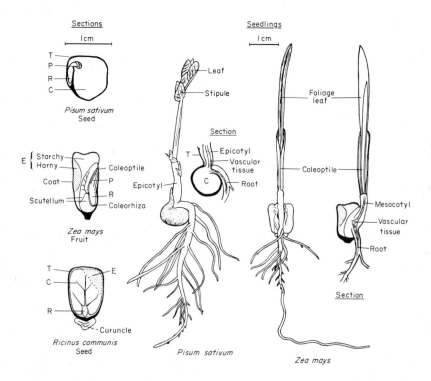

Fig. 2.1 Some examples of seeds and seedlings: the pea, *Pisum sativum*, a
dicotyledon with cotyledonary reserves; the castor bean, *Ricinus communis*, a
dicotyledon with endospermic reserves; and maize, *Zea mays*, a monocotyledon
with endospermic reserves. In the *Ricinus* seed section, part of the cotyledon is
cut away to show the endosperm (stippled). C, cotyledon; E, endosperm; P,
plumule; R, radicle; T, testa.

Nearly all seeds contain some reserve nutrient; in some cases this may
make up 85–90% of the seed by weight. Even in small seeds, such as
those of lettuce (*Lactuca sativa*), weighing only a few mg, the reserves
can support embryo growth for several days. In seeds like peas and beans,
weighing up to 1·5 g, the stores suffice for several weeks, while coconut

(*Cocos nucifera*) seedlings have been found to deplete only one-half of their reserve during 15 months of growth in darkness. The reserves may be found (as is common in the dicotyledons) in the cotyledons, in the endosperm (as in the Gramineae), or more rarely in the perisperm (e.g. in some Liliaceae and Piperaceae). Usually one type of storage tissue is present in any one seed, but this is not universally so. Both perisperm and endosperm are for instance present in the nutmeg (*Myristica fragrans*).

Table 2.1 The chemical composition of some seeds of economic importance. The percentages are based on the fresh (air-dry) weights of the seeds, except for Date palm, where the percentages are expressed on a dry weight basis.

Species	Family	Nature of reserve tissue	Per cent content Carbo-hydrate	Protein	Lipid
Maize (*Zea mays*)	Gramineae	Endosperm	51–74	10	5
Wheat (*Triticum vulgare*)	Gramineae	Endosperm	60–75	13	2
Pea (*Pisum sativum*)	Leguminosae	Cotyledons	34–46	20	2
Peanut (*Arachis hypogaea*)	Leguminosae	Cotyledons	12–33	20–30	40–50
Soybean (*Glycine* sp.)	Leguminosae	Cotyledons	14	37	17
Brazil nut (*Bertholletia excelsa*)	Lecythidaceae	Hypocotyl	4	14	62
Castor bean (*Ricinus communis*)	Euphorbiaceae	Endosperm	0	18	64
Date palm (*Phoenix dactylifera*)	Palmae	Endosperm	57	6	10
Sunflower (*Helianthus annuus*)	Compositae	Cotyledons	2	25	45–50
Oak (*Quercus robur*)	Fagaceae	Cotyledons	47	3	3

The chemical composition of some seeds is given in Table 2.1. The analysis reflects mainly the composition of storage tissues. The high lipid contents are noteworthy; no other plant organs achieve such high lipid levels. Lipids provide the highest amount of potential energy per unit weight. All the basic protoplasmic components are present in seeds, including nucleic acids, amino acids, vitamins, coenzymes and minerals. The phosphorus content is often high; the element occurs most commonly

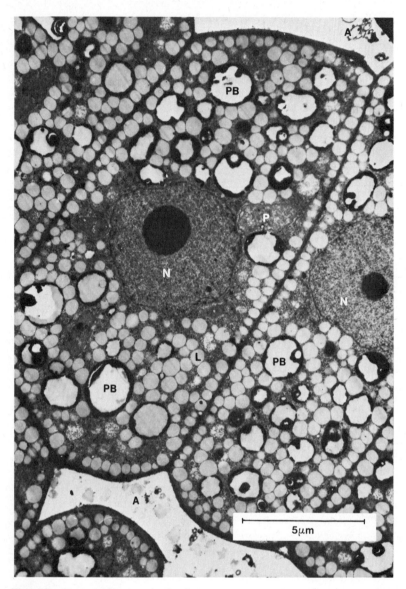

Fig. 2.2 Electron micrograph of cells in the embryonic coleoptile of an imbibed but ungerminated grain of rice (*Oryza sativa* L.). The cells contain many lipid vesicles (L, small, electron-transparent) and fewer but larger protein bodies, PB. The concentration of protein body contents around their peripheries may be a fixation artifact. A, air space; N, nucleus; P, plastid. Fixation in glutaraldehyde and osmium tetroxide. × 6700.

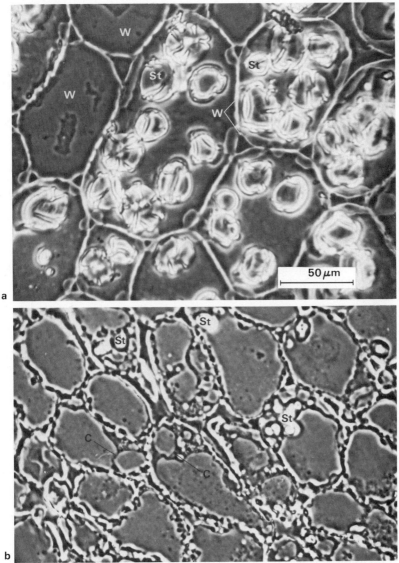

Fig. 2.3 (a) Photomicrograph of reserve-packed cells from a mature, ungerminated cotyledon of bean (*Phaseolus vulgaris*). St, starch grain; W, cell wall (which is seen in surface view in two cells at top left). (**b**) Cells from same tissue after 11 days' germination at 25°C. The reserves have been digested; the cells are empty except for some cytoplasmic strands, C, and small starch grains; many cells are quite empty and dead. Scale as (**a**); the cells look smaller because of shrinkage and collapse.

as phytin (salts of inositol hexaphosphate). All seeds contain protein as a protoplasmic component, but in some cases, e.g. in legumes, large quantities of special reserve proteins, with a distinctive chemical composition, are also stored. Chlorophyll is usually absent.

The reserves are found in the storage cells mostly as insoluble compounds. Small amounts of soluble sugars are usually present, but are concentrated mainly in the growing parts of the embryo. Carbohydrate occurs chiefly as starch or hemicelluloses. Starch is stored as grains up to 50 μm in diameter, formed in amyloplasts. Hemicelluloses are normal cell wall components in all tissues and where they form a major seed reserve they are laid down as heavy cell wall thickenings which almost fill the cell lumen, as in seeds of the date (*Phoenix dactylifera*) and ivory nut palm (*Phytelephas macrocarpa*). Reserve lipids are deposited as droplets of varying size enclosed within a limiting membrane though this does not show the usual unit membrane structure. The storage proteins occur as membrane-enclosed protein bodies (aleurone grains) or more rarely as crystals. The cells of reserve tissues are packed full of storage materials, and even the embryonic tissues of seeds are rich in reserve granules (Figs. 2.2 and 2.3).

Seeds often contain unusual amino acids which are not constituents of proteins and these can act as a nitrogen store, being present to the extent of several per cent of the seed dry weight, and often containing a high proportion of nitrogen in the molecule. Pyrazol-1-yl-alanine, found in seeds of some members of the Cucurbitaceae, has a nitrogen content of 26%; the nitrogen content of canavanine, a constituent of seeds of the legume *Canavalia ensiformis*, amounts to 32%. (An average protein contains about 16% nitrogen by weight, though in seed reserve proteins the value may reach 19%). The non-protein amino acids are often toxic to animals and are thought to fulfil also the role of repellents against seed-eating animals. Caterpillars and mice have been noted to refuse a diet containing 5% canavanine, the percentage normally present in *Canavalia* seeds, and similar experimental results have been obtained with other non-protein amino acids of seeds. Moreover it has been observed that, in nature, leguminous seeds with toxic amino acids are avoided by insects and other seed-eating animals.

The metabolic rate of ungerminated seeds is usually extremely low. The factor responsible for this is the low water content, 5–20% on a fresh weight basis, compared with 80–95% for most plant tissues in an active state. Most of the water in 'dry' seeds is moreover firmly bound to colloids, inaccessible for hydrolytic reactions, unfreezable, and removable only by temperatures approaching 100°C or by storage in high vacuum. Due to this dehydration, the cells and subcellular organelles in dry seeds are often shrunken and angular.

Germination is the resumption of metabolic activity and growth by the seed tissues, involving rehydration, utilization of nutrient reserves, and the gradual development of synthetic systems which enable the young plant to assume an autotrophic existence.

HYDRATION PHASE OF GERMINATION

The first process that occurs in germination is water uptake, involving both *imbibition* and *osmosis*. Colloidal imbibition is dominant in the initial phase of water uptake and, since this is not dependent on metabolic activity, it will occur under anaerobic conditions, and, albeit slower, at temperatures too low to permit subsequent development; even dead seeds take up water. The magnitude of the force of colloidal imbibition is at first very high; 'dry' seeds can develop suction forces of 1000–2000 atm. As the water content rises, the imbibitional force rapidly decreases, so that the rate of water uptake slows down, and osmotic forces become relatively more important and determine the final water content reached in the hydration phase.

During this hydration phase, the testa is frequently the limiting factor and in such cases removal or puncturing of the testa significantly speeds up the rate of water uptake. Imbibition causes swelling of the seed and this is often greater in the living cells than in the dead coats, so that the coats are consequently ruptured during the hydration phase. The micropylar pore and the hilum may be the chief areas of water entry; for example in beans (*Vicia* and *Phaseolus*) the micropyle is responsible for 20% of the water entry in the first 24 hours. In the seed of horse chestnut (*Aesculus hippocastanum*) and the peanut (*Arachis hypogaea*), the testa is more permeable to water from the outside inwards than in the opposite direction, thus showing some adaptation to water uptake. The testa of the lima bean (*Phaseolus limensis*) is impermeable to water from the outside until it has been wetted from the inside by water entering through the hilum.

Inside the seed, hydration normally proceeds inwards, cell layer by cell layer, so that in a partially imbibed seed the hydration is not even. Water movement is faster in the embryonic tissues than in the storage regions. In the castor bean, the cotyledons which are embedded in the middle of the endosperm are quickly hydrated and conduct water to the endosperm, which thus gets hydrated from two sides.

The initial hydration phase brings the water content of the seeds to 50–60% of their fresh weight, a value determined by the presence of a high proportion of storage cells which do not necessarily become vacuolated at this stage. This is in consequence lower than the water content of 80–95% generally characteristic of mature tissues not packed with storage material and of the embryo axis itself at the completion of the hydration phase. The cells and subcellular organelles regain the size and shape they had before the drying out which occurred during ripening of the seed. As the protoplasm becomes hydrated, it resumes metabolic activity.

A dry seed contains a certain complement of enzymes, coenzymes and substrates. Diverse enzyme activities have been detected in extracts prepared from air-dry seeds. Enzymes are activated by hydration, but the water content at which activity becomes evident varies for different enzymes. In wheat grains (*Triticum vulgare*), proteinases, transaminases, and glutamic decarboxylase are activated when the average water content of the seed is 15%, while respiratory dehydrogenases need over 25% water for activation. Whether this reflects real differences in the degree of hydration required by these enzymes, or whether it results from uneven hydration on a subcellular level, some enzyme sites becoming hydrated before others, is not known.

Under certain conditions, the seed's development may be arrested at the stage of completed hydration. The light-sensitive seeds of foxglove (*Digitalis purpurea*), of certain varieties of lettuce (*Lactuca sativa*), and of tobacco (*Nicotiana tabacum*) will in the dark undergo hydration associated with a limited activation of their metabolism. However, only when the seeds are illuminated does their metabolism become further activated and their germination proceed. Seeds can also be maintained in the hydrated state without embryo growth and development at low temperature (this is one technique of vernalization, see Chapter 12).

PHASE OF ACTIVATED METABOLISM AND GROWTH

Hydration is followed by a stage of intense metabolic activity. Development now follows a different course in the two functional regions of the seed. In the embryo, cells begin to elongate and divide; according to species, either of these processes can start first, or both simultaneously. The metabolism of the growing regions of the embryo is directed towards the synthesis of new cell components and structures. Growth is usually visible in the radicle before the plumule; the emergence of the radicle is frequently taken as the criterion of germination. The radicle is positively geotropic (see Chapter 10), and thus grows downwards, irrespective of the position in which the seed has happened to fall. In the grasses, the radicle is enclosed in a protective sheath, the coleorhiza, as it emerges. The plumule grows out later, when the seed has already been anchored to the substratum by the radicle. The plumule grows upwards, being negatively geotropic and positively phototropic. In its natural habitat, a seed frequently is covered by soil or leaf litter by the time it germinates, and the delicate growing tip of the plumule is protected while the seedling pushes through this covering. In the grasses, protection is afforded by a plumular sheath, the coleoptile. In dicotyledons, the young leaves are folded round the tip, and in many cases the plumule axis is bent into a hook, which meets the soil resistance, the more delicate tip trailing after it. The straightening of the hook and unfolding and expansion of the leaves occur only in the light. The greening of seedling tissues also takes place only in those parts exposed to light. Germination is classed as *epigeal* if the cotyledons come above ground; in that case the plumule tip can receive further protection by being enclosed by the cotyledons; the main region of elongation in early germination is then the hypocotyl, the internode below the cotyledons, and the hypocotyl forms the hook. If the cotyledons stay underground, the germination is *hypogeal*, and the hooked epicotyl, the internode above the cotyledons, is the main region of elongation.

The metabolism of the storage tissues is now directed to a hydrolysis of the storage reserves, and translocation of the resulting soluble products to the growing regions. There is as a rule no cell division in the storage tissues, and cell expansion is limited to that associated with rehydration. The activity of the storage tissues during germination is thus the reverse of that which occurred during ripening, when they received soluble compounds by translocation and converted them into insoluble reserve materials. Storage tissues of parent origin, endosperms and perisperms, die when their reserves are exhausted; their metabolic activity during germination is high but brief. Reserve-carrying cotyledons, too, may die quickly, or they may become green and persist for some time as the first photosynthetic leaves of the plant.

Respiration during germination

The intense metabolism of germinating seeds is accompanied by high rates of respiration per unit weight of tissue both in the embryonic and the storage regions. Respiratory enzymes are already present in the dry seeds, and hydration leads to a steep rise in respiration rate, once a critical water content has been passed (Fig. 2.4). The respiration rate of storage organs destined to die during germination typically rises to a peak and then falls as their senescence sets in. This rise to a peak is observed whether measurements are made on a basis of per organ, per cell, or per unit weight. The overall course of development and metabolism in the growing tissues is more complex. For the growing axis as a whole, the total respiration continues to increase throughout germination. The axis, however, soon comes to contain regions of different structure, function and age, within each of which the respiration per cell or unit weight reaches a peak and then decreases again to a more or less steady value characteristic of maturity. Respiratory metabolism during germination involves changes in pathways as well as quantitative changes, as is illustrated by considering the changes in respiratory quotient during germination.

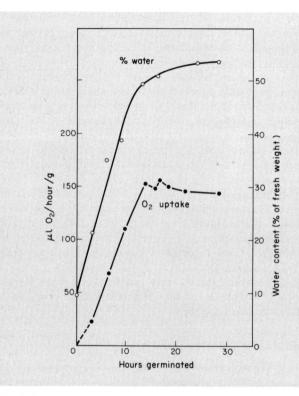

Fig. 2.4 The activation of respiration, measured as oxygen uptake, in cotyledons of bean (*Phaseolus vulgaris*) during germination. After the initial hydration is completed (at about 50% water content), the respiration rate remains constant for some hours.

Respiratory quotient during germination

The respiratory quotient (RQ) of germinating seeds has been studied extensively. The RQ is defined as the fraction:

$$\frac{\text{Volume of } CO_2 \text{ evolved}}{\text{Volume of } O_2 \text{ absorbed}}$$

For the aerobic oxidation of carbohydrate, the $RQ = 1 \cdot 0$; for lipids, $0 \cdot 7$–$0 \cdot 8$, according to the chemical structure of the lipid molecules; for proteins, $0 \cdot 8$–$1 \cdot 0$, according to the degree of completeness of amino acid oxidation. During anaerobic respiration, CO_2 evolution takes place without O_2 uptake, giving an RQ of infinity; hence the simultaneous occurrence of aerobic and anaerobic respiration will give RQs above unity.

Mature plant tissues respire aerobically on a carbohydrate substrate and with an RQ of about 1. During germination however the RQ deviates widely from unity and changes rapidly. In the first hours of imbibition, very many seeds exhibit RQ values above unity, which fall quickly once hydration has proceeded to a critical extent. For intact seeds of pea (*Pisum sativum*), RQ values of up to 8 have been reported at the very beginning of germination. Such initially high RQ values have, in certain cases, been interpreted as indicative of anaerobic metabolism, conditioned by O_2 shortage resulting from the diffusion resistance of the incompletely hydrated testa. If the testa is removed from germinating peas, the RQ drops from $8 \cdot 0$ to $1 \cdot 5$. In two species of pine, the oxygen uptake of decoated seeds was found to be 3 to 4 times higher than in seeds with intact coats. However not all seeds have testas highly impermeable to oxygen and in seeds of dwarf French bean (*Phaseolus vulgaris*), the RQ is unaffected by removal of the testa and oxygen uptake is increased by only 10%.

A second factor restricting oxygen access to the cells is the diffusion resistance offered by incompletely hydrated tissues, which frequently lack air spaces until the cells swell and become rounded. Dry tissue also does not become wetted easily, and water films form on the surfaces of seeds hindering gaseous exchange. Rapid fluctuations of the RQ between $0 \cdot 5$ and $1 \cdot 5$ in germinating barley grains have been interpreted as due to uneven wetting of tissue and consequent obstruction of gaseous diffusion. The amplitude of these fluctuations becomes smaller and smaller as hydration proceeds until by 30 hours from addition of water the RQ settles to a steady value of $0 \cdot 90$–$0 \cdot 95$. In the seeds of *Phaseolus vulgaris*, the RQ after 6 hours of germination at $25°$ is $1 \cdot 3$–$1 \cdot 5$ and the cotyledons can be seen to be unevenly hydrated. If the seeds are then enclosed in vessels without further water supply, water movement continues within the seed during the next 24 hours to give a more even distribution without change in overall water content, and as this occurs the RQ falls to below unity.

Reports of very high RQ values in germinating seeds should be accepted with caution. Considerable quantities of adsorbed air, which may be enriched with carbon dioxide (presumably accumulated during the slow respiration of the air-dry seed) can be released very rapidly when dry seeds, and any other dry plant material, living or dead, are wetted. Therefore if water is added to dry seeds and changes in gas pressure determined immediately, the release of adsorbed gas could be mistaken for a large respiratory output of carbon dioxide. There is also a possibility of carbon dioxide evolution from metabolic reactions distinct from respiration. Glutamic decarboxylase, an enzyme which splits off carbon dioxide from glutamic acid, is activated at lower water contents than many respiratory enzymes.

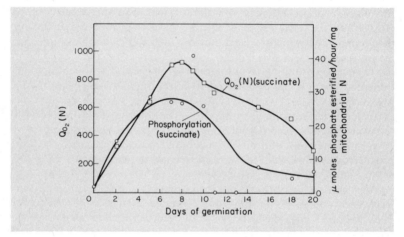

Fig. 2.5 Changes in O_2 uptake and oxidative phosphorylation rate of mito-chondria isolated from cotyledons of peanut (*Arachis hypogaea*) germinating at 30°C in the dark. Succinate was used as the substrate. The O_2 uptake is expressed as the Q_{O_2} (N), i.e. μl O_2/hour/mg mitochondrial protein nitrogen. After 10 days the cotyledons begin to senesce. (Adapted from Cherry, 1963, *Pl. Physiol., Lancaster*, **38**, 440–6.)

After the hydration phase, further increases in respiration rate are associated with increases in the amounts of respiratory enzymes in the developing embryo. In the storage tissues, where growth does not take place, there are nevertheless also increases in the activity of respiratory enzymes (Fig. 2.5). Studies with isolated mitochondria show that the oxidative activity of these organelles increases. Electron micrographs of peanut cotyledons, maize scutellum and bean cotyledons show increases in the complexity of structure and in the number of mitochondria. Maize scutellum and castor bean endosperm have yielded mitochondria which are among the most active so far isolated from plant tissues. Since the main energy-yielding reactions of respiration occur in mitochondria, the storage tissues of germinating seeds develop a high potential capacity for energy production.

The soluble sugars of the seed which serve as substrates in early germination are soon used up and respiration comes to depend on the hydrolysis of the reserves. The metabolism, including the respiration, of the storage tissues is primarily related to the mobilization of their reserves. The RQ drops below unity, especially in the storage tissues, reaches a minimum lasting some days, and then rises again. An explanation of these RQ changes in terms of underlying physiological processes is not easy. The oxidation of fats and proteins produces RQ values below unity, and the usual and probably generally valid explanation put forward is that, in germinating seedlings, these compounds rather than or in addition to carbohydrates serve as respiratory substrates. The occurrence of RQ values as low as 0·3 has been explained as due to a conversion of lipid to carbohydrate proceeding concurrently with lipid and carbohydrate oxidation. This conversion is an oxidative process not accompanied by carbon dioxide release and thus has an RQ of zero. Lipid-rich seeds generally have RQs lower than those of carbohydrate-storing seeds. Yet there are instances of seeds with high lipid contents in which the RQ never falls far below unity, and seeds low in lipid may have very low RQs. Products of fermentation such as alcohol and lactic acid may accumulate during a period of oxygen shortage and the oxidation of these can lower the RQ.

In pea seeds, for example, alcohol and lactic acid accumulate during soaking and disappear when the testa is ruptured, the RQ during the oxidation of the alcohol and lactic acid being close to 0·53. Again there is the possibility of carbon dioxide fixation reactions lowering the RQ; such 'dark' fixation of CO_2 has been demonstrated in germinating seeds. The RQ is therefore clearly not a value determined by one single process, but the resultant of a number of biological reactions involving oxygen and carbon dioxide.

In the embryo axis, the RQ value deviates much less from unity than in the storage tissues. In the lipid-storing castor bean seed, the RQ of the embryo, after a brief minimum immediately after the hydration phase, stabilizes at 0·8–1·0 in contrast to the endosperm which has an RQ of 0·4–0·5. It may be concluded that the RQs of storage tissues reflect their special type of metabolism, concerned with the hydrolysis and further chemical modification of reserves, while the growing regions receive their respiratory substrate from the storage cells largely in the form of soluble carbohydrates.

Mobilization of food reserves

The first stage in the utilization of the nutrient reserves is hydrolysis. Table 2.2 lists the enzymes responsible for the hydrolysis of the chief classes of reserves and the primary products of the hydrolysis. The cellulose walls of storage cells usually remain undigested, but enzymes promoting cellulose breakdown have been detected in germinating barley.

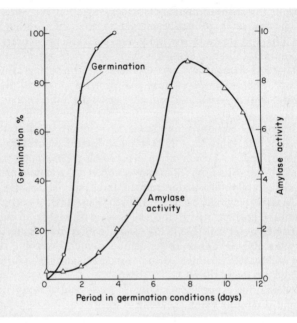

Fig. 2.6 The increase in amylase activity in germinating grains of barley (*Hordeum vulgare*). The activity is expressed as mg starch digested in 2 minutes by a volume of extract equivalent to half a grain. The emergence of the radicle was taken as the criterion of germination. (From Drennan and Berrie, 1962, *New Phytol.*, **61**, 1–9.)

It is interesting to note that while amylases and lipases are not species-specific, i.e. the amylase of one species will hydrolyse the starch from another, the seed proteinases show considerable specificity, being much more efficient in hydrolysing the proteins from the same species. A proteinase preparation from cabbage (*Brassica*) seed, for instance, has been found to be completely inactive towards the proteins from the seeds of bean (*Phaseolus*).

Enzymes indispensable to energy metabolism, such as respiratory enzymes, are present in the dry seed at quite high levels, and need only hydration to become active. By contrast the activity of many of the hydrolytic enzymes is low or absent in dry seeds; the appearance of activity or increase in the initial low activity of the hydrolytic enzymes begins some hours or even days after the hydration phase, and continues for several days (Fig. 2.6).

Increases in enzyme activity in a tissue may come about either by release of an enzyme present in an inactive form, or by enzyme synthesis. Both processes contribute to increases in enzyme activity in germinating seeds. In cereals, an appreciable amount of β-amylase is present in the ungerminated seed in an inactive form. In extracts of ungerminated seeds

Table 2.2   The main classes of hydrolytic enzymes involved in the mobilization of the food reserves of seeds.

Reserve compound	Enzymes	Products of hydrolysis
Starch	α- and β-amylase Maltase Phosphorylase	Maltose, glucose Glucose Glucose-1-phosphate
Hemicellulose	Cytases	Hexoses, pentoses
Lipid	Lipases (esterases)	Fatty acids and glycerol
Protein	Proteinases Peptidases	Amino acids, peptides Amino acids
Phytin	Phytase	Inorganic phosphate and inositol
Ribonucleic acid	Ribonuclease	Ribonucleotides
Cellulose	1. Cellulase 2. Cellobiase	Cellobiose Glucose

this enzyme can be activated by treatment with a proteinase; *in vivo*, the increase in activity may be presumed to be elicited by native proteinases. Similarly, some lipases may occur in an inactive state in ungerminated seeds.

On the other hand, it has been shown that in the cotyledons of germinating peas, increases in the activity of α-amylase result from enzyme synthesis. The rise in activity of this enzyme is inhibited by the application of chemicals known to inhibit protein synthesis and by 2,4-dinitrophenol (DNP), which prevents the transfer of respiratory energy to synthetic processes. A similar synthesis of α-amylase in germinating barley grains has been followed by measuring the incorporation of ^{14}C-labelled amino acids into the enzyme protein.

The physiological activity of seed storage tissues during germination has been described as being catabolic, or degradative, in contrast to the anabolic or synthetic activity of the growing regions of the embryo. The foregoing paragraphs however emphasize that in the storage tissues there occurs synthesis of protein. Nucleic acid synthesis also occurs (Fig. 2.7) and an increase in the number and activity of mitochondria. Xylem and* phloem elements differentiate in cotyledons; even short-lived cotyledons become green and produce chloroplasts if they come above ground. The mobilization of food reserves is therefore the consequence not of a purely degradative self-digestion of the storage cell contents, but a process also involving complex, energy-dependent syntheses.

There are a number of puzzling features concerning the activities of hydrolytic enzymes in germinating seeds. There is often no obvious proportionality between the level of activity of a particular enzyme and

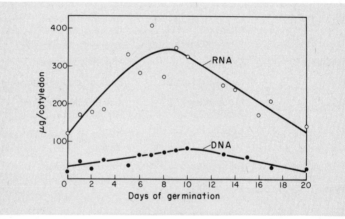

Fig. 2.7 Changes in DNA and RNA content in cotyledons of germinating peanut; conditions and source of data as for Fig. 2.5. Comparison with the latter figure shows that the period of increase in nucleic acid content coincides with the period of increasing mitochondrial activity, and the fall in nucleic acid content commences as the respiratory activities begin to fall, and senescence sets in.

the quantity of its substrate. For example, soybean seeds are rich in β-amylase, but contain little or no starch; seeds with high lipase activity are not necessarily rich in lipid. Activities of particular enzymes frequently continue to rise after their substrates are depleted. This suggests that the complex control mechanisms which operate in growing cells may be impaired in the senescent storage cells.

The hydrolysis of reserves does not proceed uniformly throughout the storage tissues and, correlated with this, certain enzymes have been shown to have characteristic distribution patterns. In the cotyledons of leguminous plants, digestion begins in areas furthest away from the ramifying vascular bundles. The cells where hydrolysis first starts are dead before digestion becomes evident in the cells next to the bundles. Lipid hydrolysis in castor bean endosperm proceeds simultaneously from the outside inwards and from the site of the cotyledons outwards. In cereals, the endo-

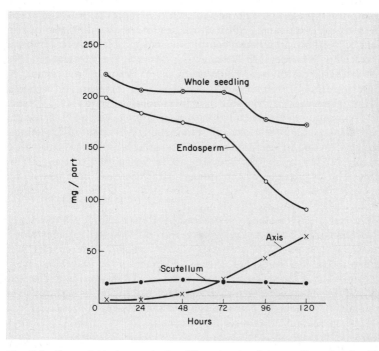

Fig. 2.8 Dry weight changes in the different parts of the seedling of maize (*Zea mays*) germinating at 25°C in the dark; the weights are given as mg/seedling or mg/seedling part. (From Ingle, Beevers and Hageman, 1964, *Pl. Physiol.*, *Lancaster*, **39**, 735–40.)

sperm is differentiated into the metabolically active aleurone layer cells and the endosperm cells which are dead or of very low metabolic activity. In resting cereal grains, proteinase, peptidase, esterase and phytase activities are confined to the aleurone layer and the embryo. The aleurone cells contain the protein and phytin reserves. However β-amylase is found in the endosperm and is absent from the aleurone layer, being at its highest concentration just outside this layer. During germination, the aleurone layer secretes other enzymes, e.g. α-amylase, into the endosperm and digestion in the endosperm starts in its vicinity. This digestion is also promoted by the secretion of enzymes by the scutellum (Fig. 2.1). In the date seed, the tip of the cotyledon burrows into the endosperm, secreting a cytase which digests the hemicellulose reserves.

The secretion of enzymes raises the question as to whether the secreted enzymes move from cell to cell via protoplasmic connections (plasmodesmata), or whether they are discharged from the secreting cells and diffuse through the walls and intercellular spaces to the storage cells. There is no satisfactory evidence that proteins are readily absorbed by plant cells. Although isolated aleurone layers and isolated cereal embryos do discharge amylases into their bathing medium, this does not establish that discharge occurs to any significant extent in the intact germinating grain.

Hydrolyses convert insoluble reserves to soluble derivatives. In maize, the proportion of soluble compounds rises from 2% to 25% of the dry weight during the first 5 days of germination. A fraction of the soluble products is used in respiration and for syntheses in the storage tissues themselves, but by far the greater part is transported to the growing parts. The dry weight of the storage parts decreases and that of the growing parts increases (Fig. 2.8). As their reserves are exhausted, storage cells collapse and die (Fig. 2.3b).

The transport is assumed to proceed by diffusion from cell to cell and by phloem translocation. Endosperm does not develop vascular tissue, and reserves from it are absorbed where it makes close contact with embryonic tissues. In cereals, the scutellum acts as an absorbing organ; it absorbs the glucose arising from starch breakdown in the endosperm and converts the glucose into sucrose, which is the form of sugar involved in phloem transport. In date and coconut the cotyledons grow deep into the endosperm and act as absorbing organs.

Utilization of food reserves for seedling growth

The utilization of the products of hydrolysis for synthetic reactions in the embryo necessitates extensive interconversions of metabolites since the chemical composition of the new cells formed in growth is very different from that of the storage cells. In particular most of the stored lipid is converted to carbohydrate. Table 2.3 shows an analysis of the lipid and carbohydrate content of germinating castor bean seeds, which at the beginning of germination contain 60–70% lipid. The conversion occurs in the storage tissue and the sucrose formed is translocated to the embryo. The biochemical pathway for this conversion is the glyoxylate cycle and the two enzymes unique to this cycle, isocitratase and malate

Table 2.3 Changes in lipid and carbohydrate content in castor beans during germination at 25°C in the dark.
(Data of Desveaux, R. and Kogane-Charles, M., 1952, *Annls Inst. natn. Rech. agron., Paris,* **3**, 385–416.)
The increase in total dry weight results from the incorporation of water and oxygen during the conversion of lipid to carbohydrate.

Days germinated	Weight per 100 seedlings (g)		
	Lipid	Carbohydrate	Total dry weight
0	26·2	1·51	37·6
4	25·0	5·10	39·0
6	10·8	18·2	45·1
8	5·40	23·3	43·9
11	1·78	17·7	38·4

synthetase, are only found in high activity in the tissues of fatty seeds during the period of lipid breakdown. They appear on germination and disappear again when the lipid is used up.

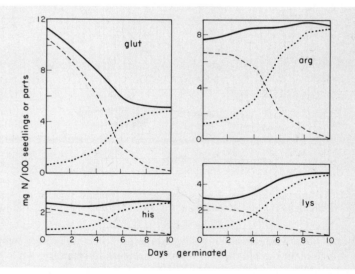

Fig. 2.9 Changes in the quantities of four amino acids in seedlings of barley germinated in the light at 22·5°C without an external nitrogen source. Continuous line—whole seedling; dotted line—embryo; broken line—endosperm. For all the acids there is an increase in the embryo and a decrease in the endosperm, but the total quantity per seedling decreases in the case of glutamic acid (glut), remains almost constant for histidine (his), and increases for arginine (arg) and lysine (lys). (Adapted from Folkes and Yemm, 1958, *New Phytol.,* **57**, 106—31.)

The protein metabolism of seedlings includes interconversions between amino acids. The amino acid composition of the storage proteins differs from that of the proteins of the growing embryo. Fig. 2.9 shows changes in some nitrogenous compounds in barley seedlings germinated without an external nitrogen supply. As the amount of protein in the endosperm falls, the amount in the embryo increases and the overall protein content of the seedling does not change markedly, but this is not true of the

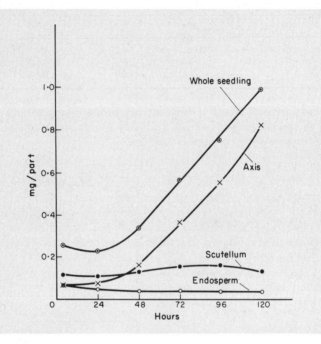

Fig. 2.10 Changes in content of nucleic acids in various parts of the maize seedling during germination; conditions and source of data as for Fig. 2.8.

amounts of individual amino acids. Glutamic acid and proline, which are abundant in the endosperm reserve, decrease in quantity, while the amounts of aspartic acid, alanine and glycine increase. The amino acid conversions (transaminations) responsible for the changes proceed in the tissues of the embryo.

As soon as growth begins in the embryonic regions, the synthesis of nucleic acids, both RNA and DNA (deoxyribonucleic acid) commences there. Knowledge of the nucleic acid interconversions occurring during seed germination is at present very limited. Dry seeds have low nucleic acid contents and both RNA and DNA levels per seedling increase early in germination (Fig. 2.10). This implies nucleic acid synthesis from non-nucleic acid material. However, the storage tissues do contain some nucleic acid, particularly RNA, and increases in the activity of ribonucleases (enzymes which hydrolyse RNA) in seed storage tissues have been reported to occur during germination. This suggests that breakdown products of storage tissue RNA may be used in RNA synthesis in the embryo. It has even been claimed that intact RNA molecules are translocated from storage tissues to the growing regions. It seems however that the amounts of RNA lost from the storage cells would in most cases supply only a small fraction of the RNA formed in the growing areas, and in certain cases it has been shown that the RNA content of the storage tissues does not fall until after a considerable increase in the RNA content of the embryonic regions has taken place. The first change in RNA content of the storage tissue is, in fact, an increase (Fig. 2.7), probably connected with the onset of synthesis of the hydrolytic enzymes. In the growing regions, the rise in DNA content parallels the increase in cell number. Few data are available for changes in DNA content of storage tissues. In maize scutellum, the DNA content is stated to remain constant during germination. In peanut cotyledons, though cell number does not increase, radioactive phosphate is incorporated into DNA and total DNA content rises (Fig. 2.7). This may be related to increase in the number of mitochondria which contain DNA.

Activation and control of protein synthesis

Protein synthesis plays an important part in germination, as the foregoing paragraphs show. According to the current hypothesis, protein synthesis requires a complex synthetic apparatus. The cytoplasmic sites of protein synthesis are the *ribosomes*, particles composed of *ribosomal* RNA and protein. Amino acids are transported to these ribosomes by *transfer* RNA molecules. The synthesis of each different kind of protein is finally directed by a specific *messenger* RNA which attaches to the ribosomes, linking them into functional units or *polysomes*. The primary structure (amino acid sequence) of the protein is coded in the base triplets of the messenger RNA and is 'translated' into the protein amino acid sequence during synthesis on the ribosome. The master code for the protein resides, however, in the nuclear DNA from which it is 'transcribed' into the messenger RNA. Many authors have asked the question: do dormant seed tissues possess a complete protein synthesizing system needing only hydration for its activation, or must some of the components of the synthesizing system itself first be synthesized?

Ribosomes can be clearly seen in dry seeds, both in embryonic and storage regions and the density of ribosomes per unit volume of cytoplasm may be very high in the embryonic regions. An 'almost complete' disappearance of ribosomes from castor bean endosperm during seed maturation, and their reappearance during early germination, has been claimed, but this claim was based on isolation and the observation may simply reflect the inadequacy of the isolation method when applied to dry tissue. The presence of ribosomes in dormant tissues is generally accepted. Some earlier work indicated that dry seed tissues lacked messenger RNA, but all other components of the protein synthesis machinery were present and the synthesis was activated by the formation of messenger RNA during early germination and the binding of ribosomes into polysomes. However, evidence for the presence of some messenger RNA in dry seeds has also been obtained. It has been isolated from dry wheat embryos and at least one group of workers has claimed, from the results of feeding in radioactive amino acids and radioactive precursors of RNA, that protein synthesis of wheat embryos, as measured by the incorporation of radioactive amino acids into protein, started immediately on imbibition, while transcription of messenger RNA did not begin until 24 hours later. In barley embryos protein synthesis, again measured by radioactive amino acid incorporation, has been found to be unaffected by the application of actinomycin-D, an inhibitor of transcription, during the first four hours; by eight hours, however, protein synthesis was inhibited by 50% and eventually growth stopped. These results suggest that a certain amount of messenger RNA is present in the dry tissues, but this suffices to support protein synthesis only for a limited time after which more must be transcribed, probably including new molecular species not present in the dry state. Ribosomal and transfer RNA are also eventually synthesized, especially in regions where growth takes place.

However, there is not universal agreement about the sequence of events. Other workers have claimed that in wheat embryos messenger RNA synthesis is detectable *first*, to be followed by protein synthesis, DNA synthesis, ribosomal RNA synthesis and transfer RNA synthesis, in that order. The study of protein and nucleic acid synthesis in early germination involves difficult experimental techniques and more data are needed. The sequence of events might even vary from tissue to tissue and some dormant tissues could contain appreciably greater stores of messenger RNA than others. There is also uncertainty as to which kinds of proteins are the first to be synthesized. While much emphasis has been placed on enzyme synthesis during germination, some recent work has suggested that the first proteins to be made are more likely to be structural membrane proteins. The fine structure of dry seeds is characterized by a low membrane content and some membrane increases occur very rapidly. In the rye

(*Secale cereale* L.) embryo, increases in mitochondrial cristae are apparent within two hours of the start of imbibition and endoplasmic reticulum has proliferated extensively within five hours; in pea radicles, endoplasmic reticulum shows appreciable increase by eight hours. Golgi apparatus, a site of membrane formation, is also absent or sparsely represented in dry seeds, becoming apparent during early germination.

INTERRELATIONSHIP BETWEEN THE GROWING SEEDLING AND THE STORAGE TISSUES

The growing regions of the seedling exert a close control over the activity of the storage tissues. Recent work with pea seedlings has shown that the increases in enzyme activity which normally occur in the cotyledons fail to take place if the embryo axis is removed and that under these conditions mitochondria in the cells of the cotyledons soon lose their activity. The finding that aqueous extracts of embryo axis tissue stimulated normal development of excised cotyledons pointed to the operation of a chemical regulator originating in the embryo. By excision of the embryo axis after varying periods of germination at 25°C, evidence was obtained that the regulator moves from the axis into the cotyledons between 24 and 48 hours. The subsequent senescence of the pea cotyledons was also shown to be dependent on the presence of the axis: if the axes are removed after 48 hours of germination, the cotyledons remain alive and healthy for at least 6 weeks instead of dying within about 2 weeks.

Work on barley suggests that the regulator may be a gibberellin, possibly gibberellic acid. (For description of the structure and other functions of gibberellins see Chapter 9, p. 186; Fig. 9.3, p. 161 and Chapters 11 and 12.) The embryo synthesizes a gibberellin and production of α-amylase by excised aleurone layers and endosperm halves of barley grains can be stimulated by applied gibberellic acid. The synthesis of certain other enzymes in germinating barley is also stimulated by gibberellic acid treatment. In the pea, however, gibberellic acid produces no stimulation of enzyme synthesis in the cotyledons. In cotyledons of *Cucurbita maxima*, cytokinins promote the synthesis of proteolytic emzymes while gibberellic acid is again ineffective. The role of the gibberellin (or some other hormone), secreted by the embryonic tissues, may be to induce the synthesis in the storage cells of the messenger RNA needed to initiate enzyme synthesis. By contrast there seems to be no mechanism for 'switching off' the synthesis: enzyme activity, once induced, may continue to increase after its substrate has been depleted from the storage cells.

A negative feedback control via endproduct inhibition sometimes operates. The increase in protease activity of pea seeds is inhibited when the seeds are germinated in a mixture of amino acids, the products of protease activity. In other cases, too, inhibition of storage protein breakdown by amino acids and of starch hydrolysis by sugars has been noted, though the activities of the hydrolytic enzymes were not measured.

It is not known whether any specific stimulus is required, during germination, to induce the embryo axis to embark upon synthetic activity and growth. Cell division, cell elongation and the increase in dry weight begin very suddenly, and not simultaneously in the radicle and plumule. The suddenness with which these processes take place has suggested to various workers the operation of a specific 'trigger' substance, but it is equally possible that hydration initiates a predetermined programme of reactions, leading the cells to start division and elongation when some sequence of reactions is completed.

Certain aspects of the close interrelationship between the growing regions and the storage tissue have clearly yet to be elucidated. It is evident that the embryo axis is dependent on the storage tissues for its nutrient supply. The developmental changes in the storage tissues, which result in this supply becoming available as required, are dependent on stimuli, probably of hormonal nature, from the embryo axis.

Gradually, the root system of the seedling becomes able to absorb and supply mineral ions to the developing plant; the photosynthetic apparatus develops and takes over the production of organic compounds. The heterotrophic seedling becomes an independent autotrophic plant and germination is complete.

FURTHER READING

AMEN, R. D. (1968). A model of seed dormancy. *Bot. Rev.*, **34**, 1–31.
BEEVERS, L. (1975). *Nitrogen Metabolism in Plants*. Contemporary Biology Series, Edward Arnold, London.
HAYWARD, H. E. (1938). *The Structure of Economic Plants*. Macmillan, New York.
JAMES, W. O. (1953). *Plant Respiration*. Clarendon Press, Oxford.
LANG, A. (1965). Effects of some internal and external conditions on seed germination. In *Encyclopedia of Plant Physiology*, ed. RUHLAND, W., **15** (2), 848–93. Springer-Verlag, Berlin.
MAYER, A. M. and POLJAKOFF-MAYBER, A. (1963). *The Germination of Seeds*. Pergamon Press, Oxford.

SELECTED REFERENCES

CHEN, D. and OSBORNE, D. J. (1970). Ribosomal genes and DNA replication in germinating wheat embryos. *Nature, Lond.*, **225**, 336–40.

CHERRY, J. H. (1963). Nucleic acid changes in the storage tissues of seeds during germination. *Biochem. biophys. Acta*, **68**, 193–8.

DOBRAZANSKA, M., TOMASZEWSKI, M., GRZELCZAK, Z., REJMAN, E. and BUCHO-WICZ, J. (1973). Cascade activation of genome transcription in wheat. *Nature, Lond.*, **244**, 507–9.

FOLKES, B. F. and YEMM, E. W. (1958). The respiration of barley plants. X. Respiration and the metabolism of amino-acids and proteins in germinating grain. *New Phytol.*, **57**, 106–31.

HALLAM, N. D., ROBERTS, B. E. and OSBORNE, D. J. (1972). Embryogenesis and germination in rye (*Secale cereale* L.). II. Biochemical and fine structural changes during germination. *Planta*, **105**, 293–309.

INGLE, J., BEEVERS, L. and HAGEMAN, R. H. (1964). Metabolic changes associated with the germination of corn. I. Changes in weight and metabolites and their redistribution in the embryo axis, scutellum and endosperm. *Pl. Physiol., Lancaster*, **39**, 735–40.

MARCUS, A. (1969). Seed germination and the capacity for protein synthesis. *Symp. Soc. exp. Biol.*, **23**, 143–60.

VARNER, J. E., BALCE, L. V. and HUANG, R. C. (1963). Senescence of cotyledons of germinating peas. Influence of axis tissue. *Pl. Physiol., Lancaster*, **38**, 89–92.

VARNER, J. E. and RAM CHANDRA, T. (1964). Hormonal control of enzyme synthesis in barley endosperm. *Proc. natn. Acad. Sci. U.S.A.*, **52**, 100–6.

3

Energy Economy

INTRODUCTION

At the level of cellular physiology and biochemistry, energy economy would imply the free energy changes involved in metabolic reactions and mechanisms of energy transfer at the molecular and atomic level. In ecology it would be concerned with energy flow between the individuals and populations which make up living communities and between the plants and their environment. Here we shall confine our discussion to a consideration of energy flow within the whole plant and between the plant and its environment.

The photosynthesis of green plants is the means by which the thermo-nuclear energy of the sun transmitted to the earth as electromagnetic radiation is transformed into the chemical energy of organic substances. The rate and efficiency of this conversion process are therefore central to any consideration of the energy relationships of plants. The efficiency of photosynthesis can be thought of in terms of the whole earth, of populations of plants (semi-natural vegetation or agricultural crop), of the whole plant, of the individual photosynthetic organ (leaf or other green organ), of the chloroplasts or of the photo- and thermochemical reactions involved. Thus when considering the whole of photosynthesis on earth it must be borne in mind that about one-third of the input of solar energy is involved in the evaporation of water, that considerable parts of the land surface are bare of vegetation, that only radiation within a narrow wavelength range (400 to 700 nm—closely corresponding to the visible range of the human eye) is utilizable in photosynthesis and that the rate of recycling of carbon limits the availability of carbon dioxide (the air contains some 3 parts in 10 000 by volume of CO_2).

CHAPTER 3

Similarly when assessing the photosynthetic efficiency of leaves one must consider the extent to which they shade one another, how much of the light striking the leaf is reflected and how much absorbed, how much of the total absorption is effected by the chloroplasts, how far the photosynthetic activity of the chloroplasts is limited by carbon dioxide availability and so on. 'Literally thousands of individual calculations are needed to compute what happens when sunlight illuminates a cornfield' (Duncan 1967). Our principal concern is to consider the main factors which operate to determine photosynthetic efficiency. Elsewhere certain other ways in which solar energy enters into plant physiology will be considered (Chapters 4, 11 and 12).

At one end of a complex chain we have the total available energy within the wavelength range utilizable in photosynthesis, at the other end either an energy gain in the form of living matter, or, at the level of the human economy, a utilizable end-product, the actual commercial harvest of plant material. At each step in this chain some energy loss will occur; the ultimate efficiency will be compounded of the efficiencies of the separate component processes. Only then by attempting to assess the efficiency of these separate steps can we hope, as experimentalists, to recognize where and how improvements may be achieved in the energy conversion machinery represented by the living green plant.

ENERGY FLOW IN THE PLANT

Photosynthesis leads to the formation of organic compounds from water and carbon dioxide and in flowering plants the first stable products are predominantly sugars. Such sugars form the starting point for the synthesis of other organic plant constituents including macromolecules such as those of proteins, polysaccharides and nucleic acids. These and many other organic molecules are involved in cellular architecture. Thus we must consider the efficiency with which the energy of the sugar molecules, formed in photosynthesis, is retained in the multitude of different organic substances of the living cell. During respiration the energy of these sugar molecules becomes redistributed among the intermediates of sugar breakdown (sugar phosphates and organic acids) and certain cell constituents (such substances as ATP, adenosine triphosphate) whose special function is to act as the energy currency of the plant. Energy-rich molecules, such as those of ATP, are not only required in many of the chemical reactions involved in the synthesis of cell constituents but, again through chemical processes, as energy sources which enable the cells of the plant to do work (growth, movement, transport of solutes and so on). Here again the efficiency with which, at this stage, the energy derived from the primary sugar molecules is used in the performance of work represents an important aspect of the energy economy.

The flow of chemical substances between the separate organs and tissues of the plant can also be considered in terms of energetics. Clearly all the tissues which are not photosynthetic depend upon the photosynthetic cells for their primary supply of energy. Sugars and substances derived from them flow from the expanded leaves to the developing parts of the shoot system (leaf and stem primordia, secondary growth regions of the stems, flowers and fruits) and to the root system. This, however, is not entirely a one-way traffic. The root for instance is the site of synthesis of organic substances which are not only involved in root metabolism but are transported to the shoot. In a land plant the root is also responsible for almost all water and mineral salt absorption and the water and minerals then move from the absorbing regions of the root to supply all other parts of the growing plant. In any attempt to evaluate the patterns of energy flow resulting from the movement of chemical substances account must be taken of the evidence that plants not only exchange heat with their surroundings but also lose to their external environment appreciable quantities of materials: water vapour and gases by diffusion and air movement, chemical substances, including essential organic cell constituents, by the solvent action of rain and soil moisture and entire parts of their body by abscission (e.g. leaves, petals, fruits) and by death or mechanical damage (almost any part of their root or shoot system).

The energy flow patterns within the plant and between the plant and its environment must proceed in a highly co-ordinated way if they are to be compatible with the normal growth and development of the organism. A complex control system must determine the energy flow patterns. Our knowledge of the control systems which regulate cellular metabolism is far from complete. Still less can we identify and describe the mechanism of action of the control systems which in complex organisms are superimposed on those regulating particular metabolic pathways. Clearly in plants, growth-regulating substances (plant hormones) represent a very important element in this organismal control of energy-flow as will be appreciated by a study of Chapters 8–12.

ENERGY CONVERSION IN PHOTOSYNTHESIS—QUANTUM EFFICIENCY

The overall process of photosynthesis can be expressed by the Van Niel equation:

$$CO_2 + 2H_2O \longrightarrow (CH_2O) + H_2O + O_2 \quad \Delta G = 117 \text{ kcal} \quad (3.1)$$

where ΔG is the change in free energy (G).

This reaction in the direction of the arrow involves a gain in free energy (ΔG has a positive value) and in photosynthesis this energy is fed in as radiant energy. The gain in free energy occurring in the Van Niel equation can be calculated for defined conditions. The reduction of one gram molecule of CO_2 in accordance with this equation, assuming the concentration of reduction product (sugar) to be 0·05 M and oxygen and carbon dioxide concentrations to be those normally present in air, involves a gain in free energy of 117 kcal. However we now know that radiant energy is involved in photosynthetic phosphorylation reactions which can be summarized thus:

$$2H_2O + 3ADP + 2NADP^+ + 3P_i \longrightarrow$$
$$3ATP + O_2 + 2NADPH + 2H^+ \quad \Delta G = 135 \text{ kcal} \quad (3.2)$$

(P_i = inorganic phosphate, ATP = adenosine triphosphate, ADP = adenosine diphosphate, NADP = nicotinamide adenine dinucleotide phosphate), and that subsequently the ATP and reduced adenine nucleotide (NADPH) effect CO_2 reduction. At normally operating concentrations this overall reaction of photosynthetic phosphorylation involves per gram molecule of oxygen evolved a gain in free energy of about 135 kcal.

If we take such a figure as indicative of the gain in free energy of the primary or photochemical acts of photosynthesis we can go on to determine experimentally how effectively radiant energy is transformed into chemical energy by photosynthetic cells or plant organs.

Although we can think of light as a continuous wave motion, the energy of light comes in discrete units or packets termed *photons*, each associated with a quantum of energy. Quanta are indivisible and photochemical reactions involve molecules or atoms activated by the absorption of a single quantum or, in successive steps, of several quanta. The quantum is not a constant; its energy value is inversely related to the wavelength of the radiation. The magnitude of the quantum (E') is given by the equation

$$E' = h v \text{ ergs} \quad (3.3)$$

where v is the frequency of the radiation ($v = c/\lambda$ where c = velocity of light, 3×10^{10} cm/s and λ = wavelength in cm) and h is Planck's constant ($= 6·62 \times 10^{-27}$ erg-seconds).

The quantum (E') relates to the energy unit absorbed by an individual molecule or atom. To convert this to the level of the gram molecule it must be multiplied by Avogadro's number (the number of molecules per gram molecule $= 6·02 \times 10^{23}$) for which the symbol is N. Therefore:

$$E'N = h v N = E \text{ (the Einstein) ergs} \quad (3.4)$$

This is the amount of energy acquired by 1 gram molecule when each individual molecule absorbs 1 quantum.

To express the Einstein in kilocalories its value in ergs is divided by 4.18×10^{10} thus

$$E = hvN = \frac{6.62 \times 10^{-27} \times 3 \times 10^{10} \times 6.02 \times 10^{23}}{\lambda \times 4.18 \times 10^{10}} \text{ kcal}$$

For red light of wavelength (λ) 670 nm ($= 6.7 \times 10^{-5}$ cm) we have

$$E = \frac{6.62 \times 10^{-27} \times 3 \times 6.02 \times 10^{23}}{6.7 \times 10^{-5} \times 4.18} = 42.7 \text{ kcal}$$

For blue light of wavelength 400 nm, $E = 71.5$ kcal.

The smallest whole number of Einsteins of red light which can supply the energy needed to effect the evolution of a gram molecule of O_2 by equation 3.2 is 4 (equivalent to $4 \times 42.7 = 171$ kcal). If only 4 Einsteins are needed per gram molecule O_2 evolved by a photosynthetic cell or organ, then this aspect of photosynthesis is proceeding with 100% efficiency (although an energy loss is involved since the free energy gain in equation 3.2 is only 135 kcal). In so far as more than 4 quanta are required the efficiency is below 100%, and the quantum yield (number of O_2 molecules released per quantum) is less than 0.25.

To determine the quantum efficiency or quantum yield the concentration of CO_2 must be sufficiently high so that it does not operate as a limiting factor and the light intensity must be low, working within the range where photosynthesis rate rises most steeply with rise in light intensity. The main experimental difficulties are: (1) the correction for simultaneous respiration; (2) the problem of undefined periods in light and in near darkness when using dense stirred algal suspensions and low incident light intensity to eliminate loss of light by scattering; (3) calculation of light scattering where this is a quantitatively important factor; (4) demonstration that an equilibrium rate of O_2 evolution has been established. However, despite these difficulties it has been found by a variety of methods and with both single-celled algae and with leaves that 8–12 quanta are needed per molecule of oxygen (quantum yield: 0.125– 0.084 moles/quantum). Against a theoretical requirement of 4 quanta/ molecule O_2 this implies a quantum efficiency of 30–50%. Further it has been shown that the quantum efficiency is more or less constant over the range of wavelength 400–670 nm, so that, in terms of kilocalories, red light is most efficient. For instance if the quantum requirement is taken = 10 per O_2 molecule and the value $E = 42.7$ kcal, the percentage efficiency calculated for equation 3.2 is c. 32%, and from equation 3.1 c. 27%. In explanation of these findings on efficiency it should be emphasized that a proportion of the absorbed radiation will be transformed into kinetic energy causing a rise in temperature and loss of long wavelength heat waves and that this effect will occur in many other kinds of molecules than those of the chloroplast pigments. Again a proportion of the activated chloroplast pigments lose their energy of activation within 10^{-8} to 10^{-6} seconds by emitting fluorescent radiation.

PHOTOSYNTHESIS OF A CROP—CROP EFFICIENCY

If we now turn our attention to estimates of the photosynthetic efficiency of whole plants or of a crop it is very important to consider the time scale. Values may be based upon a period of photosynthesis on a bright summer day, a whole 24-hour period, a growing season or over a year. Again we have to consider whether photosynthesis has been measured directly (e.g. by O_2 evolution or CO_2 uptake) or in terms of dry weight gain or crop yield.

The radiation reaching the surface of the earth from the sun has a maximum intensity of about 1·6 cal/cm² per minute. Forty-seven per cent of this energy is in the 400–700 nm wavelength range and therefore utilizable in photosynthesis.

In a study of photosynthesis under field conditions in a field of maize undertaken at the time of maximum coverage at Ellis Hollow, New York, it was found that, with incident solar radiation of 1·0 cal/cm²/min, the recorded CO_2 uptake was $0\cdot3 \times 10^{-6}$ g/cm²/s, or corrected for respiration $0\cdot345 \times 10^{-6}$ (and converted to moles CO_2, $0\cdot08 \times 10^{-7}$ moles CO_2/cm²/s or $4\cdot8 \times 10^{-7}$ moles CO_2/cm²/min). From these data the quantum yield (molecules of CO_2 fixed per quantum) can be calculated from the expression:

$$\text{Quantum yield} = \frac{\text{moles converted}}{\text{Einsteins absorbed}} \qquad (3.5)$$

$$= \frac{4\cdot8 \times 10^{-7} \text{ moles/cm}^2/\text{min}}{(0\cdot47 \times 1\cdot0 \text{ cal/cm}^2/\text{min}) (16 \times 10^{-6})}$$

$$= 0\cdot064$$

where 0·47 is the fraction of the incident solar energy between 400–700 nm, and $16 \times 10^{-6} = R$, the Einsteins absorbed per incident calorie. The value 0·064 is to be compared with the best laboratory values for quantum yield of 0·125.

The value of 0·064 corresponds to 16 quanta per molecule of CO_2, i.e. about 50% of the efficiency achieved in determining the minimum quantum requirement. This implies from equation 3.1 an efficiency of 14% of the visible radiation or some 6·6% of the total incident radiation.

This however is the photosynthetic efficiency and, to work out the efficiency of net fixation of CO_2 per day, we have to reduce the figure by the respiratory loss of CO_2 throughout the 24 hour period. This reduces the figure by 30–50% even under conditions of a high photosynthetic rate during the day. Thus at the time when the crop is at maximum efficiency we can expect only 3–4·5% efficiency of carbon gain relative to incident utilizable energy falling on unit crop area per day. Using the data for the maize crop quoted above and with total radiation per day taken as 500 cal/cm² (this would be just over 8 hours at 1·0 cal/cm²/min), and assuming a respiratory loss of carbon equivalent to 33% of that fixed by photosynthesis then the calculated net gain is just over 20 g C/m²/day. This value can be compared with actual values averaging the carbon gains per day over the growing season for various 'crops' (Table 3.1).

Table 3.1   Carbon gains per day averaged over the year or growing season for some natural, semi-natural and cultivated plant communities. (Data quoted by Westlake, D. F., 1963, Comparisons of plant productivity, *Biol. Rev.*, **38**, 385–425.)

Vegetation	g C/m²/day (mean for growing season)
Marine phytoplankton, Denmark	0·32
Birch forest, England	2·2
Tropical rain forest	7·6
Maize crop, Minnesota	8·1
Sugar cane, Java	11·1

Lowered photosynthetic efficiencies due to such factors as water stress, limiting temperatures, mineral deficiency, disease and limiting CO_2 availability are involved in these actual seasonal averages. However of great importance in actual yields are: (1) the fact that over much of the growing season energy strikes bare ground, not the leaves of the crop, and that at the height of growth (time of maximum leaf area index, i.e. ratio of total leaf area to the ground area occupied) many leaves may be so shaded that they have very low net photosynthesis; (2) the seasonal energy input which at many times may be limiting carbon fixation; a cloudy sky reduces the mid-day light intensity to between 5–15% of that from a cloudless sky. Latitude and season limit the maximum input at different points on the earth's surface. The maximum value at the latitude of London varies from 980 cal/cm²/day in summer, down to 170 cal/cm²/day in winter.

When all the actual losses are taken into account we begin to be able to predict the finding that, even under conditions of intensive agriculture, crop yields expressed as dry matter production relative to total incident energy work out at less than a 1% conversion of total available radiant into chemical energy. When it is further recognized that only a fraction of the dry weight yield is utilizable as food or in manufacture, the energy of the harvest may be as low as 0·2–0·5% of the solar energy input. Averaged out over the year the conversion will normally have a still lower value.

Studies in crop growth in relation to plant habit, climate and soil factors are now being carried out by techniques which reveal the factors limiting energy conversion in the growing crop. Thus in studies on the corn crop in the United States it has been shown that the leaf area index reaches a value of 4 but computer calculations indicate that a value of 8 is needed for maximum production. However to be effective this increased leaf area index will require plants not with horizontal or drooping leaves but with near vertical leaves. The plants with vertical leaves, if the plant breeder can provide them, will need to be planted at a higher density than now used and to be planted equidistant from one another rather than in rows. Again yield in corn is limited by the 35 days during which the grain grows; if this could be extended grain yield would be increased (a greater proportion of the dry matter would appear in the harvested grain). An effective crop plant should be rapidly growing and capable of close planting so that an effective leaf area index is rapidly established and the period reduced when the radiation strikes bare earth. Avoidance of water stress is important not only for rapid growth but to ensure that diffusion of carbon dioxide is not restricted by stomatal aperture. Under high light intensity fully open stomata are needed for maximum photosynthesis. From appropriate monitoring of such moisture stress, transpiration loss and light intensity, irrigation can be programmed to be most effective. At high light intensity the natural carbon dioxide level is often a limiting factor in photosynthesis and there are many instances reported of large yield increases of greenhouse crops from increasing the carbon dioxide level often up to values of c. 0·5%. There is however no good evidence that the low natural levels of carbon dioxide are seriously depleted within growing crops under conditions of high light intensity; the level of 0·03% in the air above the crop may, within the crop, fall to 0·027% during the day and rise to 0·042% during the night. Only under exceptional climatic conditions are bigger fluctuations than this recorded.

Photorespiration

There is evidence that at high light intensities photosynthesis is limited by the rate of CO_2 diffusion and by the affinity of the carboxylating enzyme, ribulose diphosphate (RUDP) carboxylase.

Maize, sugar cane, sorghum and other tropical grasses have at high light intensities rates of photosynthesis 2–3 times greater than sugar beet, tobacco, wheat and most other crop plants. The first group of plants can lower the external CO_2 level to a CO_2 compensation point which is almost zero (less than 5 p.p.m.), and the second group only to about 50 p.p.m. A steeper diffusion path of CO_2 is maintained in the first group and they are capable of higher rates of photosynthesis particularly under conditions when limited water stress may increase the diffusion resistance of the stomata. These plants are often referred to as C_4 plants because they fix CO_2 predominantly via phosphoenolpyruvate (PEP) carboxylase leading to formation of C_4 acids (particularly malic acid). After transport to the site of RUDP carboxylase some of the malic acid molecules release CO_2 which is assimilated by the normal photosynthetic carbon reduction (Calvin) cycle. The remainder of the acid molecules are reconverted to PEP, in reactions utilizing photosynthetic energy, which can again participate in CO_2 assimilation. The efficiency of PEP carboxylase in scavenging CO_2 enables these plants to achieve a very low CO_2 compensation point. The efficiency of the system is further improved by the structural organization of the plants. Many C_4 species have the PEP carboxylase system concentrated in the mesophyll cells, which are the outer cells of the photosynthetic tissue, while the Calvin cycle is mainly localized in the bundle sheath cells surrounding the vascular bundles. Thus the escape of CO_2 from the leaf is prevented by the highly efficient fixing system in the outer cells, and the final conversion to sugars and starch occurs in the bundle sheath, whence the products can be easily translocated away.

The plants in the second group (referred to as C_3 or Calvin cycle plants) fail to achieve this low compensation point; at high light intensity and lowered CO_2 availability at the site of RUDP carboxylase, much of their RUDP suffers breakdown, through the oxygenase activity of RUDP carboxylase, to give 3-phosphoglycerate and a C_2-compound phosphoglycoaldehyde. This latter compound then suffers dephosphorylation and oxidation first to glycollic acid and then to glyoxylic acid and finally decarboxylation with the loss of CO_2. These reactions (termed *photorespiration*), leading to the loss of some of the newly fixed CO_2 in light, are enhanced at high O_2 and low CO_2 concentrations and at high temperature (photorespiration can increase up to 8-fold by a rise in the temperature from 20 to $30°C$). Under such conditions photorespiration may reduce net photosynthesis by up to 50%. When this photorespiration is inhibited, e.g. by α-hydroxy-2-pyridinemethane sulphonate, the rate of photosynthesis in individual tobacco leaves and leaves of other C_3 species can reach the high values characteristic of C_4 plants (Table 3.2). Experimental and genetic repression of photorespiration might therefore be of importance in improving energy conversion in a number of important crop plants. However

Table 3.2 CO_2 budget for a tobacco leaf at 25° and 35 °C in high illumination and 300 p.p.m. CO_2. (Data from Zelitch, I., 1971, *Photosynthesis, Photorespiration and Plant Productivity*, Academic Press, New York.)

	mg CO_2 dm^{-2} hour^{-1}	
	25°	35°
Gross photosynthetic CO_2 uptake	− 25.0	− 47.0
CO_2 output from dark respiration	+ 3.0	+ 6.0
CO_2 output from photorespiration	+ 7.0	+ 26.0
Net CO_2 uptake observed	− 15.0	− 15.0
When photorespiration inhibited net CO_2 uptake observed	− 22.0	− 41.0

this hypothesis interprets photorespiration as having no useful purpose. If this is the case it is difficult to understand why it has not been eliminated by evolution. The alternative view is that the C_4 plants are such good crop plants not because they lack photorespiration but because they effectively return to the carbon reduction cycle, via the action of the PEP carboxylase of their mesophyll cells, the CO_2 evolved by respiration (including photorespiration).

Conversion of photosynthetic products into plant dry weight

When as in Table 3.1 we quote average C gain per day per m^2 of crop we are taking account not only of photosynthetic carbon fixation but of loss of carbon mainly by respiration and also in part by shedding of aged leaves or other organs and leaching out of metabolites by rain or soil moisture. CO_2 release in respiration is an index of energy release by the equation:

$$C_6H_{12}O_6 + 6O_2 \longrightarrow 6CO_2 + 6H_2O + 689 \text{ kcal} \qquad (3.6)$$

which indicates a release of some 2600 cal per g CO_2 evolved. This energy may be built back into the system by biosynthesis of new plant constituents, may be utilized to do work (ion accumulation, movement of substances within the plant and so on) or be lost as heat. Using the symbol E_{CO_2} for the energy release indicated in equation 3.6 we can write

$$E_{CO_2} = W + S + H \qquad (3.7)$$

W = physical work, S = synthesis, H = heat.

There are many examples in the literature indicating that 90–99% of E_{CO_2} is liberated as heat and that a very low percentage is used in biosynthesis and physical work. However most of these measurements relate to mature or senescent organs which have ceased growth or in which cell structure is being degraded. An interesting experiment is quoted by J. A. Richardson (*Physics in Botany*: Pitman and Sons, London, 1964) where E_{CO_2}, heat release and decrease in calorific value (E_{CV}) were followed during the first 6 days of germination of wheat grains. S in equation *3.7* above was calculated from $E_{CO_2} - E_{CV}$, and W from $E_{CV} - H$. Both values proved to be less than 3% of E_{CO_2}. If these values are accepted they indicate that a very small proportion of the energy released in respiration is used to transport sugars, amino acids and other metabolites from the endosperm to the embryo, to convert these into new embryo mass and to overcome the physical forces resisting embryo growth. They also suggest either that respiration is inevitably a highly wasteful process or may proceed in certain plant tissues at an unnecessarily high rate. In so interpreting equation *3.7* we are regarding heat release as a measure of energy wastage. However the living cell is a system of low entropy (a highly organized system) and the maintenance of this low entropy state (prevention of increasing chaos or randomness) will require the continuous expenditure of energy not reflected in net synthesis or recognizable work. The through-put of energy for this purpose could be measured as heat loss.

Various workers have studied the efficiency with which glucose is converted into mycelial dry weight or glucose carbon is converted into mycelial carbon in fungi. The relevance of such 'economic coefficients' to an understanding of the fate of the energy release in respiration is not always apparent since CO_2 evolution is often fermentative, or partly derived from fermentation and partly from aerobic respiration, and metabolites are often released in large amounts into the culture medium and hence do not contribute to mycelial dry weight or carbon content. In a study of carbon-balance in a culture of *Aspergillus niger* producing citric acid it was reported that the efficiency of conversion of glucose carbon to mycelium carbon ranged from 17–8% as the fermentation proceeded. Many values for the economic coefficients of fungi grown in dilute media for no longer than is necessary to utilize the supplied carbohydrate fall within the range 20–35%. In certain instances however very high efficiencies of sugar utilization have been recorded; yeast dry weights equal to 50–60% of the sugar consumed can apparently be achieved in cultures of Torula yeast (*Candida utilis*).

It seems clear that further critical work is required on the efficiency of utilization of the products of photosynthesis in green plants and of organic substrates by fungi. Such studies should reveal how far plants and plant tissues differ in this respect and reveal at what points in metabolism these differences arise.

FURTHER READING

SAN PIETRO, A., GREEN, F. A. and ARMY, T. J. (eds.) (1967). *Harvesting the Sun*. Academic Press, New York.

WHITTINGHAM, C. P. (1974). *The Mechanism of Photosynthesis*. Contemporary Biology Series, Edward Arnold, London.

ZELITCH, I. (1971). *Photosynthesis, Photorespiration and Plant Productivity*. Academic Press, New York.

4

Water Relations

Liquid water is absolutely necessary for life as we know it. Firstly it is the solvent and reaction medium of the cell; secondly it is a reactant in many metabolic processes and thirdly, as the hydration water associated with macromolecules, it forms part of the structure of protoplasm, existing as 'liquid ice' in an ordered but labile structure. The physico-chemical properties of water are unique; even heavy water (deuterium oxide, D_2O or deuterium hydroxide, DHO) is toxic. Additionally in plants, the turgor pressure of water-filled vacuoles gives mechanical rigidity to thin-walled tissues and some plant movements occur as a result of turgor pressure changes.

Although certain plant tissues may be able to endure periods of almost complete desiccation (see Chapter 7), they are while 'dry' metabolically inactive. When in an active state, most plant tissues contain 70–95% water. Plant cells can grow only when they are turgid and even small decreases in water content below full saturation may result in decreased growth rates. In the fungus *Polystictus versicolor*, the growth rate of the hyphae is directly proportional to their degree of hydration. Not only quantitative but qualitative changes in metabolism can be brought about by changes in water content. For example hydrolysis of starch to sugar occurs in many plant tissues as their water content decreases (Chapter 7).

WATER RELATIONS OF PLANT CELLS

The amount of water present in a plant cell (or tissue, or whole plant) at any one time will be determined by a balance between internal forces promoting water entry and environmental factors tending to withdraw water. According to fundamental thermodynamic principles, any system tends to assume the state of lowest possible free energy. If there are two water-containing systems in contact, and the free energy of water differs in the two systems, water will move *from the system of higher free energy to that of lower free energy*, till the free energy of water is equal in both systems; at equilibrium, there will be no net change in the water content of either system, though an exchange or flux of water, equal quantities moving in each direction per unit time, may still proceed. We can thus say when:

Free energy of cell water < free energy of external water then net flux will be *into* the cell, whereas when
Free energy of cell water > free energy of external water net flux will be *out of* the cell.

In order to predict the direction of movement of water into/out of plant cells, we thus need a measure of the free energy of the water.

Concept of water potential

The amount of free energy of water contributed by every mole of water in a system is the ***chemical potential of water*** (μ_w). This chemical potential cannot be measured directly, but the chemical potentials of water in different systems can be compared using for comparison the chemical potential of pure water (μ°_w) at 1 atm pressure and at the same temperature as the system being studied. We then define the ***water potential***, ψ (psi), of a system as the difference between μ_w, the chemical potential of water in the system and μ°_w, the chemical potential of pure water:

$$\psi = \frac{\mu_w - \mu^\circ_w}{\bar{V}_w}$$

The term $\bar{V}_w$ is the partial molal volume of water, i.e. the volume of 1 mole water (18 cm³). By dividing through by this value, the water potential (ψ) is obtained in convenient units (energy per mole water/volume per mole water; energy per unit volume; force per unit area or pressure). Thus water potential can be expressed either in energy units, e.g. erg/cm³, or pressure units, e.g. atmospheres or bars (1 bar = 10⁶ dynes/cm², or 0.978 atm).

Since the vapour pressure of water depends on its chemical potential, the water potential can also be expressed in terms of vapour pressure:

$$\psi = \frac{RT \ln \frac{e}{e^0}}{\bar{V}_w}$$

where R is the gas constant, T the absolute temperature, e the vapour pressure of water vapour in the system and e^0 the vapour pressure of pure water at the same temperature. Measurements of vapour pressure can therefore be used to obtain the water potential. Only if the cell is completely water-saturated (when the free energy of the cellular water equals that of pure water, i.e. $\mu_w = \mu^\circ_w$ and $\mu_w - \mu^\circ_w = 0$) does $\psi = 0$. This situation may naturally obtain in a submerged aquatic in equilibrium with almost pure water. Any decrease of the chemical potential of cellular water below that of pure water makes $(\mu_w - \mu^\circ_w)$ negative and hence ψ is negative (a positive value for ψ of a cell is possible only under the unlikely circumstance that the cellular water is at a higher chemical potential than pure water).

The water potential of a cell is determined by three forces: (i) **hydrostatic pressure**, P, in excess of 1 atm; this *increases* the free energy; (ii) **osmotic forces**, π (pi); these *decrease* the free energy; (iii) **colloidal** (matric, interface, imbibitional) **forces**, τ (tau); these also *decrease* the free energy. Hence:

$$\psi = P - \pi - \tau$$

where in a plant cell, P is represented by the turgor pressure of the cell wall (wall pressure), which tends to squeeze water out; π by the osmotic effects of low molecular weight solutes, mainly vacuolar, and τ by forces of colloidal hydration of protoplasmic (and where appropriate also vacuolar) macromolecules. Thus the water content of plant cells is maintained by osmosis and by colloidal hydration (imbibition). Osmosis, which depends upon the presence of solutes and the semi-permeable properties of the plasmalemma and tonoplast, controls water uptake and loss in vacuolated cells of high water content. Imbibitional forces are only important in controlling water uptake and retention by tissues of really low water content such as those of 'dry' seeds. Some workers have cited experimental observations apparently indicative of the development of hydrostatic pressures in vacuolated cells in excess of those to be expected from osmosis and reported water movement into growing cells in opposition to the expected direction of net water movement from osmotic considerations. On the basis of such observations it has been proposed that an 'active' pumping of water into plant cells can occur. However the evidence for such an 'active' component in water movement is inconclusive and will not be further discussed here.

Since the imbibitional forces are of little importance in highly vacuolated cells, the imbibition force component of their water potential is often ignored; considering the cell simply as an osmotic system one can write:

$$\psi = P - \pi.$$

Water movement can then be considered as resulting from a balance between osmotic forces tending to draw water in and the hydrostatic or turgor pressure of the wall opposing water entry. In older terminology, water relations of plants have often been expressed in terms of the diffusion pressure deficit, DPD, defined by:

$$\text{DPD} = (\text{osmotic pressure}) - (\text{wall pressure})$$
$$= \pi - P$$
$$= -\psi$$

Thus, numerically, water potential and DPD have the same value, but opposite signs.

A cell with a positive turgor pressure is said to be, to some degree, turgid. When the cell is at full turgor, its water uptake capacity is saturated; it no longer has a negative ψ or tendency to take up water. The osmotic pressure of the cell contents is then being balanced by an equal and opposite turgor pressure:

$$\psi = 0 \quad \text{and} \quad \pi = P.$$

On the other hand, as water is lost from the cell, its ψ decreases, both as a consequence of concentration of solutes in the cell, and of the reduction of turgor pressure. When the stage is reached where the protoplast no longer presses against the cell wall, the cell is said to be flaccid; then:

$$P = 0 \quad \text{and} \quad \psi = -\pi.$$

A plant part in which the cells are flaccid is wilted. If still more water is removed, the effect on the cell depends on the mode of removal. If this is accomplished by immersion in a solution of high osmotic pressure, plasmolysis results; the protoplast shrinks away from the wall, letting the external solution fill the space left between it and the wall. If water is removed by evaporation, the protoplast generally remains adpressed to the wall, and the walls cave in as the contents shrink. The degree of flexibility of the wall may then determine the amount of water that can be removed. Loss of water beyond a certain limit, which varies with the particular cell and with factors such as the rate of dehydration, is fatal (see Chapter 7).

Measurement of water potential

The water potential of a tissue can be measured by exposing replicate samples of the tissue to a graded series of water potentials, either by immersing the samples in solutions of known water potential, or by enclosing them in atmospheres of known vapour pressure. In a solution there is no excess hydrostatic pressure and the water potential is determined solely by osmotic forces:

$$P = 0 \qquad\qquad \psi = 0 - \pi = -\pi.$$

The water potential of a solution equals its **osmotic potential** (this is numerically equal to osmotic pressure, but with a minus sign). Water will move out of a tissue into solutions with water potentials more negative than that of the tissue and will move into the tissue from solutions with water potentials less negative than that of the tissue; in a solution whose water potential equals that of the tissue, there is no net change in tissue water content. Changes in the water content of the tissue are estimated by weighing the samples before and after immersion. If immersion of tissue in liquid is thought to be undesirable—errors can arise by penetration of liquid into tissue air spaces, giving misleading weight increases—the tissue samples can be exposed to atmospheres of known vapour pressure by suspension above the solutions in small chambers. The water potential in the atmosphere of each chamber will equal that of the solution in it and the tissue will react just as to the solutions, although equilibration with a vapour phase takes longer than when immersed in a solution.

Another method for measuring water potential is by means of the **thermocouple psychrometer**. The tissue is arranged to line the walls of a small chamber in which a thermocouple junction is enclosed, and which is incubated at a constant temperature. Water evaporates from the tissue into the chamber until, at equilibrium, the water potential of water vapour in the chamber is equal to the water potential of the tissue. A small drop of pure water is then introduced on to the thermocouple junction. As the water evaporates it cools the thermocouple, causing a current to flow and the magnitude of this is recorded. The current is proportional to the rate of cooling; the rate of cooling depends on the rate of evaporation which in turn depends on the vapour pressure in the chamber. The instrument is calibrated by measuring the currents produced in a series of atmospheres of known water potential and the water potential of the tissue can be accordingly obtained from the current reading.

WATER RELATIONS OF WHOLE PLANTS

The water relations of a whole plant are more complex than those of the individual cell. The concept of ψ can still be applied to the whole plant, though the formulae given above are meaningful only at the cell level. A plant contains cells differing in their capacities for water uptake and with different ψs at any given moment. Only the epidermis of a flowering plant is in direct contact with the environment; the environment of the inner cells consists of the surrounding cells and of the intercellular air space system. Stomata and air spaces allow atmospheric gases to penetrate tissues, but the composition of the atmosphere in these spaces is modified by the encompassing tissues; the concentration of water vapour is higher than outside and is determined by the ψs of the inner cells and the rate of diffusion of water vapour.

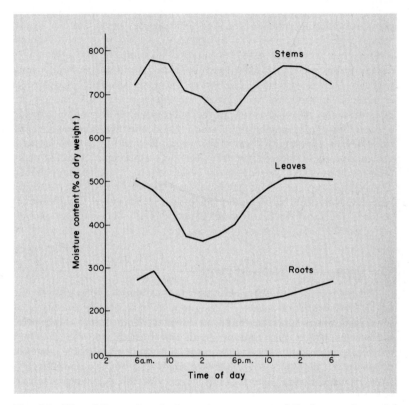

Fig. 4.1   Diurnal fluctuations in the moisture content of the leaves, stems and roots of field-grown sunflower, *Helianthus annuus*. (From Wilson, Boggess and Kramer, 1953, *Am. J. Bot.*, **40**, 97–100.)

Flowering plants are essentially land plants; the aquatic species represent a secondary evolutionary return to water. The evolution of land plants has depended upon the evolution of systems for the absorption, conduction and conservation of water. Their water is usually obtained by a root system invading a soil. Some tropical epiphytes absorb rainwater through special aerial roots and through scales and hairs on their leaves, and a few flowering plants such as *Tillandsia usneoides* derive their water entirely from atmospheric rain, mist and dew.

The photosynthetic mode of life of flowering plants requires the development of a large surface area for light absorption and for gaseous exchange, and in consequence of a large surface from which there is continual water evaporation or **transpiration**. The water potential of the atmosphere is nearly always very much more negative than that of the plant—often by several hundred atmospheres—and hence there is a great tendency for water loss from the plant. This loss of water by transpiration must be made good by absorption from the soil; there is a flow of water, the transpiration stream, from the roots to the transpiring surfaces. Only a very small fraction of the water absorbed by the roots is retained in the plant. For maize, an annual plant, this fraction has been estimated at less than 1% of the water absorbed during its growing season. During one single bright, sunny day, leaves may transpire several times their own weight of water. For example, a leaf of *Senecio jacobaea* growing on a sand-dune can transpire its own weight of water in 45 minutes. The water content of the aerial organs of a plant is generally lower in the daytime, when transpiration is higher, than during the night when the water content rises, the deficit being made good. The amount of water in the roots fluctuates much less (Fig. 4.1). If water loss exceeds water uptake, wilting ensues and death may follow.

The absorption of water by roots

The root systems of plants are often very extensive. Roots may extend much further underground than the shoot spreads into the air (Fig. 4.2). The roots of an apple tree may go down to about 10 m; and even in herbaceous plants this kind of depth can be reached, e.g. in alfalfa (*Medicago sativa*). Some measurements on the root system of a 4-month-old plant of rye (*Secale cereale*) grown singly in a box are reproduced in Table 4.1. The total external surface area of the rye shoot was only

Table 4.1 The extent and average daily growth rate of the root system of a 4-month-old plant of rye (*Secale cereale*) grown singly in a box. (After Dittmer, H. J., 1937, *Am. J. Bot.*, **24**, 417–20.)

Surface area of total root system (hairs included)	639 m^2
Area of root hairs	402 m^2
Length of total root system (hairs excluded)	622 km
Length of root hairs	10 620 km
Average daily growth rate of roots (hairs excluded)	4·99 km
Average daily growth rate of root hairs	89 km

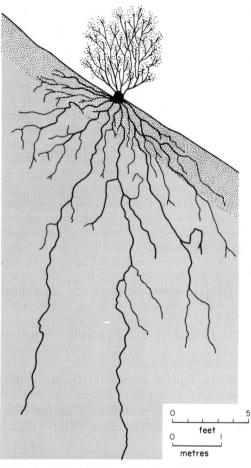

Fig. 4.2 Diagrammatic sketch of root system of a Californian woody shrub, the chamise (*Adenostoma fasciculatum*). (From Hellmers, Horton, Juhren and O'Keefe, 1955, *Ecology*, **36**, 667–78.)

4·61 m². If to this is added the internal surface area of the shoot, that is, the area of cells bordering the internal air spaces, then the total surface area of the shoot was 27·9 m². The root surface area was 22 times this value. Root hairs contribute considerably to the surface area of the root. Root hair area is included in the root area quoted in Table 4.1; estimated separately, it was 1·7 times that of the remainder of the root surface. In other species, root hair areas amounting to 8–12 times that of the rest of the root have been recorded although many of these observations have been made on roots grown in moist air when the root hairs are more abundant than in the soil. Not only do the root hairs increase the absorbing surface, but they make very intimate contact with the soil, bending round soil particles and penetrating into crevices. The extent to which soil is filled by roots may be appreciated from the fact that the entire root system of the above-mentioned rye plant was contained in less than 0·06 m^3 of soil.

Most of the absorption takes place near the growing root tips where the epidermis (piliferous layer) is thin-walled and root hairs are present. As the root tissues mature, the epidermis with its root hairs is replaced by a more impermeable suberized periderm. For most efficient water uptake, root growth must continuously regenerate the absorbing zone behind each growing root apex. Continuous growth is also necessary to enable roots to invade new soil. This can be very important under conditions of water stress for there is very little movement of water in soil beyond downward drainage directly after water addition. Water will not move to a substantial extent to the roots, and the only way in which the roots can reach a further supply of water is by growth. Positive hydrotropism may be important in directing root growth towards soil water (see Chapter 10). Roots can grow very rapidly; a rate of 10 mm per day is stated to be common for grasses; maize roots can extend 50–60 mm per day. The average daily increase in length of the total root system of the rye plant (Table 4.1) was calculated to be almost 5 km per day.

Though the root hair zones provide the chief absorbing surfaces water uptake through older regions is still appreciable, particularly during conditions of water shortage and at times when root growth is slow, such as winter. Points of emergence of lateral roots break the suberized layers and make regions of entry for water.

The route of water movement

The main channel for upward movement of water in the plant is the *xylem*. When the tissues outside the xylem in a short length of woody stem are peeled off, the conduction of water beyond the stripped region continues unimpeded. The xylem vessels at least in young wood are filled with a watery sap and dyes and Indian ink can be seen to move in the xylem. During the later nineteenth century, several workers, notably Eduard Strasburger, demonstrated that the water passes through non-living tissues by showing that strong poisons moved up to the leaves of trees, and that a second aqueous solution could move up after the passage of the poisonous solution, which would have killed any living cells in its path. Water conduction continues through heat-killed stems. Chilling has no effect on the rate of water movement, as long as the temperature is kept above the freezing point of the xylem sap. When xylem vessels are experimentally blocked by mercury or cocoa butter, water movement is strongly inhibited. The chief conducting elements of the xylem are considered to be the vessels which can be regarded as well suited for mass flow of liquid. The diameters of vessel units range from 20 to 400 μm; even 500–600 μm is attained in some lianas. Vessel lengths range from a few centimetres to many metres; in some trees, some continuous vessels run right from the crown down to the roots. In woody perennials, the older parts of the xylem lose their conducting capacity; the vessels become air-filled or blocked by tyloses and deposits of gums and resins. The water moves then only through the young sapwood elements. In ring-porous species, conduction is usually confined to the current year's growth; in diffuse-porous wood, the few outermost annual rings are utilized.

The rate of water movement is very variable; Table 4.2 gives examples of maximum rates attained in a number of species. In any one plant the rate is also highly variable, depending on environmental conditions. Among the species quoted in Table 4.2, the order of increasing speed of movement is also the order of increasing anatomical development towards wider and more numerous vessels in the xylem. In conifers, which lack vessels and depend on tracheids only for transport, water movement is much slower than in angiosperms and the conductivities for water of conifer woods are much lower than those of the woods of most angiosperms.

Since the xylem of the root is a central core of tissue, water must pass through the epidermis (piliferous layer), cortex, endodermis and pericycle to reach the xylem vessels (Fig. 4.3). It is still disputed whether this radial movement proceeds mainly through intercellular spaces, cell walls, cytoplasm or vacuoles. Movement through intercellular spaces does not appear very likely, since the spaces are generally air-filled. In the epidermis and the endodermis the cells are closely packed without air

Table 4.2 The mid-day maximum speeds of the transpiration stream, measured by observation of dye movement or heat conduction. (After Huber, B., 1956, *Encyclopedia of Plant Physiology*, ed. Ruhland, W., **3**, 541–82, Springer-Verlag, Berlin.)

Species	Speed, metres/hour
Evergreen conifers	1·2
Mediterranean sclerophylls	0·4–1·5
Deciduous diffuse-porous trees	1–6
Deciduous ring-porous trees	4–44
Herbaceous plants	10–60
Lianas	150

spaces; in these tissues at least, water must pass through some part of the cells. The radial walls of the endodermal cells at the level of most active water absorption of the root develop Casparian strips which resemble suberin in chemical reactions. It has therefore been frequently suggested that at the endodermis, if nowhere else, water is forced to pass through the protoplasts of living cells, and that this layer of cells

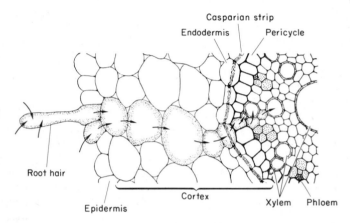

Fig. 4.3 Diagram of root cross-section, showing the tissues through which water and minerals move when passing from the soil solution to the xylem. (From Esau, 1960, *Plant Anatomy*, Wiley, New York and London.)

thereby regulates water movement from soil to xylem. Direct measurement of the water permeability of endodermal cell walls has not yet been achieved, but there is evidence which supports the above suggestion. There is a view that the cytoplasmic contents of all the cells of the root constitute a continuous unit, the symplast, and that once water has entered the cytoplasm of a root cell, it can move from cell to cell via plasmodesmata without the necessity of crossing any more outer cell membranes (see also Chapter 5 and Fig. 5.2, p. 80).

In a herbaceous plant with separate vascular strands, any part of the root system normally supplies those parts of the stem and its append-ages which are directly above it, these being the parts with which it is in direct vascular connection, so that lateral movement does not occur or is very restricted. If, however, part of the root system is deprived of water, the overlying aerial parts then receive their water supply from other root sectors indicating an activation of lateral movement. In trees with a continuous cylinder of wood, dye injection has shown that the path of water movement frequently winds in a spiral round the stem, but this follows the spiral arrangement of the conducting cells in the wood and involves longitudinal not lateral movement.

The motive forces in water movement—Root pressure and transpiration pull

The movement of water in the xylem vessels must involve either pumping under pressure or pulling (lifting) under tension. Capillary rise (a surface tension phenomenon) could not account for a rise of more than 1 metre in the finest vessels (many plants are much taller than this, some reaching 90–100 m!) and would still require the operation of an extracting force.

In certain circumstances, evidence has been obtained that the xylem sap is under positive hydrostatic pressure. Evidence in favour of this from inserting manometers into the wood has been questioned on the grounds that the pressure registered is an exudation pressure from injured living cells of the xylem not directly involved in water movement. However in a number of instances (when such pressures have been recorded) it has also been shown that decapitation of the plants just above ground level leads to continuing exudation from the exposed vessels in the root stump. A manometer fitted over such a bleeding root stump records the pressure known as the *root pressure*. In many cases root pressures of up to 1–2 atmospheres have been recorded. In excised tomato roots in culture root pressures apparently of up to 7–8 atmospheres occur. The development of this pressure is dependent on conditions favourable to the metabolic activity of the roots. No positive root pressure is found when the roots are subjected to treatments inhibiting metabolic activity such as lack of oxygen, addition of respiratory inhibitors, low temperatures, or starvation. Root pressure is regarded as the outcome of an osmotic mechanism: water from the soil moves through the root tissues along a gradient of osmotic potential (OP) (p. 46), a negative ψ being maintained in the xylem by continuous secretion of salts or other osmotically active substances into the xylem sap (see Chapter 5). In cases where root pressure can be demonstrated it has been shown that the OP of the xylem sap is more negative than that of the external solution (Table 4.3). When the OP of the solution external to the root is suddenly decreased, the rate of exudation falls and may become negative (liquid is drawn into the vessels at the cut surface); roots maintaining a root pressure have been described as behaving like sensitive quick-response osmometers.

Drops of liquid sometimes appear at leaf tips and edges when plants are maintained in a humid atmosphere: this phenomenon, termed *guttation*, results from the forcing out of xylem sap under pressure through pores overlying vein endings (see Chapter 6). The salt concentra-

Table 4.3   The effect of varying the osmotic potential (OP) of the solution bathing the roots on the osmotic potential of the exudate from the stumps of decapitated plants of tomato (*Lycopersicon esculentum*). (After Kramer, P. J., 1959, *Plant Physiology*, ed. Steward, F. C., **2**, 607–730, Academic Press, New York and London.)

	Normal salt plants			Low salt plants
	May 24	May 25	May 26	June 5
OP of culture solution, atm	−0·49	−0·54	−0·60	−0·82
OP of stump exudate, atm	−2·40	−1·50	−2·18	−2·21

tion in the guttated fluid is nevertheless lower than in the xylem sap (suggesting some absorption of salts by the leaf cells) although markedly dependent upon the composition of the solution bathing the roots. Both bleeding from exposed root stumps and guttation exhibit a repeating rhythm during successive 24 hour periods, with maxima usually at mid-day (Fig. 4.4).

Although the development of positive root pressure is well authenticated, there are many cases where it cannot be invoked to account for water movement. The observed pressures are as a rule too low to raise and move water against a frictional resistance to the required level. Some species apparently never develop root pressure. In deciduous trees of temperate habitats, root pressures are measurable in the spring before the leaves open; however, once the leaves expand and rapid transpiration starts, positive root pressures can no longer be detected. The *quantity* of water that can be moved by root pressure seems to be very limited. Wheat seedlings, which can transpire 2·6–3·0 ml water per hour, can exude by root pressure only 0·5 ml per hour. In many cases maximum bleeding rates are only 1–2% of the rate of water loss occurring by transpiration. Root pressure persists only whilst the water yielding capacity of the soil is high. In beans, root pressure uptake was stopped when the OP of the solution external to the isolated roots had a value of −1·9 atm whereas intact plants could extract water from a solution of −14·7 atm OP. Moreover, during periods of rapid water movement, the evidence indicates that the xylem sap is not under positive pressure but under tension (negative pressure). If, when this is the case, a cut is made into the xylem under a dye solution, the dye moves instantaneously into the xylem and travels very rapidly both upwards and downwards from the cut. Lateral shrinkage of tree trunks detected by sensitive calipers (the dendrograph), and shrinkage of individual xylem vessels observed microscopically, have been reported to occur as water movement begins or is speeded up by enhanced transpiration. These observations accord with the development of longitudinal tensions in the conducting vessels.

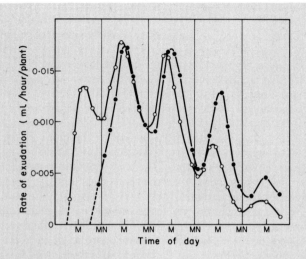

Fig. 4.4 Diurnal rhythm in the rate of exudation of de-topped sunflower plants (*Helianthus annuus*). Plants were decapitated at different times of day, as indicated by the broken lines, but the time of decapitation did not influence the rhythm, which shows maxima at midday (M) and minima at midnight (MN). (From Grossenbacher, 1939, *Am. J. Bot.*, **26**, 107–9.)

There is a diurnal pattern of water movement in trees, water movement beginning in the morning (as transpiration begins) and starting first in the upper branches. In conformity with this there occurs a downward moving wave of contraction in diameter of the branches and trunk. It has been demonstrated that transpiring twigs can pull water against an artificial resistance more effectively than can a vacuum pump; for instance leafy twigs can raise a column of mercury to heights significantly in excess of an atmosphere (76 cm). On the basis of such evidence it is generally accepted that water movement in plants, and particularly in tall woody species, occurs primarily as a result of the water being pulled up to replace that lost in transpiration. We are therefore faced with the need to explain how water can be pulled up under tension to the height of the topmost leaves of a tall tree.

The transpiration–cohesion theory

A theory of the ascent of sap based on the cohesive properties of water was advanced independently by Dixon and Joly (1894) and Askenasy (1895), although earlier writers had postulated on less convincing arguments that water movement under tension was involved. The transpiration–cohesion theory visualizes that cells in contact with the external atmosphere or with the internal air space system of the plant are constantly losing water by evaporation. Their ψ decreases and as a result water moves to them by osmosis from the more deeply-seated cells with which they are in contact. These in turn replenish their loss from still deeper-lying cells, till water is extracted from the xylem by cells in contact with the conducting vessels, especially at the veinlet endings in the leaf. This removal of water from the xylem can be made good only by the further uptake of water from the soil by the roots. There is thus considered to exist an uninterrupted column of water moving under tension from the soil to the leaves. The energy for the movement comes from solar heat, which causes water to evaporate continually by supplying the latent heat of evaporation.

In the classical account given above osmosis has been postulated to cause movement of water between the fine vein endings and the inter-cellular spaces of the mesophyll. However here, as in the case of the radial movement of water across the root from soil to xylem, it is disput-able whether the water leaving the xylem passes mainly through cell walls, cytoplasm or vacuoles. Osmosis operates only where passage across cellular membranes is involved. According to one recent estimate, movement would be too slow if water had to diffuse from cell to cell; hence it is held that a large proportion of water movement passes through cell walls, which can deal with a movement of up to 50 times that which could flow under a similar tension through the protoplasts. Altogether, a view is emerging which regards the water in the plant as a continuous system but divided into a number of compartments: vacuolar, cyto-plasmic, xylem sap, cell wall and extracellular water. Exchange of water between all these compartments and the environment is possible, but the rapidity of such movement is limited by protoplasmic membranes and cell walls. The extracellular water is the most accessible to environmental influences, the vacuolar water the least accessible. When transpiration induces water movement in the plant, water will move by preference along routes where it does not encounter the resistance of cell membranes, that is on the outside of cells if extracellular water is present, otherwise within cell walls, and in the xylem. Only if the transpiration rate is high, and there is a shortage of water in the plant, will water move from the less accessible compartments into the flow.

The maintenance of water columns under tension depends, according to the cohesion theory, on the cohesive attraction of water molecules. Theoretically, this cohesion is very great; pure water, under appropriate conditions, should withstand at least 1300 atm tension. Dixon and Joly claimed to have demonstrated the development of tensions of 200–300 atm in sealed glass capillaries before the water columns in them cavitated (collapsed with vaporization). Later workers have queried the calculations of Dixon and Joly and concluded that the tensions developed in such capillaries are much lower. A more recent calculation taking into account the diameter of the xylem vessels, the nature of their walls, and the presence of solutes and dissolved gases in the xylem sap, puts the tensile strength of xylem sap *in situ* at only about 30 atm. A tension of 1 atm will raise water against an average resistance to flow in the xylem to a height of about 5 metres; thus a tension of 30 atm would suffice to raise water to 150 metres and even the lower estimate given above for the tensile strength of xylem sap *in situ* is sufficient to allow water movement into the crowns of the tallest trees by a transpiration pull. The maintenance of water columns under tension also requires a high tensile strength of the xylem cell walls to avoid collapse.

The direct measurement of tensions in the xylem *in situ* in intact plants has so far proved physically impossible, since the water column under tension is immediately disrupted by the insertion of any instrument. Xylem tensions have, however, recently been estimated on cut branches. On cutting, the sap retracts from the cut as the tension is released; the branch is then enclosed in a pressure chamber with the cut end protruding, and gas pressure is applied until sap re-appears at the cut end. The pressure necessary to achieve this is taken to be numerically equal to the original xylem tension. With this technique, tensions of 5 to 80 atm have been measured, the highest values occurring in halophytes and desert plants. The tension is greater in higher branches of trees than lower ones. Another indirect method is to measure the ψs of leaf cells or of living stem cells in contact with the xylem. In wilted plants of tomato (*Lycopersicon esculentum*, privet (*Ligustrum lucidum*) and cotton (*Gossypium barbadense*), leaf ψs have been found to reach -41, -70 and -77 atm respectively, while values of up to -143 atm have been obtained for wilting desert plants. The xylem sap is then assumed (without direct proof) to be under a tension of the same magnitude, since the tension must be balanced by the leaf cells if water is to move into the leaves. In the ivy (*Hedera helix*), leaf ψs decrease progressively up the plant, in accordance with the expected tension gradient. Such numerical values for the *in situ* tension thus support the cohesion theory.

Criticisms of the transpiration–cohesion theory

Reluctance in accepting the transpiration–cohesion theory has arisen because the great stability of the water-conducting system under natural conditions seems at variance with the metastable state of water columns under tension. Any break in the water column, or any introduction of an air bubble into a vessel, ought to stop the flow of sap through it; indeed, the breaking of a single twig might be expected to let air spread throughout the xylem of the whole plant. Yet clearly this does not happen in nature, nor do experimentally produced breaks in the column of xylem sap necessarily disrupt water movement. Twigs which are cut so as to allow air into the vessels will resume water uptake when the severed end is placed in water. Cuts can be made in woody stems, overlapping from opposite sides, one above the other, and impermeable barriers inserted in the cuts; sap movement in the xylem still continues, transpiration rate is unchanged, nor do the leaves above the cut show any sign of water stress—provided the cuts are a certain minimum distance apart (see below). In the winter xylem sap may freeze; the dissolved air is then trapped as bubbles in the ice and should remain as bubbles when the sap thaws—yet sap flow is resumed in the spring. Moreover water columns under tension in capillary tubes cavitate on the slightest mechanical shaking or tapping and the movement of plants by wind might therefore be expected to cause cavitation in the xylem. The hydrophilic nature of the vessel walls has been invoked as giving stability to the water columns but experiments have indicated that xylem sap in grapevine stem segments is much less stable towards tension than water in glass capillaries of comparable diameters. The xylem segments cavitated on centrifugation at tensions of 1–1·5 atm, rarely enduring 3 atm, whereas water in the capillaries withstood 10–17 atm. A technique has been developed by which cavitation can be demonstrated in intact plants or organs. The minute and quite inaudible 'noise' produced by the cavitation of a single xylem vessel is amplified by means of suitable electronic equipment to an audible click. The clicks can then be counted and/or tape-recorded to give a record of the course of cavitation. With this method it has been shown that cavitation occurs in intact plants when water is withheld from the roots or when water uptake is inhibited by chilling the roots (Fig. 4.5). During rapid drying out one can count several hundred clicks per minute in a wilting leaf; the cavitation starts well in advance of any visible wilting. When the water supply is restored the cavitation ceases and the plants recover from wilting, showing that water uptake is resumed in spite of the preceding cavitation. Cavitation has been observed in the field under natural conditions. All these observations are difficult to reconcile with the cohesion theory. However, no more satisfactory theory has been forthcoming and workers in this field have therefore considered how far such observations might still be compatible with a cohesion theory. It is quite clear that air *can* be introduced into the xylem in nature (by freezing, by cavitation due to water stress, by accidental breaks), or experimentally, without permanently or even temporarily stopping the overall flow. How is this to be reconciled with the need of continuous columns for the movement?

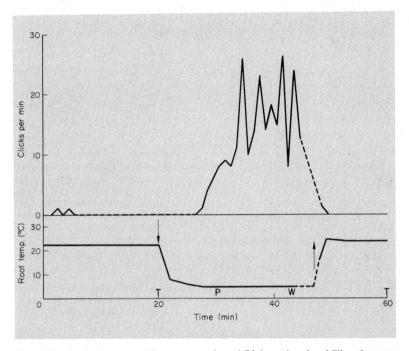

Fig. 4.5 Cavitation caused in a water-cultured *Ricinus* plant by chilling the roots to induce a water shortage. After 20 min at 22°C, during which almost no cavitation occurred, the roots were cooled to 5°C and clicking, indicating cavitation, began after a short delay. On raising of the root temperature to 25°C, the clicking quickly ceased. The state of the plant is indicated on the time axis as T=turgid; P=partially wilted and W=wilted. (From Milburn, 1973, *Planta*, **112**, 333–42.)

To account for the resumption of sap flow in the spring after freezing the suggestion has been made that air bubbles introduced into the xylem by freezing and thawing might be gradually forced into solution again by root pressures, which are highest in early spring, though the root pressures actually measured in trees have in general been too low to make this possible. Another proposition is that the old vessels in which air bubbles have developed do not resume conduction in the spring, their function being totally taken over by the newly differentiating vessels each season. Some studies of dye transport support this view. Scholander (1958) has made the interesting suggestion that the xylem should be regarded as 'a flooded continuous micropore system scattered with elongated macrocavities (vessels)'. The 'micropore system' is represented by the xylem cell walls from which water cannot be centrifuged out at 1700 **g** but can be

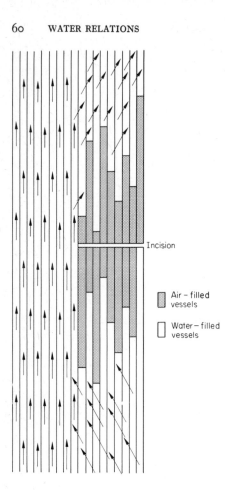

Fig. 4.6 Suggested pattern of sap- and air-filled vessels and the water flow pathways (arrows) after a stem incision, as seen in longitudinal section. Cross walls of uncut vessels are not shown. To allow sap flow in the presence of two overlapping cuts, the cuts must be spaced widely enough to leave some intact vessels between the cuts. (From Mackay and Weatherley, 1973, *J. exp. Bot.*, **24**, 15–28. By permission of the Clarendon Press, Oxford.)

squeezed out under pressure. As long as the whole system is water-filled, water movement is regarded as proceeding largely through the vessels since these offer the paths of least resistance. If however an airlock develops in a vessel, the water flow can proceed round it in the wall micropores. In support of this concept Scholander cites experiments on lianas, where the introduction of air into the xylem did not diminish the *rate* of water transport, but did increase the *resistance* to flow; this was presumably compensated by the development of correspondingly lower ψs in the leaves. Moreover, the airlocks in these lianas did not spread along the whole length of the vessels, suggesting the operation of valves, confining the air to segments about 60 cm to over 100 cm long. These valves can hardly be anything else but vessel cross-walls. These are perforated, but the pores, being very small, may stop the receding meniscus of a broken water column and prevent the next vessel unit from becoming air-filled. This mechanism is clearly of great importance as demonstrated by the experiments on overlapping cuts mentioned above. To allow water flow in the presence of such cuts, these must be separated by a minimum distance which depends on the vessel length of the species: the distance must be long enough to leave some intact vessels between the cuts. Apparently only the vessels actually cut through become air-filled, the flow of sap passes sideways around these and continues in the intact vessels at the side of each cut (Fig. 4.6). The cohesive system as a whole would not be seriously reduced in cross-sectional area by the presence of air in occasional segments. Further the total amount of xylem in a plant is generally much in excess over that needed to satisfy the water needs of the plant, as shown when large amounts of wood are removed. Cuts in stems severing up to 90% of the cross-section can be made without any detectable change in leaf water potential or transpiration; only the velocity of sap flow near the cut is increased.

When water movement is controlled by transpiration pull, roots act as passive absorbing surfaces. The roots offer a resistance to water movement as evidenced by the observation that the transpiration stream moves faster when the roots are cut off under water, or killed by heat. An active role was at one time postulated for the roots, on the grounds that transpiration is slowed down by chilling the roots, by depriving them of oxygen and by treating them with carbon dioxide or respiratory inhibitors. However these findings can be explained on the basis that all these treatments decrease the permeability of roots to water and a lowering of temperature additionally increases the viscosity of water. As the suction tension applied to the roots increases, their resistance decreases, so that regions further back from the tip are utilized under strong tensions. It has also been suggested that if rapid withdrawal of water from the roots causes flaccidity of root cells then spaces between the cells are opened up, facilitating water entry.

It therefore seems that under conditions when transpiration is rapid, the transpiration pull developed is responsible for water movement. Positive root pressures if developed will be of importance only when transpiration is slow, at night, and in spring before leaf expansion. A movement of sap in trees and shrubs in spring can also occur by osmotically motivated flow within the stems. In a number of tree species water moves from the inner regions of the xylem into the bark and into buds before any root pressure develops. Such movement occurs also in rootless shoots: the inner wood then becomes quite dry; normally it would have received water by a 'slow movement' from the roots. Associated with this outward flow of sap there is a conversion of starch to sugar in the bark. A similar conversion in the xylem parenchyma and medullary rays of woody plants in spring may promote water uptake.

Since submerged aquatic plants are able to absorb water over the entire plant surface, there would seem to be no need in such plants for water conduction. Notwithstanding this there is a slow movement of water in their xylem probably mediated by a root pressure. The movement could function to transport ions, or it may be an evolutionary relic with no physiological significance.

Factors controlling the rate of water uptake and movement

The rates of water absorption, water loss and consequently of water movement through the plant, are determined by a combination of plant and environmental factors. The environmental factors can be classified as soil and atmospheric: the amount and availability of soil water, soil temperature and soil aeration on the one hand; atmospheric temperature, humidity, wind and light, on the other. The plant factors are the number and degree of opening of stomata; the areas of the evaporating and absorbing surfaces and their ratio, and the water permeability of the absorbing and evaporating surface.

Soil conditions

The soil is a complex system of particles and pores of heterogeneous size. When a soil is saturated with water, all the pores are filled, but a well-drained soil does not remain water-saturated for long. Water drains away quickly under gravity from the larger spaces, but some is retained by capillary and surface tension forces within the smaller pores, and as adsorbed surface films around the soil particles. When a soil contains as much water as it can hold against gravity, it is said to be at *field capacity*. The amount of water present at this stage is a characteristic of the type of soil. Soils with fine particles have many small pores, and can hold more water than coarse soils. A clay soil at field capacity may hold 55% of water on a dry weight basis (i.e. 55 g water per 100 g dry soil), while a coarse sand may hold only 17% (Fig. 4.7). Once the water content has fallen to field capacity there is practically no more movement of liquid water in a soil, though water evaporates and escapes to the atmosphere. Since soil 'water' is a solution of ions, the plant must therefore absorb water from the soil against surface and osmotic forces.

The ψ of a soil at field capacity is very high, almost zero, and uptake by plants can proceed freely. As water is removed from the soil, the soil ψ decreases progressively (Fig. 4.7). At first, correspondingly lower ψs develop in the absorbing cells of the root. However as the water content of

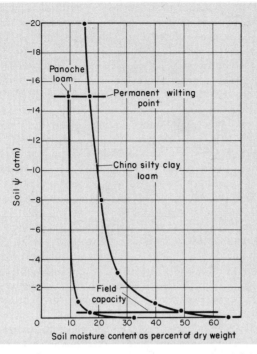

Fig. 4.7 The relation between soil moisture content and soil ψ in a sandy soil (Panoche loam) and a clay soil (Chino silty clay loam). (Adapted from Kramer, 1949, *Plant and Soil Water Relationships*. Used by permission of McGraw-Hill Book Co., New York and Maidenhead.)

the soil falls, a stage is reached when the ψ of the soil becomes so low (i.e. soil moisture stress so high) that the plant can no longer obtain enough water to compensate for transpiration losses, and it wilts. The soil moisture has reached the **permanent wilting point** (PWP), defined as the stage when the plant will not recover from wilting (even in a saturated atmosphere) unless water is added to the soil. Numerically, the PWP is expressed as the percentage of water left in the soil. Temporary wilting may occur before that, the plant wilting by day when transpiration is high, but recovering at night, when water uptake catches up with water loss. Once the PWP is reached, removals of very small amounts of water cause very large decreases in the soil ψ.

When the concept of the PWP was initially introduced, it was considered to be a characteristic of the soil rather than of the plant. Experiments seemed to indicate that different species growing in the same soil reached permanent wilting simultaneously; the soil ψ at the PWP in different soils appeared the same, about -15 atm. The water contents at which this is reached of course vary with the soil type, just as do the water contents at field capacity (see Fig. 4.7). More recent work indicates that this view is an oversimplification and the results in Table 4.4 show that each of the three species investigated reduces soil moisture to a different level at the PWP. This suggests that, for each plant, the PWP reached is when the turgor pressure of its leaf cells falls to zero. The lower leaves may reach permanent wilting before the upper. Table 4.4 shows moreover that, contrary to earlier views, there is still a measurable amount of water uptake by a plant after the PWP is passed. A progressive decrease in the ψ of the plants can be seen in the above results; the lower value of leaf ψ as compared with leaf sap osmotic potential is believed to be the result of wall tensions developed by cohesion between walls and protoplasts.

Most of the water uptake of a plant occurs when the soil moisture content is between field capacity and permanent wilting point. As the soil dries out, the forces opposing plant water uptake increase progressively and growth rate can be impaired by high water stress even before wilting is reached. This reduction of growth rate can aggravate the effect of water shortage, for the slowing down of root growth decreases the rate at which new areas of soil are tapped by the roots.

Soil aeration affects water uptake. An adequate oxygen supply is necessary for root growth and a lack of oxygen and a high concentration of carbon dioxide are reported to decrease the permeability of roots to

Table 4.4 Osmotic potential (OP) of expressed leaf sap, leaf ψ, soil ψ (all expressed in atmospheres) and soil water content as percentage of soil dry weight as three plant species were allowed to dry out gradually.
The 'first PWP' is the stage when the first leaves wilted permanently; at 'ultimate wilting' all leaves had wilted. The experiment was concluded when the plants were dying. (Adapted from Slatyer, R. O., 1957, *Aust. J. biol. Sci.*, **10**, 320–36.)

Species	At first PWP				At ultimate wilting		At conclusion of experiment			
	Leaf		Soil		Leaf	Soil	Leaf		Soil	
	OP Sap	ψ	ψ	Water con-tent %	ψ	ψ	OP Sap	ψ	ψ	Water con-tent %
Lycopersicon esculentum	-18	-19	-20	11·8	-32	-32	-35	-41	-45	9·8
Ligustrum lucidum	-47	-45	-48	9·7	-50	-60	-66	-70	-110	6·9
Gossypium barbadense	-38	-43	-38	10·2	-48	-50	-67	-77	-107	7·0

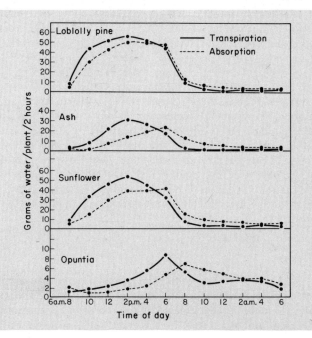

Fig. 4.8   The relation between the rate of transpiration and the rate of absorption of water by plants. (From Kramer, 1937, *Am. J. Bot.*, **24**, 10–15.)

water. Temperature similarly affects root growth and root permeability, both being decreased at low temperatures. Since the viscosity of water increases as the temperature is lowered, low soil temperature may, for this reason, under certain conditions, considerably reduce the water uptake via the root resulting from transpiration pull. Active water uptake leading to positive root pressures develops only in well-aerated soils of favourable moisture content and temperature.

Atmospheric conditions

The daily course of water absorption closely follows, with a time lag, the course of transpiration (Fig. 4.8). Thus the atmospheric factors which determine the rate of transpiration also determine the rate of water uptake. Transpiration rate increases with increasing temperature. Evaporation is faster the higher the temperature, and a rise in temperature results in a steeper concentration gradient of water vapour from the leaf air spaces to the atmosphere. The atmosphere in the leaf air spaces is at a *relative humidity* (RH) near saturation (100% RH). Since the absolute concentration of water vapour at a given RH increases with increasing temperature the concentration of water vapour in the leaf air spaces increases with temperature so that a high RH is maintained whereas the RH of the external air tends to fall. The steepness of the diffusion gradient from leaf to air increases. A temperature rise of 10°C approximately doubles the steepness of the gradient. Wind speeds up transpiration by sweeping away water vapour from the plant surfaces thus maintaining a steep diffusion gradient. By causing leaf bending it may cause mass flow of air into and out of the leaf thereby enhancing water loss. Light has no direct effect on water loss, but through the control it exerts over stomatal opening (see below), it has a profound effect on the water relations of plants. Atmospheric conditions thus tend to promote higher transpiration rates by day than by night, and in summer than in winter.

Plant factors

The plant factors which control the rate of passage of water through the plant are to a great extent those that control the rate of transpiration. However, the water uptake capacity of the roots can become limiting, as shown in Fig. 4.9; when half the leaves are removed from a plant, the remainder transpire more rapidly, being now able to draw on the whole root system for water. Plants also differ in the ψs they can develop (Table 4.4).

If comparison is made between plants of different species, or different individuals of the same species, the following shoot characters are found to favour rapid transpiration: an outer surface with a thin cuticle and devoid of hairs; a high stomatal frequency (number of stomata per unit area), and a large surface area. The area of cells exposed to internal air spaces may be determinative rather than the external surface area. Table 4.5 shows that the *Citrus* species with the higher ratio of internal

Table 4.5 The effect of internal and external leaf surface area on the rate of transpiration, measured over a period of two months. (After Turrell, F. M., 1936, *Am. J. Bot.*, **23**, 255–64.)

Species	Transpiration g/dm^2 of external surface	Ratio of internal to external surface	Transpiration g/dm^2 of internal surface
Citrus limonia	45·57	22·2	2·05
Citrus grandis	37·91	17·2	2·15

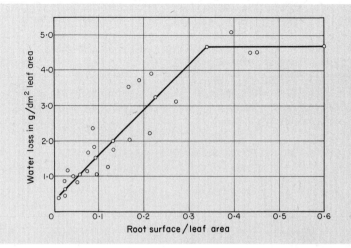

Fig. 4.9 Effect of variation in ratio of root surface to leaf area on rate of transpiration of rooted lemon (*Citrus limonia*) cuttings. Transpiration was reduced in proportion to reduction in root surface below a root surface to leaf area ratio of about 0·35, but independent of root surface above this ratio. (From Kramer, 1956, *Encyclopedia of Plant Physiology*, ed. Ruhland, **3**, 188–214. Springer-Verlag, Berlin.)

to external leaf surface area has the higher rate of transpiration as calculated per unit of external surface, although per unit of internal surface the transpiration rates are almost equal.

If on the other hand the water relations of an individual plant under different environmental conditions are considered, the degree of opening of the stomata is often the most important single factor controlling the rate of transpiration. By far the greater proportion of the water lost comes from the leaf air spaces via the stomata, although the stomatal area may be only 1–2% of the total leaf surface. This can be seen by comparing the rates of transpiration with the stomata open and closed (Fig. 4.10). Where there is a mid-day closure of stomata this is always accompanied by a reduction of transpiration rate. The transpiration of leaves with stomata confined to the lower surface shows a much greater reduction of rate when the lower surface is vaselined than results from vaselining the upper surface. The great efficiency of stomata in gaseous exchange stems from the fact that diffusion through small apertures is fastest at the edges, where the diffusing molecules can fan out. For the same total surface area, many small pores are therefore more efficient than one large one, the small pores having more total 'edge'. In plants

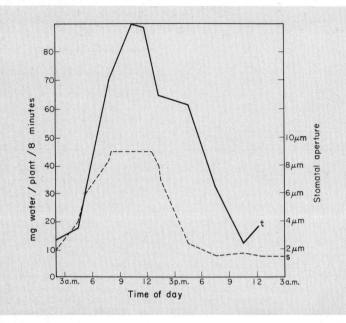

Fig. 4.10   The relationship between the daily course of transpiration and stomatal aperture in *Verbena ciliata*. The rate of transpiration, t, follows closely change in stomatal width, s. (From Lloyd, 1908, *The Physiology of Stomata*, Carnegie Institution, Wash.)

with a thick cuticle, like *Laurus nobilis*, water loss through the epidermis itself, the 'cuticular transpiration', may be as low as 2% of total transpiration. When the cuticle is thinner, cuticular transpiration can constitute 5–45% of the total and the 'average' cuticular transpiration for mesophytes is 10–25% of the total. Closing of the stomata will therefore, according to species, reduce transpiration to 2–45% of that occurring when the stomata are open.

Transpiration is most rapid when stomata are fully open and slowest when they are fully closed. At intermediate apertures, other factors determine whether the degree of stomatal opening affects transpiration rate or not. If the atmospheric conditions do not favour rapid transpiration, the full transpiration rate may be reached when the stomata are only partly open. But when external factors favour rapid transpiration, the rate increases with increasing stomatal aperture right up to maximum opening (Fig. 4.11).

The width of the stomatal pore is directly determined by the turgidity

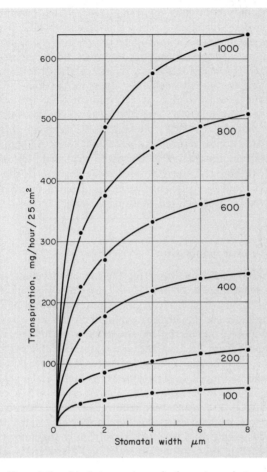

Fig. 4.11 The relationship between transpiration rate and stomatal aperture in birch (*Betula pubescens*), under different conditions of evaporation. The number on each curve represents the rate of evaporation of water, in mg, from 25 cm² blotting paper surface under the same conditions. At low rates of evaporation, full transpiration rate is reached at a stomatal aperture of only 2 μm; at higher rates of evaporation full transpiration rate is scarcely reached with a stomatal aperture of 8 μm. (From Stålfelt, 1932, *Planta*, **17**, 22–85.)

of the guard cells: the higher their turgidity, the wider the opening. Wilting, therefore, induces stomatal closure, and this cuts down further water loss. The early stages of wilting, however, are often accompanied by a widening of the stomatal aperture, the guard cells being pulled apart by the wilting of surrounding epidermal cells, which lose water more rapidly. In extreme wilting also, the shrinking epidermal cells can again pull the pores open. Stomata are highly sensitive to the water status of the plant, and even before wilting occurs, water stress begins to induce stomatal closure. Other factors influencing stomatal aperture act indirectly via turgor changes. Stomata generally open in the light and shut in darkness. Light acts primarily by its influence on the intercellular carbon dioxide concentration; stomata open when this falls below a critical level, and, in the light, photosynthesis achieves this decrease in carbon dioxide concentration. A direct light effect on stomata, independent of carbon dioxide, has also been reported. Of the several hypotheses as to how the above stimuli cause changes in the turgor of the guard cells, none is truly satisfactory. A detailed discussion of the problem is given by Meidner and Mansfield (1968).

The necessity of transpiration

Is transpiration really necessary for the life of the plant, or is it an unavoidable consequence of the plant structure needed to permit photosynthesis to take place but carrying with it the danger of fatal water loss? This question can be further explored by asking whether water could be transported efficiently by any other mechanism available to plants as we know them; and whether transpiration fulfils any other vital function in the plant besides motivating water transport. It would seem that water could be moved up as a cohesive column under tension even without the existence of transpiration. As long as there is a continuous column of water in the plant, any removal of water from it, for biochemical reactions or for cell expansion, should cause water movement. The movement would then be much slower, only the amount actually used and retained in the plant being taken up. There are no short term ill effects of preventing transpiration by a saturated atmosphere.

It has been argued that transpiration is a protection against overheating of plants by the sun. The cooling effect of evaporation is however rather small, the leaf temperature rarely falling more than 2–5°C below that of the ambient air, and this effect is therefore of doubtful biological significance. In this connection it is interesting to bear in mind that the major resistance in the path of the flow of water from the root surface to the external atmosphere is evaporation of water into the air space system of the leaf. In a rapidly transpiring plant this conversion of liquid water into water vapour is the rate-limiting step.

Ions as well as water normally move in the transpiration stream and a slowing down of water movement therefore would cause a corresponding slowing down of the movement of ions (in the xylem). However ions are also transported in the phloem so there seems no *a priori* reason why such transport should not render ion movement in the transpiration stream unnecessary. It is difficult to find any convincing evidence that transpiration fills some essential positive role in plants; it appears rather to be an inevitable result of an organization evolved primarily in relation to photosynthetic efficiency.

The outstanding impression which emerges from a survey of the water relations of the flowering plant is that of the efficiency with which water supply is maintained to the delicate, highly hydrated photosynthetic cells of leaves exposed to the hazard of a warm dry atmosphere and the drying actions of high winds. This efficiency is achieved by the special structure and extent of the xylem and the strength and elasticity of plant cell walls. Cellulose cell walls can withstand the required tensions. Xylem provides appropriate channels for the existence of water columns under tension and their longitudinal flow and protects the whole system from being jeopardized when individual columns cavitate. In perennial plants, new conducting tissue is formed year by year through the activity of a vascular cambium. The xylem, more than any other tissue, gives mechanical strength to the shoot system, thereby enabling it to grow without the mechanical support afforded by immersion in water, and in the extreme case to the height of the tallest tree.

FURTHER READING

DAINTY, J. (1969). The water relations of plants. In *Physiology of Plant Growth and Development*, ed. WILKINS, M. B., 421–52. McGraw-Hill, London.

DIXON, H. H. (1914). *Transpiration and the Ascent of Sap in Plants*. Macmillan, London.

FOGG, G. E. (ed.) (1965). The State and Movement of Water in Living Organisms. *Symp. Soc. exp. Biol.*, **19**.

KRAMER, P. J. (1969). *Plant and Soil Water Relationships: a Modern Synthesis*. McGraw-Hill, New York.

MEIDNER, H. and MANSFIELD, T. A. (1968). *Physiology of Stomata*. McGraw-Hill, New York and Maidenhead.

MEYLAN, B. A. and BUTTERFIELD, B. G. (1972). *Three-dimensional Structure of Wood*. Chapman and Hall, London.

STOCKING, C. R. (1953). Histology and development of the root. *Encyclopedia of Plant Physiology*, ed. RUHLAND, W., **3**, 173–87. Springer-Verlag, Berlin.

STREET, H. E., ELLIOTT, M. C. and FOWLER, M. W. (1975). The Physiology of Roots. In *Interactions between Soil Microorganisms and Plants*, ed. DOMMERGUES, Y. and KRUPA, S. (in press). Elsevier Sci. Pub. Co., Amsterdam.

SUTCLIFFE, J. (1968). *Plants and Water*. Studies in Biology, No. 14, Edward Arnold, London.

SELECTED REFERENCES

GREENIDGE, K. N. H. (1958). Rates and patterns of moisture movement in trees. In *The Physiology of Forest Trees*, ed. THIMANN, K. V., 19–41. Ronald Press, New York.

MACKAY, J. F. G. and WEATHERLEY, P. E. (1973). The effects of transverse cuts through the stems of transpiring woody plants on water transport and stress in the leaves. *J. exp. Bot.*, **24**, 15–28.

MILBURN, J. A. and MCLAUGHLIN, M. E. (1974). Studies of cavitation in isolated vascular bundles and whole leaves of *Plantago major* L. *New Phytol.*, **73**, 861–71.

SCHOLANDER, P. F. (1958). The rise of sap in lianas. In *The Physiology of Forest Trees*, ed. THIMANN, K. V., 3-17. Ronald Press, New York.

THUT, H. F. (1932). Demonstrating the lifting power of transpiration. *Am. J. Bot.*, **19**, 358–64.

ZIMMERMANN, M. H. (1964). Effect of low temperature on ascent of sap in trees. *Pl. Physiol., Lancaster*, **39**, 568–72.

5

Mineral Nutrition

INTRODUCTION

Isolated studies related to plant nutrition were conducted during the 16th and 17th centuries by chemists such as van Helmont, Boyle, Glauber and Mayow. Their studies indicated the importance of water and of minerals for plant growth and formed the basis for work in the 18th century (particularly by Duhamel du Monceau in 1758 and by Horne in 1762) which confirmed the essentiality to plants of minerals derived from the soil and from natural waters. The 19th century witnessed the emergence of agricultural chemistry and the use of artificial fertilizers (the studies of Boussingault in France, of Liebig in Germany and of Lawes and Gilbert in Britain) and also the development of water and sand culture techniques leading to the recognition of the elements which are essential for plants (de Saussure, 1804; Salm-Horstmar, 1848, 1851; Sachs, 1860; Knop, 1860–1865; Wolf, 1866; van der Crone, 1904). The mixed salt solutions used by Sachs, Knop and van der Crone are, in slightly modified form, still in use today.

The pioneer sand cultures of Salm-Horstmar indicated that nitrogen, phosphorus, sulphur, calcium, potassium, magnesium, silicon, iron and manganese were needed for the healthy growth of cereals. The many water culture experiments of Sachs showed, for a range of plant species, the essentiality of nitrogen, phosphorus, sulphur, potassium, calcium, magnesium and iron.

Although Salm-Horstmar noted the beneficial effect of manganese and gave a description of the now well-known manganese-deficiency disease of oats ('grey-speck') it was not until 1922 that manganese was shown to be an essential element for a range of species. Mazé in 1914 demonstrated that zinc is essential for maize; later workers confirmed its equal essentiality for other species. Studies by Aghulon (1910), Mazé (1919) and Warington (1923) established the essentiality of boron. The elements manganese, zinc and boron, although essential, were shown to be required in very small amounts only (parts per million in the culture solution) and were hence termed micro-nutrient elements. To complete the list of the essential micro-nutrient elements we must add iron, copper, molybdenum and chlorine. In contrast to these elements are those required in much larger amounts—the macro-nutrient elements, nitrogen, phosphorus, potassium, sulphur, calcium and magnesium.

The elements listed above are now regarded as probably required by all plants on the grounds that no plants that have been tested can complete their growth in their absence. Certain other elements (this applies to sodium, iodine and silicon) at present appear to be essential for some plants but not for others. Still other elements appear to have the status of beneficial elements, this beneficial effect usually being recorded only for certain plant species. Thus selenium appears to be beneficial to *Lupinus albus*, *Phleum pratense* and to species of *Astragalus*, and aluminium to a number of grasses, to tea (*Camellia sinensis*), *Miscanthus sinensis* and *Polygonum sachalinense*.

To establish clearly that an element is an essential plant nutrient certain criteria must be met. The criteria of essentiality now generally accepted are: (1) the plant cannot complete its life cycle without the element; (2) its action must be specific and cannot be replaced by another element; (3) its effect on the plant must be direct. This last criterion means that the element must not be acting by promoting or retarding the uptake of some other essential or toxic element. Often it is difficult to be sure that this last criterion is met.

MINERAL NUTRIENTS IN THE SOIL

Soils are of many kinds and are always complex physical, chemical and biological systems. Special experimental techniques for the study of the soil have been developed and in consequence knowledge of its origin, structure and function in plant nutrition has grown rapidly. Today a knowledge of this soil science is needed to appreciate fully the way in which soils function as sources of plant nutrients and how the soil is modified by plant growth and by application of mineral and organic fertilizers.

Pure silica sand can be regarded as biologically inert and is used in sand culture to give physical support to the growing plant and, by allowing free drainage, to ensure very simply an adequate aeration of the root system. Once a sand is enriched by natural additions of inorganic and organic matter it begins to take on the properties of a soil. Natural soils contain organic matter and clays and it is these which confer upon the soil its capacity to hold ions by adsorption, to show an *ion exchange capacity*. These soil constituents usually carry a net negative charge. Positively charged cations (Ca^{2+}, Mg^{2+}, H^+, K^+, Na^+ and NH_4^+) are adsorbed at the points where negatively charged groups occur in the clay and organic particles. In consequence such adsorbed cations account for most of the exchangeable ions of the soil. These exchangeable ions are not held rigidly at the surface of the soil particles but are held in a field of force arising at the surfaces by the ionization of reactive groups and are surrounded by water molecules. They are freely exchangeable for other ions and can be extracted by washing the soil in a strong solution of a salt such as NH_4NO_3 when the NH_4^+ ions will displace the other cations from the surface of the soil particles.

The exchangeable soil cations, Ca^{2+}, Mg^{2+} and K^+ are quantitatively important in that order. Exchangeable Na^+ may be either larger or smaller in amount than exchangeable K^+ according to the nature of the soil. By contrast the adsorption of anions is relatively unimportant and effectively the anions Cl^-, NO_3^- and SO_4^{2-} are entirely free in the soil solution. Hence these ions are very readily leached from soil and availability of NO_3^- and SO_4^{2-} depends particularly upon the rate of decomposition of soil organic matter. The situation with regard to phosphate ions is more complex. They are to some extent adsorbed at soil particle surfaces (note the high charge density of the trivalent phosphate ion), they can replace hydroxyl and silicate ions in clays and can react with iron (Fe^{3+}) and aluminium (Al^{3+}) ions. Exchangeable phosphate is however only of significance in acid soils of low Ca^{2+} content, where the very low soluble phosphate level is maintained by continuous release from almost insoluble, more complex, phosphates.

The mineral elements which pass from the soil into the plant can be regarded as derived directly from the displaceable liquid phase of the soil, the *soil solution*. The concentration of this soil solution rises as the water content of the soil falls but except under dry conditions is always very dilute. In several instances it has been shown that a solution corresponding in ionic composition to the soil solution will support good growth of crop plants provided it is frequently renewed or applied as a flowing solution so that it does not become depleted. Thus for instance the content of phosphate in the soil solution is always low: 1 p.p.m. or less. Nevertheless plants can meet their phosphate requirement in water culture solutions containing as little as 0·1 p.p.m. However with such low soluble phosphate levels it is essential that phosphate ions are continuously released from the solid phase of the soil as they are removed by plant roots from the soil solution. It has been calculated that the phosphate of the soil solution may have to be renewed 10 or more times a day to meet the phosphorus demand of a growing crop. Because nitrate is almost entirely present in the soil solution and is rapidly absorbed by plants its rate of renewal is often quite critical. This renewal involves release of the cation NH_4^+ from the organic fraction of the soil and its rapid conversion to nitrate by nitrifying bacteria. In soils of acid pH the soil solution is normally low in calcium and high in iron, manganese and aluminium. Problems of calcium deficiency and of manganese and aluminium toxicity are therefore often encountered in such soils. By contrast in alkaline soils we have the reverse situation of high calcium level and low levels of iron, manganese and certain other metal ions—hence the well-known phenomenon of lime-induced chlorosis (yellowing of leaves due to low chlorophyll content). This is, in part, due to iron deficiency induced by the almost complete absence of iron from the soil solution at neutral and alkaline pH, particularly in soils of low organic content. Soluble organic substances tend to protect iron and other metals from precipitation due to the formation of soluble co-ordination complexes or chelates, stable under neutral and mildly alkaline conditions.

Soils as media for plant nutrition vary according to: (1) the composition of the soil solution; (2) the capacity of the solid phase to renew the solution by ion exchange (release of essential cations in exchange for H^+ or of essential anions for OH^- or HCO_3^-), by chemical decomposition or by microbial action; (3) the degree of aeration of the soil (availability of O_2 and rate of release of respiratory CO_2); (4) the physical resistance of the soil to root penetration. In consequence within any climatic region each distinctive soil type supports a characteristic flora. These soil (edaphic) factors are thus of importance in plant distribution and in the development of plant communities. The problems raised here are therefore usually studied in more detail in Ecology.

Cation exchange

Uptake of ions by plant roots has been shown to consist of two phases, adsorption and absorption (accumulation). The adsorption phase is a physicochemical phenomenon, is non-metabolic and is predominantly concerned with cations. It is an exchange process, H^+ generated by respiration being released into the soil solution in exchange for metal cations. The cation exchange properties of roots appear to depend upon cell wall constituents, particularly the uronic acids of the cell wall. In general, cation exchange values are higher for the roots of dicotyledons than for those of monocotyledons. For instance if we express the cation exchange capacity in milli-equivalents of cation adsorbed per 100 g dry weight of root the value for wheat is 9·0, and for larkspur (*Delphinium ajacis*) it is 94·0. Roots with a high exchange capacity have a higher affinity for calcium relative to potassium than roots with a low exchange capacity.

Clearly the movement of cations from soil colloids to the root will depend upon the relative binding capacity of the soil colloids and the cell wall colloids and the rate at which ions are moved from the cell walls into the protoplasts of the root cells. The relative binding of cations by soil colloids is strongly influenced by the complex of cations adsorbed. Thus the extent to which a given cation (say Ca^{2+}) can be exchanged depends upon the other cations adsorbed. If these other cations (complementary ions) are strongly bound, the Ca^{2+} will be more completely released than if they are weakly bound. Thus with a clay from a chernozem soil it was shown that NH_4^+ displaced Ca^{2+} more completely when the second ion bound was Na^+ than when the second ion was either Mg^{2+} or H^+.

The most generally accepted concept of the path of ions from soil to root postulates an intervening liquid phase represented by the soil solution. However in 1939, two workers, Jenny and Overstreet, put forward the theory that when a root surface makes contact with a soil particle interchange of ions takes place by contact-exchange. In support of this view they quoted evidence that the uptake of certain cations (such as Na^+) proceeds more rapidly from a clay suspension than from a sodium salt solution of equal cationic concentration. However, the significance of such contact-exchange remains very doubtful and many results can be quoted in support of the older view that the ionic environment of the root is best represented by the composition of the soil solution.

SALT UPTAKE AND TRANSPORT WITHIN THE ROOT

Inorganic ions move across cellular membranes into cells and cell organelles (plastids, mitochondria, vacuoles). This process is normally one of salt accumulation, the movement taking place despite a high free salt concentration in the cell and a lower concentration in the bathing medium. Such accumulation can take place from very low external concentrations as evidenced by phosphate and sulphate uptake. The uptake is always selective; the relative concentrations of different ions inside the cells differ, often strikingly, from their relative concentrations in the external medium (Fig. 5.1). The uptake of a particular ion is often markedly affected by the presence of other ions in the soil or culture solution; various groups of ions can be distinguished, the members of which compete with one another in the uptake process (e.g. Ca^{2+} and

Mg^{2+}) but not with members of other groups. Salt accumulation is linked to cell metabolism; the energy released in respiration is used to power the accumulation process. This is what is implied when we describe salt accumulation as an 'active' process. Further consideration of possible mechanisms of the membrane transport of ions will not be developed here; it is an important aspect of cellular physiology and biochemistry.

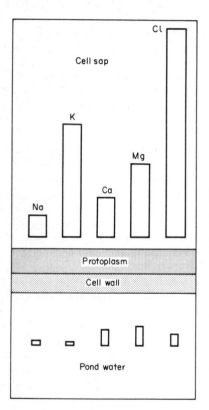

Fig. 5.1 Relative concentrations of different ions in pond water and in the vacuolar sap of the cells of the alga *Nitella* growing in the pond. (From Hoagland, 1944, *Inorganic Plant Nutrition.* Chronica Botanica, Waltham, Mass.)

Salts move from the soil into the xylem vessels of the root and are therein transported to the shoot. The movement of salts across cellular membranes into the root cells, discussed above, is one component of this transport system. To reach the xylem vessels ions must enter the epidermis (piliferous layer) of the root, and move through the cortex, endodermis and stelar parenchyma (Fig. 4.3, p. 52). Ions required for the growth and metabolism of the root cells will be retained, surplus ions being released into the transpiration or root pressure stream.

From studies on the ease with which ions can be washed out of plant tissues it has been found that some cations and anions are very easily removed by water, that some cations not readily removed by water are rapidly exchanged for other cations and that still other ions are retained by the tissues and only very slowly released. The ions quickly released into water are described as occupying the 'water free space' (WFS) and this seems to correspond in volume to that of the water-saturated cellulose cell walls of the tissue. The readily exchangeable cations appear to be associated with fixed anions in the cell walls and at the protoplast surfaces. Such cations are often described as occupying the 'Donnan free space' (DFS), named after Donnan who first described the equilibria established when inorganic ions are separated by a membrane permeable to such ions but impermeable to large organic anions present in one compartment of the system. The ions which are retained by cells will then be those which have been transported across cellular membranes by the salt accumulation process.

The above interpretation of the WFS and DFS of plant tissues is not universally accepted. It is nevertheless based upon a body of evidence that normally the membrane at the surface of the protoplast (the plasmalemma) is an effective diffusion barrier to ions and that it is across this membrane that primary ion accumulation takes place. Some workers however consider that it is only the ions that are in the vacuoles (beyond the tonoplast) or in the membrane-enclosed plastids and mitochondria that are retained and that the ground mass of the cytoplasm is part of the free space of the tissue. As will presently appear, this controversy is not unimportant in relation to the pathway of salt transport across the root.

The protoplasts of the living cells of the piliferous layer, cortex, endodermis, and stelar parenchyma are interconnected by fine cytoplasmic strands (plasmodesmata) and hence we can conceive of a protoplasmic continuum or symplast (Fig. 5.2). Assuming this and that the plasmalemma is an effective diffusion barrier to ions, then we can visualize that ions can move by diffusion into the cell walls of the piliferous layer and cortex, can be accumulated into the cytoplasm and pass from cell to cell by protoplasmic streaming within each cell and across the cell boundaries by diffusion through the plasmodesmata, and when retained within the root are withdrawn from the cytoplasm into cell organelles (particularly the vacuoles). On this interpretation a significance can be assigned to the Casparian strip in the walls of the endodermal cells. By preventing ion and water movement through the longitudinal and transverse radial walls, it ensures both that moving solvent and solutes must at the endodermis enter the symplast and that any hydrostatic pressure developed in the stele can be maintained by a protoplasmic resistance to the 'back-flow' of water (see Chapter 4, p. 52).

The final step in the salt transport path, the release of salts into xylem vessels, has been regarded by some workers as an active secretory process and by others as a leakage due to an inability of the symplast at the centre of the root to retain salts accumulated under the more aerobic conditions existing at or near the root surface. The concentration of salts established in the xylem fluid (usually assessed by analysis of bleeding xylem fluid under conditions where there is a positive root pressure) is much lower than in the root cells but usually many times that in the soil solution. The concept of an active secretion of salts into the xylem vessels (as against leakage due to an impaired ability to retain salts in the symplast) is supported by the observation that metabolic inhibitors like dinitrophenol and chloramphenicol not only inhibit salt uptake but

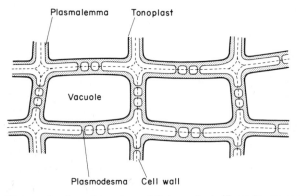

Fig. 5.2   Diagram to show the nature of the symplast. (From Brouwer, 1965, *A. Rev. Pl. Physiol.*, **16**, 241–66.)

also salt transport into the xylem vessels. The concept that salts leak into the xylem vessels from the stelar parenchyma is supported by the observation that the freshly isolated root stele separated from the cortex by shearing along the line of the endodermis will, in contrast to the freshly separated cortex, rapidly release its ions into a bathing solution. If the stele is maintained in aerated water for some time its capacity for salt retention increases; a similar development of a capacity for salt accumulation is well known to occur if discs of storage tissue (potato tuber discs or carrot root discs) are washed in aerated water.

When the rate of water transport from the soil to the xylem is increased, particularly by enhanced transpiration, salt uptake and transport are also increased. A generally accepted explanation of this is still lacking. It has been suggested that the additional ions entering the xylem represent a mass flow of ions in the water stream—a passive flow of ions in a water current. Alternatively it has been suggested that at low transpiration rates the concentrations of ions in the xylem vessels are high enough to limit ion movement into them, whereas at a higher transpiration rate the xylem fluid is more dilute and hence salt release takes place at a higher rate. On this explanation the increased water flow is considered to increase the 'active' movement of ions from the symplast. A still further possibility is that the tension generated by a high transpiration rate lowers the resistances to water and salt movement thereby increasing salt release whether this is a metabolically controlled secretion or a leakage due to impaired 'active' salt retention. Certainly there is evidence that tensions developed in the xylem vessels are transmitted across the root diameter.

MINERAL ELEMENT DEFICIENCIES

A number of economically important and symptom-characteristic plant diseases are now recognized as due to mineral element deficiencies. Examples of such diseases are 'tea-yellows' (sulphur deficiency); 'grey-speck' of oats, 'marsh spot' of peas and 'speckled yellows' of beet (all due to manganese deficiency); 'exanthema' of fruit trees, 'mottle leaf' of *Citrus*, 'white bud' of maize and 'sickle-leaf' of cocoa (all due to zinc deficiency); 'heart-rot' of beet, 'stem-crack' of celery, 'brown heart' of swede, 'corky core' of apple, 'top-sickness' of tobacco (all due to boron deficiency); and 'scald' disease of beans and 'whiptail' of *Brassica* crops (due to molybdenum deficiency). Even where the symptoms of a particular element deficiency have not been given a disease name, the symptoms are usually characteristic for the species and a reliable means of identifying the deficiency. However such identification may only be possible by the time the crop is virtually ruined and earlier diagnosis may often be achieved by rapid techniques of leaf analysis or by studying the curative effects of foliar applications of salt solutions.

The symptoms of mineral deficiencies in a wide range of crop plants have been accurately described and recorded by colour photography to assist rapid diagnosis (*The Diagnosis of Mineral Deficiencies in Plants— By Visual Symptoms*, T. Wallace, H.M.S.O., London, 1951). Certain plant species which rapidly develop characteristic deficiency symptoms for particular elements are now used as *indicator plants* for testing soils suspected of being mineral deficient.

The recording of mineral deficiency symptoms, visual, microscopical, physiological and biochemical, provides the evidence on which our understanding of the role of each element in metabolism is based. Particularly at the physiological and biochemical levels experimental work requires careful comparison with normal tissues. At present although we have some knowledge of the role of all the essential elements, in many cases our understanding is very incomplete. In summary it can be said that many of the essential roles of nitrogen, sulphur, phosphorus, manganese, iron, copper and zinc are well established. Thus nitrogen and sulphur are essential constituents of protein molecules, sulphur compounds are important in the regulation of oxidation-reduction potentials, phosphorus is present in nucleic acids, phospholipids and in such substances as adenosine polyphosphates (ADP and ATP), and so on. Similarly iron, copper, zinc, manganese, magnesium, molybdenum and chlorine are known to be either parts of the prosthetic groups (cofactors) of enzymes or in ionic form are specific activators of enzyme reactions.

One difficulty often encountered, and well illustrated by potassium, is the identification of the particular aspects of metabolism in which an element is *essential* (no other element can substitute). Sodium for instance appears to be able to substitute for some of the activities of potassium, but cannot completely replace the need for this element. Many enzymes can, with different effectiveness, be activated by either magnesium or manganese ions although both elements have other activities where the one cannot substitute for the other. Again the demonstration of one essential role, such as the essentiality of zinc as a component of the enzyme carbonic anhydrase, does not exclude it having other essential roles in enzymes (e.g. in alcohol dehydrogenase) or in other essential metabolites.

The roles of boron

It would clearly be beyond the scope of the present volume to examine in detail our knowledge regarding the roles of each essential element. Very brief statements purporting to summarize such knowledge are often very misleading, particularly where there are various contending hypotheses. To illustrate the difficulties involved and the incompleteness of present knowledge we have chosen rather to consider the possible roles of a single element. For this we have selected boron because, despite considerable research, no essential role of the element has been identified with certainty.

In 1923, Miss Warington demonstrated the essentiality of boron for broad bean (*Vicia faba*), and reported as a prominent feature of the deficiency the death of the shoot apical meristems (Fig. 5.3c). Many other studies have emphasized the importance of boron for the proper functioning of plant meristems: the apical meristems of roots and shoots, the secondary vascular and cork cambia, and the meristems of leaf primordia. In the affected meristematic regions severe necrosis (death of cells) often occurs and is frequently associated with blackening of the tissues. Flowering is often completely suppressed and flowers fall without producing seed. Microscopic study shows that meristems in deficient

(a)   (b)

Fig. 5.3 (a) Root of broad bean (*Vicia faba*) grown in presence of boric acid. (b) Root of a plant of similar age, with boric acid omitted. (c) Shoot showing new growth (left) subsequent to the addition of boric acid after death of the main axis (right) typical of boron deficiency. (From Warington, 1923, *Ann. Bot.*, **37**, 629–72.)

(c)

plants function only for a short time and are replaced by further meristems whose function is also limited in duration. The cells derived from such meristems often fail to complete their normal differentiation, and may become abnormally enlarged and thin walled. Prior to the cessation of cell division in the meristems, the interphase between mitoses is increased.

Anthers appear to be especially sensitive to boron deficiency, breakdown occurring particularly in the sporogenous tissue or at the tetrad stage of pollen grain formation. Pollen germination is often dependent upon a supply of boron and pollen tubes arising in absence of boron show abnormal swelling and burst. Boron deficient roots lose their geotropic sensitivity. Both these effects could be attributed to the deficiency of boron disturbing growth hormone synthesis or distribution.

Complexes readily form between the borate ion and *cis*-polyhydroxyl configurations such as occur in certain sugars and sugar alcohols. Boron deficiency is associated almost without exception with increased concentrations of sugars and starch in leaves and there is evidence that this accumulation takes place before the phloem becomes non-functional by failure of phloem differentiation and necrosis of sieve tubes. These observations led Gauch and Duggar (in 1953) to advance the hypothesis that the main role of boron is to facilitate the translocation of sugars by formation of sugar-borate complexes, an essential step for their movement across cell membranes. To answer the criticism that at any one time very little of the sugar could be complexed with borate it was suggested that the boron was located in the cell membranes (was a carrier molecule or part of such a molecule). Gauch and Duggar then explained the characteristic necrosis of terminal buds and root tips as a consequence of sugar starvation due to impaired sugar translocation. Although it is also possible to explain other symptoms of boron deficiency on this hypothesis there are a number of observations which do not accord with it. For example although a decrease in the rate of sugar translocation from leaves occurs fairly rapidly when plants are transferred to boron-free medium, other symptoms of the deficiency occur even more rapidly. Various workers have also shown that the meristematic activity of root cells ceases following transfer to boron-free media while the sugar concentration in the root is still quite normal.

No enzymes have been shown to be specifically activated by boron. However, in various investigations boron-deficient cells have been reported to exhibit enhanced activity of such enzymes as polyphenol oxidase, aldehyde oxidase, catalase and peroxidase. Such enzymes could be responsible for the browning of the cells. From such observations it has been suggested that boron is either an inhibitor of these enzymes or, in appropriate cases, acts by reducing the levels of their natural substrates by forming borate-diphenol complexes. However enhanced activity of these enzymes is observed in a number of other mineral deficiencies and may well be a secondary consequence of the onset of necrosis. Cellular disorganization could well lead to increases in the levels of phenols and hence to adaptive increases in the enzymes for which they are substrates.

There is no convincing evidence that boron is essential for fungi. This has suggested that boron might be involved in the formation of the pectins and cellulose of plant cell walls. Studies of the influence of boron-deficiency upon cell wall composition and upon the levels of soluble pectins and pentosans have however not revealed any consistent picture.

One of the most rapid effects of lowered boron availability is the decline of meristematic activity in root meristems (Fig. 5.3, **a** and **b**), an effect which can be detected within 6 hours of transfer to boron-free solutions. There is considerable evidence that this decline is not due to an effect on mitosis itself but on the events immediately following mitosis when normally the cell prepares for further division or, in the absence of boron, embarks upon premature vacuolation and aberrant differentiation. Hence in absence of boron the cells mature precociously and the meristem virtually 'differentiates' itself away. From such reasoning it can be suggested that boron controls the level in the cells of a hormone which determines whether the cells remain meristematic or embark upon maturation. Evidence that meristematic activity in roots is under the control of such an 'ageing' hormone has been obtained by a quite independent line of enquiry. The fact that boron application can, in certain cases, promote the rooting of stem cuttings either with or without the simultaneous application of an auxin also suggests that boron may be implicated in some aspect of hormonal control.

Clearly hypotheses abound when established facts are lacking. 'Although approximately a dozen different functions have been postulated for boron in the plant cell, the mechanism by which this trace element exercises its effect has not been elucidated. In certain respects boron presents a challenge to the plant physiologist in terms of clarifying and describing its exact mechanism of action in the living plant' (NASON, A. and MCELROY W. O. in *Plant Physiology*, Vol. 3, ed. STEWARD, F. C., Academic Press, New York and London, 1963).

TOLERANCE TO HEAVY METALS

Metal-contaminated areas occur naturally (serpentine soils and surface mineral deposits) or are man-made (by mining and ore extraction, use of agriculture sprays, lead from 'anti-knock' additive of petrol contaminating roadside verges). The main elements involved are copper, zinc, nickel and lead. Study of the colonization of areas of high heavy metal content shows establishment of a characteristic flora (containing typical species which have been termed metallophytes), provided heavy metal levels are not completely toxic and the physical and nutritive conditions are not too severe. Some species are naturally confined to sites of abnormally high heavy metal content and are resistant to high levels of more than one heavy metal, e.g. *Viola calaminaria, Thlaspi alpestre, Minuartia verna.* Such species are at a high competitive advantage on such sites but the heavy metals are in no sense directly beneficial to them. Many species (covering a wide range of flowering plant families, certain mosses and liverworts, lichens and microorganisms) occur in the flora of contaminated sites as tolerant ecotypes or races. We know that some of these ecotypes have evolved naturally over relatively short periods (often in less than 100 years); it is possible to select for heavy metal tolerance in *Agrostis tenuis* within one generation! These metal-tolerant races have no requirement for nickel or lead or for higher than normal levels of copper and zinc. In most cases they do not survive by exclusion (reduced absorption) of the toxic metal. Although in no case has the physiological basis of tolerance been fully elucidated there is evidence that a major factor is the affinity of the cell walls for the heavy metal and that a subsidiary factor may be ability to store within the vacuoles excess metal entering the cell protoplasts. In agreement with the tolerance, the binding sites in the cell walls are specific; thus races can be obtained tolerant to copper (but not to zinc), to zinc (but not to copper) or to both elements. The genetics of the tolerance have not been critically analysed but it seems that in most cases the inheritance of tolerance is polygenic. Metal-tolerant races may show associated morphological characters and sometimes are also adapted to growth under conditions of low fertility or adverse physical conditions (marked fluctuations in temperature and available moisture). In view of the speed of evolution of metal tolerance and the ease of experimental selection of tolerant genotypes their study is of particular interest for higher plant physiological genetics. On the practical side the development and transplantation of metal-tolerant races of grasses and cover plants is already proving the key to the revegetation of many areas of industrial dereliction.

FURTHER READING

BROUWER, R. (1965). Ion absorption and transport in plants. *A. Rev. Pl. Physiol.*, **16**, 241–66.

HEWITT, E. J. (1966). *Sand and Water Culture Methods used in the Study of Plant Nutrition*, 2nd edition. Commonwealth Agricultural Bureaux, Farnham Royal.

HEWITT, E. J. and SMITH, T. A. (1975). *Plant Mineral Nutrition*, English Universities Press, London.

HOAGLAND, D. R. (1944). *Inorganic Plant Nutrition*. Chronica Botanica, Waltham, Mass.

STREET, H. E. (1966). The physiology of root growth. *A. Rev. Pl. Physiol.*, **17**, 315–44.

SUTCLIFFE, J. F. and BAKER, D. A. (1974). *Plants and Mineral Salts*. Studies in Biology, No. 48, Edward Arnold, London.

SELECTED REFERENCES

ANTONOVICS, J., BRADSHAW, A. D. and TURNER, R. G. (1971). Heavy metal tolerance in plants. *Adv. ecol. Res.*, **7**, 1–85.

GAUCH, H. G. and DUGGAR, W. M., JR (1953). The role of boron in the translocation of sucrose. *Pl. Physiol.*, *Lancaster*, **28**, 457–66.

JENNY, H. and OVERSTREET, R. (1939). Cation exchange between plant roots and soil colloids. *Soil Sci.*, **47**, 257–72.

STREET, H. E. (1967). The ageing of root meristems. *Symp. Soc. exp. Biol.*, **21**, 517–42.

WARINGTON, K. (1923). The effect of boric acid and borax on the broad bean and certain other plants. *Ann. Bot.*, **37**, 629–72.

6

Transport of Metabolites

In unicellular organisms all aspects of vital activity proceed within the confines of a single cell. In simple multicellular plants, such as filamentous algae, all the vegetative cells are functionally equivalent. By contrast a flowering plant is a complex organism with cells and organs specialized for diverse functions; its separate parts are not self-sufficient but interdependent. Nutrients must be supplied by one part to another, and communication between distant organs via growth-regulating substances is necessary to ensure harmonious development.

The compounds transported in a flowering plant are water, organic nutrients and co-factors, mineral nutrients and hormones. Water transport has been discussed in Chapter 4 and the xylem transport of mineral ions in Chapter 5. In rooted plants xylem transport is essentially a unidirectional stream from root to shoot. Organic and mineral nutrients however undergo multidirectional movement. Organic compounds, synthesized primarily in photosynthetic organs (leaves and green stems), are exported to all non-photosynthetic parts; some of these parts may later re-export the products of their own biosynthetic activity. The mineral elements which are taken up from the soil move at first upwards into growing regions, but minerals, too, may later be withdrawn from such regions, particularly as the organs senesce, for transport to other sites. Hormones and other as yet unidentified chemical stimuli are transported, apparently in very small amounts commensurate with their high physiological activity, and in some instances in a strictly unidirectional (polarized) manner. Growth hormones are synthesized in the meristematic regions and young leaves—substances involved in photoperiodic stimuli in mature leaves. From these sites they move in defined directions, are used up in the responding regions, and are not recirculated.

In a flowering plant there is accordingly a complex traffic of chemicals in many directions, each organ simultaneously receiving some metabolites and exporting others. Over small distances, chemicals can move within and between cells by diffusion and by cytoplasmic movement supplemented by active transfer across cell membranes. Transport over longer distances however proceeds mainly in the vascular tissues. The term *translocation* has been used by some authors to include all long distance movement of compounds within xylem and phloem. Here, in common with the more general usage, we are using the term to describe the multidirectional transport which occurs in the *phloem.*

THE TRANSPORTING SYSTEM

Various observations establish that xylem and phloem are the channels of transport. Their anatomy clearly suggests such a function. They contain elongate cells in longitudinal files and penetrate intimately into all parts of the plant as an uninterrupted network. Leaves are particularly

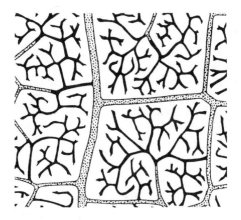

Fig. 6.1   The fine venation in a small portion of a leaf of a dicotyledon (*Ficus religiosa*). The stippled parts of the veins possess bundle sheath extensions, which are lacking in the extreme ends. (From Philpott, 1953, *Bot. Gaz.*, **115**, 15–35.)

well supplied with these vascular tissues; in leaves of many dicotyledons, the maximum distance between any mesophyll cell and a vascular bundle is only 60–70 μm in the plane of the leaf (Fig. 6.1). The highly developed vascular supply of leaves correlates with high activity of leaves in the exchange of metabolites and in transportation. During the vegetative growth of the plant its leaves are the chief recipients of water and minerals. Carbohydrates are manufactured there by photosynthesis and from the leaves flow sucrose, amino acids and other metabolites to growth centres and sites of food storage. In root tips, the apical meristem is separated from functional phloem cells by only 250–750 μm and from functional xylem elements by 400–10 500 μm. Acropetal differentiation of the vascular tissues similarly follows the upward growth of the stem apex. Within the plant axes well developed primary vascular tissues, often supplemented by differentiation of secondary vascular tissues derived from the vascular cambium, permit rapid longitudinal transport.

Visual evidence of transport in the vascular tissues comes from observations on dye movement. By appropriate choice of dye and method of application transport can be shown by this technique in both xylem and phloem. Fluorescent dyes (e.g. fluorescein), which are detectable in low concentration by virtue of their fluorescence, have been used to determine the speed of solute movement. Further information comes from experiments in which the continuity of vascular tissues is interrupted by their excision ('ringing' or 'girdling' experiments). Thus in woody plants it is easily possible to cut down to the vascular cambium and to remove the outer tissues ('bark') which include the phloem, leaving only the central xylem cylinder and pith intact. When twigs with a low carbohydrate content in the stem were defoliated along a stretch, and ringed in various positions, no starch was formed in the defoliated stem where continuity between the phloem and all leaves was interrupted. As long as phloem connections were left intact to leaves either above or below the defoliated stretch, starch deposition within the stretch occurred. This indicates that both upward and downward transport of carbohydrates from leaves occurs in the phloem. Growth of the axis and of leaves above the rings still continued, showing that minerals as well as water reached these regions through the xylem. Some decrease in growth as compared with unringed controls was noted, and interpreted to indicate that, normally, some mineral transport occurs also in the phloem. Similarly, it was found that the growth of apple fruits and of young buds was inhibited when the phloem connections were severed. Over a period of time, swelling often occurs at the edges of such rings as organic materials accumulate there and promote cell division in the outer living tissues. The more difficult operation of removing a section of the xylem, and creating a water-filled cavity inside the phloem, has also been accomplished. The growth of the shoot above such a 'bark ring' was almost equal to that of the control shoots indicating that the phloem is able to transport organic and possibly also significant amounts of mineral nutrients. These ringing experiments thus indicate that organic materials move in the phloem and that minerals are transported in both the xylem and the phloem.

THE COMPOSITION OF XYLEM AND PHLOEM SAP

Xylem sap can be obtained as an exudate from bore holes in the trunk or main stem or from decapitated root stumps at times when it is under pressure; at other times it can be sucked out with a vacuum pump. Alternatively xylem sap can be centrifuged or pressed out from lengths of plant axis. It is more difficult to obtain adequate and uncontaminated samples of phloem sap. The quantity of tissue available is smaller, and there is risk of contamination with protoplasm not only from the sieve tube elements which contain the sap, but from companion cells and phloem parenchyma. Sap does sometimes exude from cuts made into the phloem of trees. A more elegant, and at present the most reliable method, of obtaining sieve tube sap, is to use aphids to tap individual sieve tubes. These insects feed on phloem sap by inserting their stylets into sieve tubes from the outside; when the insertion has been accomplished, the insect is cut away under anaesthesia. Sap will then continue to drip from the stylets for up to several days, at a rate of 1–2 μl per hour. This liquid has been assumed to represent more or less unadulterated sieve tube sap. There is evidence that the saliva initially released by the aphid exerts no digestive function on the phloem. However even with this technique there remains the possibility of seepage of liquid from surrounding tissues into the tapped sieve tube units.

Sap analyses vary quite markedly from species to species; there are also seasonal and daily variations in sap constituents, as well as irregular fluctuations resulting from fluctuating environmental conditions. Nevertheless the composition of xylem sap always differs very significantly from that of phloem sap.

Xylem sap is a clear liquid with a viscosity close to 1·0 and with a pH of about 5. The solute concentration is low; the total dry matter does not normally exceed 1%; values of 0·1 to 0·5% are common. Its ψ is seldom below −2 atm. During periods of rapid transpiration and water uptake, the solute concentration of xylem sap falls to a very low level; since transpiration is faster by day than by night, the xylem sap is more dilute by day. Of the solids present about two-thirds to three-quarters are organic, including amino acids, amides and organic acids. The carbohydrate content is usually only 0·02–0·05%, but may be almost undetectable. The remaining solids are mineral salts. Some of the metal ions are in the form of organic chelates. In perennials, the solute concentration in the xylem sap is at a maximum in spring (Fig. 6.2). In a few trees, e.g. sugar maple (*Acer saccharum*), and birch, the xylem sap in early spring may contain up to 8% sugar. This high sugar content is however maintained only for a limited period, being derived from reserve carbohydrates stored in the stem during winter. The organic nitrogen compounds of the xylem sap are indicative of the assimilation of nitrate and ammonium ions into organic form in the root system. When nitrate occurs in quantity there is usually little organic nitrogen in the sap indicating that the shoot is synthesizing its amino acids from nitrate.

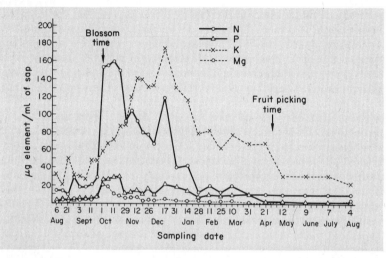

Fig. 6.2 Seasonal variation in the contents of nitrogen, phosphorus, potassium and magnesium in apple (*Pyrus malus*) xylem sap. The nitrogen is mainly present in organic combination. The data were obtained in New Zealand, so that September is spring. (From Bollard, 1958, in *The Physiology of Forest Trees*, ed. Thimann, K. V., 83–93. Copyright 1958. The Ronald Press Co., New York.)

Phloem sap is more viscous and, in contrast to xylem sap and most vacuolar plant saps, is usually alkaline (pH 7·5 to 8·6), although in perennials it may be faintly acid early in the spring. The solute concentration is much higher than in xylem sap; sugars generally make up 90% of the solids, being present at concentrations of 2 to 25% w/v. Its ψ ranges from −6 to −34 atm. In the majority of species, sucrose is the main sugar present, with traces of the oligosaccharides, raffinose, stachyose or verbascose, but in a few species one of the last sugars predominates. Amino acids are regularly present, amounting to 0·2 to 12% (exceptionally up to 50%) of the transported solutes. Mineral elements are also found in the phloem sap; the concentrations of potassium and phosphorus are particularly high, but it is not known whether these elements are there as inorganic salts or in organic combination. Phosphatases and phosphoglucomutase have been found in phloem sap. In small quantities, many other compounds have been detected including organic acids, alkaloids, vitamins, hormones, viruses, and artificially applied chemicals.

The sugar concentration of phloem sap exhibits regular daily variation. In the cotton plant, the highest concentration is recorded in the latter part of the day. In a number of trees, the highest concentration occurs at night and close to the leaves, a concentration wave moving down the tree. Such changes in concentration may reflect turgor changes in the axis as well as changes in the amount of sugars supplied by the leaves. The greatest volume of phloem exudate from cuts on trees is generally obtained on sunny afternoons. In several tree species, the greatest amount of exudate from cuts is obtained in late summer, no flow occurring till about mid-June. Marked seasonal changes are found with respect to amino acid content; this is high in spring, falls in the summer, and rises to a second peak in the autumn when leaf proteins break down prior to abscission; the nitrogen translocated out of leaves at this time is deposited in organic form in the stems where it persists during the winter.

Analyses of xylem and phloem sap thus support the evidence from the ringing experiments in pointing to the phloem as the main channel for the transport of organic materials, and to the xylem as the main path for the movement of minerals.

The movement of radioactive compounds

Radioactive labelling makes possible the detection of the labelled compound in quantities far below the limit of chemical detection, and the movement of the radioactive element is not masked by movement in the plant of the same element in the normal unlabelled form. For instance one can follow the passage of radioactive phosphorus (^{32}P) *into* a leaf rich in phosphate and from which there may be a large net export of phosphorus. The radioactivity can be measured after an extract of the plant has been prepared, or it can be detected *in situ* by scanning with a Geiger counter, or by preparing an autoradiograph (the plant material is placed in close contact with a sensitive photographic emulsion, and the site of the radiation is revealed when the photographic plate is subsequently developed).

Supplying radioactive $^{14}CO_2$ to leaves results in the appearance of radioactivity in the phloem, showing that the products of photosynthesis are exported out of leaves in the phloem; chemical analysis shows that it is the radioactivity of the carbon atoms of sucrose which accounts for most of the radioactivity of the phloem sap. A similar result is obtained if radioactive sugars are applied to the leaves. When radioactive ions are applied to the roots the radioactivity appears in both the xylem and the phloem. This might mean concurrent upward transport in both tissues, or result from lateral transfer from one to the other, for xylem and phloem are in close contact. To decide between these two possibilities, Stout and Hoagland in 1939 performed stripping experiments on young stems of house geranium (*Pelargonium zonale*) and willow (*Salix lasiandra*). Two parallel longitudinal slits were made along 22 cm lengths of stem, and the xylem and phloem separated by inserting a strip of paraffined paper; the whole treated length of stem was then wrapped in paraffined paper to protect the tissues against desiccation, and the radioactive ions— $^{42}K^+$, $^{32}PO_4^{2-}$, $^{82}Br^-$ and $^{24}Na^+$—applied to the roots. It was then found that where the xylem and phloem were left in contact, radioactivity was present in xylem and phloem alike; but in the stripped areas, only the xylem was appreciably radioactive. From this, the conclusion was drawn that the upward transport of ions occurs in the first place in the xylem, but that continual lateral transfer occurs into the phloem.

Some of the ions transported to the shoot become immobile and remain in the tissues in which they are first deposited; others move out again, passing from older to younger leaves, back to the roots, even out into the soil once more. Movement in the xylem is a strictly one-way upward traffic. Any transport of ions in the opposite direction can pass only through the phloem; when radioactive salts are fed to leaves and exported from them it is the phloem of the stem which becomes radioactive.

We can conclude that organic compounds move in both directions in the phloem and upwards in the xylem. Minerals move upwards mainly in the xylem; their downward movement is confined to the phloem. Upward transport of minerals to bud primordia may be in the phloem, due to more precocious differentiation of phloem in the bud traces.

Control of the direction of metabolite transport

The longitudinal course and interconnections between the vascular bundles in the stem and root determine between which organs transport occurs. Lateral transport from one vascular strand to another hardly occurs in either the root or the stem. Leaves export photosynthetic products to the young leaves directly above them, and to parts of the root system directly below them. This can be most readily demonstrated by applying radioactive CO_2 to a leaf and tracing the movement of radioactivity to other leaves (Fig. 6.3). If labelled CO_2 is confined to one longitudinal half of an exporting leaf, only the corresponding half-leaves above this may receive radioactivity. This applies also to xylem transport: mineral deficiencies have been induced in individual halves of tobacco leaves by withholding nutrients from appropriate parts of the root system. Lateral water transport can be induced presumably through cell walls, and then minerals move with it. *Coleus* plants have been grown with the root system separated into two halves, in separate pots. When phosphorus was withheld from one pot, leaves above that root half became phosphorus-deficient. However if this pot was left unwatered, no wilting of the leaves occurred, and phosphorus deficiency symptoms did not appear, showing that water and minerals were being transported laterally from the half receiving both water and the phosphate.

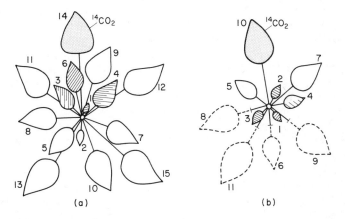

Fig. 6.3   (a) Distribution of radioactivity in leaves of a beet plant one week after supplying $^{14}CO_2$ for 4 hours to a single leaf. Shading is roughly proportional to intensity of activity. $^{14}CO_2$ was translocated to young leaves on one side of the plant only. (b) Experimental diversion of translocated materials. All fully expanded leaves were removed from one side of the plant (broken lines), and after 24 hours a single leaf on the other side was supplied with $^{14}CO_2$. Young leaves on both sides of the plant received translocated ^{14}C. Numbers indicate leaf age, no. 1 being the youngest. (From Joy, 1964, *J. exp. Bot.*, **15**, 485–94. By permission of the Clarendon Press, Oxford.)

The pattern of metabolite transport can undergo some adjustment in response to injury. In apple trees, leaves and fruits can be separated longitudinally by c. 3 m of defoliated stem without affecting the size and sugar content of the fruit. This injury response may involve development of new longitudinally directed vascular strands tending to a more complex longitudinal network. But the fact that if certain leaves are removed from beetroot plants, the young leaves above them receive radioactive nutrients from older leaves on the opposite side of the stem should not be taken to indicate that lateral transport is being induced.

Beetroot appears to be exceptional in possessing an elaborately anasto-
mosing vascular system. Generally the removal of leaves from one side
of a plant results in asymmetric growth as a consequence of one-sided
transport.

The direction of movement of compounds in the xylem is always upwards from the roots; the flow is never reversed. But the direction of
phloem translocation is variable, and is under close metabolic control.
From the mature leaves, organic materials must be supplied to all parts of
the plant that are not self-supporting. The direction is towards *growing*
regions. In a young vegetative plant, the direction of this flow is mainly
to the rapidly growing root system although some movement also occurs
to the shoot apices and developing leaves. As the plant becomes larger,
lower leaves transport predominantly to roots, upper leaves to the growing apices of the shoots; in such older plants translocation proceeds more
upwards by day and downwards at night. When the reproductive stage
is reached, practically all the transport is directed to the flowers and
fruits; this includes not only organic nutrients, but mineral elements
moving out from the leaves. At the start of the growing season, perennials
translocate nutrients from storage regions—tubers, roots, bulbs, stems—
to growing tips. Similarly in a germinating seed, translocation is from the
storage tissues to the growing regions.

Phloem translocation is often described as directed 'from source to
sink', that is from the regions of primary production to the regions of
growth or storage. This is, however, an oversimplification. No nutrients
are translocated into a mature leaf which is shaded so that it cannot
photosynthesize at a sufficient rate to meet its need for energy-rich
organic molecules; such a leaf would be expected to act as a 'sink', but in
fact it starves to death. Sugar transport in the phloem is sometimes faster
than its utilization in the storage or reproductive organs to which it is
moving, and temporary accumulation of sugar occurs in petioles or fruit
stalks without preventing or reversing the flow.

There is evidence for an order of precedence among the following
plant organs for nutrients; rapidly growing fruits > vegetative buds >
recently pollinated flowers. This order is stated to be 'at least partly
correlated' with the concentration of auxin in these organs, suggesting
that translocation proceeds towards regions of high auxin concentration.
Translocates can be attracted to a cut stem stump by applying auxin to
it, and sugar movement towards growing wheat ears can be reversed by
placing auxin on the stem at a point remote from the ears. The failure of
old leaves to obtain translocates also correlates with their low auxin
level. The mechanism by which auxin can attract a movement of sugar
to the tissues in which it occurs is unknown, but the physiological advantage of this control is obvious, for the meristematic tissues which

produce the highest concentrations of auxin are the ones which should have prior call on essential nutrients if growth is to proceed.

THE MECHANISM OF PHLOEM TRANSLOCATION

The hypothesis of mass flow driven by an osmotic gradient

For the mode of movement of any substance in solution, two possibilities exist. Either, it is carried along by a *mass flow* (bulk flow) of the solution, or else it moves by a process such as *diffusion* while the solvent remains stationary. Movement in the xylem is undisputedly a mass flow of the whole solution, and the motive force is either the tension pull of transpiration, or root pressure. The manner and mechanism of phloem transport still await satisfactory explanation. It is not certain whether mass flow of sieve tube contents occurs or whether solutes are moved independently of the liquid phase. In consequence there is equal uncertainty as to the motive force involved.

Speeds of phloem transport have been obtained by calculation from the rates of increase in weight of growing tubers and fruits, or from direct observation of the movement of fluorescent dyes and radioactive tracers. Velocities reported have ranged from 20–100 cm/hour. These values immediately rule out diffusion as the mechanism of transport, being 10^4–10^5 times too high for diffusion although more than 100 times lower than the maximum speeds of sap movement in the xylem. The total quantities translocated are also high. Sugar has been found to move into a growing pumpkin (*Cucurbita pepo*) fruit at a rate of at least 1·7 g/hour. The rate of sugar movement across 1 cm^2 of sieve tube area per hour has been calculated to be about 2 g for petioles and 20 g for fruit stalks. Phloem translocation proceeds with both a high velocity and a high rate of mass transfer (total quantity/unit time).

One of the earliest theories for the mechanism of phloem translocation was Münch's hypothesis which postulated a mass flow along a turgor pressure gradient, induced by a maintained gradient of ψ. A model for the system visualized in this theory is shown in Fig. 6.4. Two semi-permeable reservoirs A and C are joined by a connecting tube. If a concentrated solution of sugar is placed in A and a more dilute solution in C, and both are immersed in water, the water uptake into A is faster than into C. There will be a mass flow of liquid along the tube B from A to C, and water will be forced out of C; a manometer, M, inserted on tube B will register a hydrostatic pressure. The flow will stop when the concentrations in A and C have become equal. In a living plant, a continuous flow could be maintained by a continued secretion of sugar into the phloem at the leaf end (A) and removal at the site to which it is transported (C), the water being released into the xylem at C and drawn from the xylem into the system at A.

In favour of mass flow in the phloem is the fact that when a sieve tube unit is pierced by an aphid stylet, the volume of sap exuded in one hour can be 100 000 times the volume of the one sieve tube element, and the flow may continue for days. A 'surging flow' in sieve tubes of cut phloem has been described from microscopic observations. The phloem has been shown to conduct heat longitudinally in the direction along

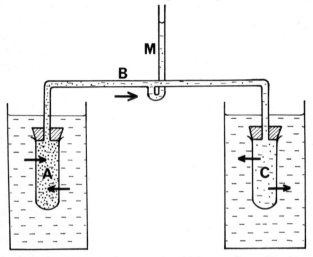

Fig. 6.4   Diagram of an osmotic system in which mass flow of liquid can occur, as postulated by Münch's hypothesis. See text for explanation.

which solutes are being translocated. Continuing exudation and visible movement in punctured or cut phloem could be artifacts caused by the wounding, but there is no explanation for a moving temperature front other than mass flow. There is considerable evidence for high turgor pressure and for a gradient of decreasing sugar concentration in the direction of flow, as required for Münch's mass-flow theory.

Some observations quoted in support of the mass-flow hypothesis are of uncertain significance. It has for instance been claimed that phloem transport is little affected by conditions surrounding the axial phloem strands, but is strongly affected by treatments modifying the metabolism of the exporting and receiving organs. The mass-flow hypothesis requires that metabolic energy be available for secretion into and removal from the sieve tubes of translocates. It is generally conceded that phloem translocation depends upon living cells and that it ceases when cells in a petiole or a stem are killed by steaming. This could be explained in terms of blocking of the conducting elements by coagulated cell material released from killed cells. However several authors have reported that translocation can be slowed down or stopped by chilling a length of stem or treating it with respiratory inhibitors and this implies that metabolic energy is required along the whole pathway of transport. Phloem tissues are reported to have high respiration rates. According to Canny (1962) 0·3–5·0% of the sucrose entering the phloem is used up in respiration during its transport.

The fact that radioactive solutes and fluorescent dyes can undergo simultaneous transport both up and down a vascular strand has been considered as contrary to expectation on the mass-flow hypothesis. This, however, is not a serious objection, for separate sieve tubes could be transporting in opposite directions. Unequivocal proof of simultaneous bidirectional transport in the same sieve tube would be extremely difficult to obtain. The difficulty is well illustrated by considering a series of experiments in which two leaves on a *Vicia faba* plant were labelled, the upper with radioactive CO_2, the lower with fluorescein, and aphids then fed on the stem between the leaves. Honeydew from a single aphid often, though not always, was simultaneously radioactive and fluorescent showing that compounds applied both above and below the feeding site were present in the same sieve tube cell. This might seem to prove bi-directional transport in the same tube, until one remembers the possibility of adjacent sieve tubes transporting in opposite directions and allowing some lateral diffusion; in *Vicia faba* there are also lateral anastomoses between separate bundles. Labelled sucrose and radioactive potassium chloride have been introduced into individual sieve tube cells of *Heracleum sphondylium* by injection from a very fine capillary pipette and the radio-activity has been found to spread both ways from the point of application at speeds of up to 450 cm/hour, yet one wonders whether the punctured phloem still functioned normally. Similarly observations that different compounds seemingly move within the phloem in the *same* direction with different speeds are not conclusive in disproving mass flow. Tritium-labelled water, fructose, radioactive phosphate and individual amino acids have been found to move each with its own speed. But different flow rates could operate in individual tubes—the methods have not permitted measurements on a level finer than a whole bundle—or substances could be separated out during flow owing to the presence of an immobile structural phase by a process analogous to chromatography. Apparent differences in speed could also be produced by different extents of lateral transport; the apparently slower rate of movement of labelled water in comparison with that of labelled solutes could well result from a higher rate of lateral diffusion of water. Further it must be borne in mind that rate measurements for separate constituents are subject to error and that, in certain instances, differences in mobility between compounds have been looked for without success.

The structure of phloem

The strongest objection to the mass-flow hypothesis comes from considerations of phloem structure. Mass flow requires continuous open channels of reasonable width; the narrower the diameter, the greater is the frictional resistance. The phloem of flowering plants consists of sieve tubes built of longitudinal files of sieve tube elements; companion cells, one or more associated with each sieve tube unit; phloem parenchyma and phloem fibres. Of these, the **sieve tubes** have a structure suggestive of a conducting function, and they are the only channels which offer a possible route for mass flow. In the mature state they usually lack normal nuclei and the cytoplasm contains few organelles; most of the lumen is filled with sap and slime, a substance containing protein, possibly as lipoprotein, and RNA. The cell diameter is 10–50 μm; this would allow mass flow, but at intervals of 150–1000 μm the tubes are interrupted by the tranverse or oblique end walls, the sieve plates, c. 0·5–2·0 μm thick, where flow would have to proceed via the much narrower sieve plate pores. The crucial question for mass flow is whether the pores are open channels, and, if so, whether their cross-sectional area is sufficient to permit transport at the observed rates.

In mature sieve tubes the pores are usually 2–6 μm in diameter but may be finer down to < 1 μm; exceptionally, as in the Cucurbitaceae, their diameter reaches 10 μm. The sieve plates and pores are usually seen to be lined with a special gluco-polysaccharide, callose, which may narrow the pore diameter to 0·1 μm. The apparent presence of callose in active phloem may, however, be an artifact since it has been shown that injury resulting from excision can cause, within seconds, callose deposition on the sieve plates.

The pore diameters are too near the limit of resolution of the light microscope to allow their contents to be examined reliably by light microscopy. Electron microscopy has so far not yielded unequivocal results and has led to a number of different models for sieve tube fine structure (Fig. 6.5). The sieve tubes are extremely delicate, highly hydrated, and susceptible to fixation injury. The cell lumen in electron micrographs typically displays fine fibrils (slime?) running parallel to the long axis of the cell; no tonoplast may be visible and it is disputable whether the contents should be regarded as cytoplasmic or vacuolar. The pores contain fibrillar material. When this is sparse, it can be taken as a continuation of the fibrillar meshwork in the lumen and mass flow through the pores would be feasible. However, the pores often seem to be blocked by very dense fibrils, and various workers have reported the presence of a lining sheath of cytoplasm and elements of endoplasmic reticulum in the pores. Proponents of the mass-flow theory regard the dense material in the pores as a precipitate formed on fixation and squeezed into plugs by the deposition of wound callose. Alternatively it is suggested that even if cytoplasm fills the pores, mass flow could proceed in the submicroscopic tubules of the endoplasmic reticulum. For an illustrated account of phloem structure the reader is referred to another book in this series by E. G. Cutter (see *Further Reading*).

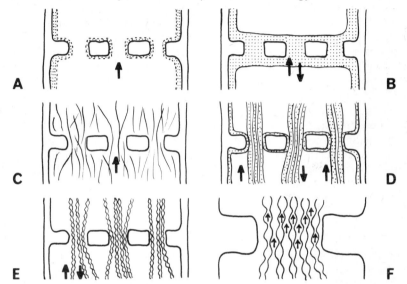

Fig. 6.5 Models of sieve tube structure showing the region of a sieve plate in longitudinal section (diagrammatic). Cytoplasm is shown stippled; arrows denote possible directions of flow. Modes of translocation possible with each model are noted.
A—empty lumen, open pores: mass flow driven by osmotic gradient.
B—membrane-covered, cytoplasm-filled pores: active transport, protoplasmic streaming, electroosmosis.
C—filamentous meshwork in lumen, open pores: mass flow, spreading along interfaces.
D—membrane-bound strands with finer contractile tubules: pumping within tubules by contractile waves; protoplasmic streaming (Thaine's model).
E (low power) and F (enlarged view of one pore)— fine contractile lipoprotein tubules: pulse flow inside tubules, mass flow outside ; spreading along interfaces (Fensom's model).
  Bidirectional transport in the same sieve tube is possible in B, D and E.

If it is assumed that the entire sieve plate pore is a hole open to flow, a hydrostatic pressure gradient of 1 atm/m has been regarded as adequate to drive mass flow at the measured rates of transport. If, however, it is accepted that there is a cytoplasmic lining to the pores, much higher pressure gradients become necessary and if the postulated conducting channels are of submicroscopic dimensions, the required forces assume impossible magnitudes. The observed pressure gradients in phloem are of the order of 0·3 atm/m, and thus seem too low to mediate mass flow even through fully open sieve plate pores.

Mass flow proceeding at 100 cm per hour involves each translocated molecule passing through 50–100 sieve plates per minute and since these plates would seem to restrict the flow it is difficult to believe that they should have been retained unless they do serve some function. One function that can be ascribed to sieve plates is that of safety devices to prevent loss of sap on wounding. From most species there is little exudation of sap from cut phloem in spite of the fact that sieve tube contents are under considerable hydrostatic pressure, for as soon as the phloem is damaged, callose deposits and slime plugs block the pores of plates near the cut. By repeated massage, the system can be desensitized so that cutting no longer induces blockage—an effect that is utilized when palms are tapped to collect the sap for palm sugar extraction. However, some hypotheses for the mechanism of translocation attempt to assign a role to the sieve plates also in the actual transport process (see below).

Alternative hypotheses for phloem translocation

The following mechanisms have been put forward either singly or in combination, as alternatives to the osmotic mass-flow hypothesis: (i) Electroosmosis; (ii) Spreading along interfaces; (iii) Protoplasmic streaming; (iv) 'Activated diffusion', or active transport. Some authors believe that some kind of 'active' translocation process may exist side-by-side with mass flow.

Electroosmosis still involves a mass flow of solution, but with the sieve plates acting as 'pumping stations'. An electric potential difference is postulated to be built up across the sieve plate by means of an active secretion of potassium ions to one side of the plate. The movement of these ions through the plates (equivalent to an electric current) would carry water and solutes with it. The potassium ions are considered to be recirculated via companion cells at the expense of more energy. This theory requires the sieve plate pores to be covered by a membrane across which a potential difference can be maintained, but which allows easy passage of water and sucrose. Experimental support for this theory is lacking and some authors discard it on the grounds that the current needed for the measured rates of translocation would be impossibly large. The concept of spreading along interfaces visualizes a process similar to the rapid spreading of oil or protein at a water–air interface to give a film of one or only a few molecules in thickness. The *molecular film* at the interface is then considered to remain intact with molecules being added at one end and removed at the other. The only experimental evidence for this hypothesis comes from observations on the spreading of certain dyes in the phloem. It is not known whether there exist, in protoplasm, surfaces over which molecules such as sucrose can spread in this manner, but since there are many membranes and fibrils in the sieve tubes, the possibility cannot be ruled out (Fig. 6.5C). The energy requirement of transport would in this case be for the main-tenance of the protoplasmic structure. However since such films are so few molecules thick many would have to be maintained to transport a major metabolite like sucrose. It would be less difficult to imagine transport of hormonal factors by some such mechanism.

Protoplasmic streaming has now been seen in sieve tubes, disproving earlier negative reports. According to one hypothesis, streaming carries compounds from one end of the sieve tube unit to the other, and at the sieve plate 'activated diffusion' transfers the compounds into the next unit cell, and so on (Fig. 6.5B). The transport of sugars across cell mem-branes is thought to require their phosphorylation, and the phloem is in fact well supplied with enzymes which phosphorylate sugar. Energy would be needed to motivate the streaming, and to provide the high-energy phosphate compounds for the sugar phosphorylation (essential to sugar entry into the sieve tubes and its activated transfer across the sieve plates).

A second hypothesis involving protoplasmic streaming has been advanced by Thaine, who claims to have observed, in living phloem, **cytoplasmic strands** 1–7 μm in thickness passing through sieve plates from one sieve tube cell to the next (Fig. 6.5D). In these strands the proto-plasm is reported to be streaming actively. Thaine postulates that these strands are continuous throughout the length of a sieve tube and contain hollow tubules with solution inside; movement of compounds can thus occur both inside the tubules in the sap, and in the streaming protoplasm on the outside. The sap could be pumped along by peristaltic waves of contraction of the tubules. In the same cell particles within strands can be seen moving in opposite directions and solution could be pumped in opposite directions in adjacent strands so that this hypothesis accommo-dates simultaneous bidirectional transport in the same sieve tube. Vari-ations in the velocities of translocation of different compounds could be explained by assuming that the rate at which solution is pumped through the tubules (say up to 300 cm/hour) is different from the rate at which components are carried in the streaming cytoplasm which by light micro-scopy has been seen to move at only up to 3·5 cm/hour. This hypothesis provides an answer to the criticism advanced against the theory of proto-plasmic streaming, namely that the streaming rates observed under the light microscope are too low. Since a mass movement of protoplasm and sugar solution is occurring, the conduction of a heat wave along the phloem would be expected. The sieve plates can be interpreted as supports for the long thin strands.

The difficulty with this theory is that, while some kind of longitudinal orientation of structures within sieve tubes is commonly seen, various authors have failed to see any streaming strands by light microscopy, or any membrane-bound strands by electron microscopy, including freeze-etching, which should give very rapid stabilization of structure. Thaine believes that this is due to the extreme fragility of the structures. After very rapid freezing of *Cucurbita* vascular bundles while they are still attached to the plant at both ends, he has demonstrated, under the light microscope, long continuous strands passing through files of sieve tube cells, and by a careful freezing technique, observed by electron microscopy, membrane-bound strands passing through sieve plate pores. Structural studies clearly are critical here.

Yet another idea, advocated by the school of Fensom, proposes that there is in sieve tubes both a 'pulse flow' inside contractile pumping lipoprotein tubules not more than 60 nm in diameter (Fig. 6.5E, F), and mass flow outside the tubules, driven either by the rhythmic contractions of many tubules pulsing in unison, or by lashing movements of contractile protein filaments attached to the tubules and beating like miniature cilia to sweep a current along. Bidirectional transport in the same sieve tube by pulse flow in different tubules would be possible, though then a mass flow could hardly be generated by the pulses. Such a mechanism could, however, coexist with an osmotically driven pressure flow and perhaps also with some spreading along interfaces, the contributions made to translocation by the different mechanisms varying between species.

The function of **companion cells** is uncertain. These cells retain their nuclei and have a cytoplasm rich in organelles. They might exercise some control over the activity of the enucleate sieve tube cells, and provide respiratory energy for the transport process. The high respiration rate of phloem may reflect the activity of the companion cells since there are few mitochondria observed in mature sieve tubes. The companion cells may be further and more directly involved in the transfer of metabolites such as sucrose and of ions into the sieve tubes. This transfer proceeds against concentration gradients, and could involve secretion into the sieve tubes from the companion cells since the enzymes (phosphatases and hexo-kinase) probably involved in sugar transport are present in the phloem and histochemical tests show very high phosphatase activity in the companion cells. The dense cytoplasm of the companion cells also suggests comparison with the cells of secretory glands. Against the concept of companion cells as fulfilling such a secretory function is evidence that radioactive phosphate and sulphate can move directly into the sieve tubes and that phloem may lack companion cells altogether.

'Transfer cells'

Present techniques permitting examination by light microscopy of plant tissue sections only 0·5–2 μm thick, coupled with electron microscopy, have revealed a special type of cell among the vascular parenchyma in certain situations, frequently adjacent to sieve tubes. These cells, termed 'transfer cells', are characterized by wall ingrowths or protuberances and a dense cytoplasm rich in organelles (Fig. 6.6). They are particularly common in the minor leaf veins of some species of Leguminosae. In leaves of *Pisum*, the transfer cells differentiate at about the same time as export from the leaves begins, and fail to develop in the dark. Transfer cells also differentiate in the cotyledons of several leguminous plants early during germination. Such cells may well be specialized for the collection of solutes and their transfer to and from the phloem. This interpretation is supported by the observation that similar wall ingrowths are characteristic of the cells of plant glands and haustorial organs, i.e. other situations where active transfer of solutes occurs.

Developmental changes in the phloem

It is generally considered that the mature sieve tube units which are enucleate and contain degenerate cytoplasm are the functional units in translocation. Some workers have proposed that by this stage in their differentiation the unit cells are already non-functional, and that translocation proceeds only through the very young sieve tube cells having abundant cytoplasmic contents. At this stage sieve pores are not formed, their sites being marked by plasmodesmata. Mass flow would not be possible in such cells, nor would Thaine's hypothesis of transcellular strands be tenable. This view that only immature sieve tube cells are involved in transport is therefore not generally accepted and some recent studies on the uptake and movement from leaves of radioactive sulphate and phosphate have indicated that the highest level of radioactivity in petioles is in the young but fully mature secondary phloem.

In most perennials with secondary growth the sieve tubes and companion cells die after one growing season, though phloem parenchyma cells and fibres survive longer. In perennial monocotyledons lacking secondary growth, the sieve tubes persist. In a few dicotyledons also, such as the lime (*Tilia*) and the grapevine (*Vitis*), the conducting cells survive for several seasons. In the lime, some sieve tube pores remain open throughout the year, though the pore diameters are restricted in the winter by callose; in the grapevine, a deposit of 'dormancy' callose closes the pores completely in the winter, but decreases when transport becomes active. Temporary depositions of callose, disappearing within

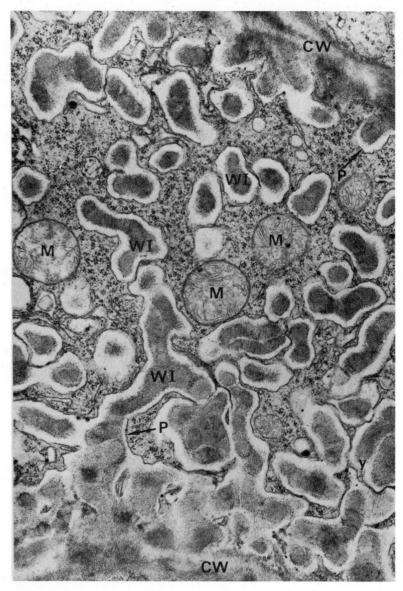

Fig. 6.6 Part of a transfer cell in the phloem of a minor vein of *Pisum arvense* L., viewed in tangential longitudinal section, showing the abundance of wall ingrowths (WI). Some ingrowths are several microns in length and repeatedly branched. Ingrowths are ensheathed in the plasmalemma (P). CW = cell wall, M = mitochondrion. × 18 000. (From Gunning and Pate, 1969, *Protoplasma*, **68**, 107–33. By permission of Springer-Verlag, Wien and New York.)

days or even hours, take place, and may be a normal means of controlling the direction of transport during the season of active translocation. Some observations on diurnal changes in the direction of translocation would become explicable if, at a particular node of the stem, the phloem becomes blocked by such callose formation for several hours during the day.

THE TRANSPORT OF STIMULI AND HORMONES

Hormones can be transported in the vascular tissues. This happens when large doses are artificially applied to plants. The synthetic hormone 2,4-dichlorophenoxyacetic acid (2,4-D) when applied to leaves moves through the phloem along with the outflow of sugars, whilst when applied to roots it moves upwards in the xylem with the transpiration stream; radioactive 2,4-D has been used as a convenient marker for both xylem and phloem transport. There is also evidence for the transport of internally synthesized hormones in vascular tissues; the bleeding sap of plants contains cytokinins and gibberellins which are apparently synthesized in roots and transported from the root to the shoot.

The movement of hormones is, however, not confined to vascular tissues, but can proceed through parenchymatous cells and it has been known for a long time that the movement of auxins involves a specific mechanism. The most striking feature of this natural auxin transport is its *polar* character (see Fig. 9.8, p. 169). In shoots auxin moves 'down' a plant, or *basipetally*, away from the apical region in which it is synthesized. The polarity is inherent in the organism and in many cases is unaffected by the orientation of the plant: when the shoot is inverted the transport still proceeds away from the apex (see also Chapter 9 and particularly Figs. 9.8 and 9.12, p. 169, p. 176). It should be noted that while net transport is basipetal, some acropetal movement does occur. In roots the polarity is reversed: the main direction of auxin movement is *acropetal* and it is believed that roots receive auxin from the shoot. Ready movement in both directions in the root has also been claimed. Not all tissues of an organ are necessarily involved in the polar transport; acropetal movement is strongly localized in the stele of maize roots and *Nicotiana* stems, the cortex and pith lacking polarity and transporting at a lower rate. On the other hand, in coleoptiles polar movement of auxin occurs in the cortical parenchyma.

The rate of polar hormone transport is much lower than the rate of transport in the vascular tissues, not reaching more than 2·0 cm/hour. The transport can occur against a concentration gradient and is generally regarded as dependent on the presence of living cells, though it has been reported that auxin moved faster in boiled *Coleus* petioles than in living; polarity was, however, completely abolished by boiling. This has led to the idea that the polarity does not involve an active transport in, say, the basi-petal direction in shoots, but rather an active inhibition of movement in the opposite direction, in living tissue. Polar transport is also dependent upon aerobic metabolism of the cells. Polar auxin transport is strongly and specifically inhibited by the 'antiauxin' TIBA (2,3,5-tri-iodobenzoic acid) and also by prolonged exposure to ethylene. Some tissues, such as the hypocotyl hook of the French bean (*Phaseolus vulgaris*) at a certain develop-mental stage, are unable to carry out the transport of auxin. The capacity for polar transport seems to diminish in tissues as they age, and its main-tenance also depends on a continued auxin supply; when the auxin-producing tip is removed from e.g. a sunflower stem, it fairly rapidly loses its capacity to transport auxin.

For a considerable time it was believed that polar transport occurred only with natural auxins and a few artificial compounds with auxin activity. More recently polar transport of gibberellins also has been demonstrated, occurring basipetally in both roots and shoots and cytokinins have been found to move basipetally in hypocotyl and petiole tissue, acropetally in roots. Very much less is known, however, of the transport of these other hormones compared with that of auxins.

The mechanism of polar transport is not understood. It is not even known whether the hormone moves in solution or, as some authors have suggested, by a surface-active movement along membranes (like spreading of sucrose along interfaces suggested as a possible means of transport in the phloem). Electric gradients have been proposed as determining the polarity; experiments, however, have indicated that these gradients may be the result of polar auxin transport, but are certainly not its cause. As the auxin moves along a longitudinal file of cells, the apical and basal ends of each cell must somehow be differentiated so that, at each cell junction, auxin moves preferentially *out of* the basal end of a cell and *into* the apical end of the next cell (in the case of basipetal transport). There is some evidence that the active secretion is localized at the basal ends of the cells, uptake by the apical ends being passive. If the hormone remains in solution in the cytoplasm, it could be carried to the basal end of the cell by cyto-plasmic streaming, ready for exit into the next cell though polar transport still occurs even if cytoplasmic streaming is inhibited. The polarity is established during cellular growth and differentiation and is probably a special aspect of the general polarity acquired by cells during their differentiation. Once established, the polarity is tenaciously maintained. In cuttings inverted and forced to root at the shoot end by hormone treatment the original polarity of IAA transport has persisted for several months, in spite of the reversal of the positions of the root and shoot apices.

The photoperiodic stimulus has not been isolated as a chemical. It is believed to be transported in phloem since it moves strictly along the path of carbohydrate transport, and the movement is enhanced by the application of sugar to a photoperiodically induced leaf (see Chapter 12), presumably because this speeds up phloem translocation from the leaf. The rate of movement is reported as 0·2–0·4 cm/hour. This is about a hundredth of the rate of carbohydrate transport (see p. 97). However since the estimation of rate of movement of the photoperiodic stimulus is based on a subsequent appearance of the flowering response, one is really measuring the time needed for accumulation of the stimulus to the level where it will elicit a response in the subsequent absence of the induced leaf or leaves. The time required for the stimulus to reach the apex is presumably much shorter, and the true rate of transport is much faster.

FURTHER READING

CANNY, M. J. (1973). *Phloem Translocation*. Cambridge University Press, London.
CRAFTS A. S. and CRISP, C. E. (1971). *Phloem Transport in Plants*. W. H. Freeman, San Francisco.
CUTTER, E. G. (1969). *Plant Anatomy: Experiment and Interpretation*. Part I. *Cells and Tissues*. Contemporary Biology Series, Edward Arnold, London.
GOLDSMITH, M. H. M. (1969). Transport of plant growth regulators. In *Physiology of Plant Growth and Development*, ed. WILKINS, M. B., 127–62. McGraw-Hill, London.
RICHARDSON, M. (1975). *Translocation in Plants*, 2nd edition. Studies in Biology, No. **10**, Edward Arnold, London.
WEATHERLEY, P. E. and JOHNSON, R. P. C. (1968). The form and function of the sieve tube: a problem of reconciliation. *Int. Rev. Cytol.*, **24**, 149–92.

SELECTED REFERENCES

BIELESKI, R. L. (1966). Accumulation of phosphate, sulphate and sucrose by excised phloem tissues. *Pl. Physiol., Lancaster*, **41**, 447–54.
BIELESKI, R. L. (1966). Sites of accumulation in excised phloem and vascular tissues. *Pl. Physiol., Lancaster*, **41**, 455–66.
CHEN, S. L. (1951). Simultaneous movement of P^{32} and C^{14} in opposite directions in phloem tissues. *Am. J. Bot.*, **38**, 203–11.
DE MARIA, M. E., THAINE, R. and SARISALO, H. I. M. (1975). Fine structure of sieve tubes prepared mainly for observation in the electron microscope by a cryogenic method. *J. exp. Bot.*, **26**, 145–60.
FENSOM, D. S. (1972). A theory of translocation in phloem of *Heracleum* by contractile microfibrillar material. *Can. J. Bot.*, **50**, 479–97.
GUNNING, B. E. S. and PATE, J. S. (1974). Transfer cells. In *Dynamic Aspects of Plant Ultrastructure*, ed. ROBARDS, A. W., 441–80. McGraw-Hill, London.
NORTHCOTE, D. H. and WOODING, F. B. P. (1966). Development of sieve tubes in *Acer pseudoplatanus*. *Proc. R. Soc., B*, **163**, 524–37.
SHAW, S. and WILKINS, M. B. (1974). Auxin transport in roots. X. Relative movement of radioactivity from IAA in the stele and cortex of *Zea* roots. *J. exp. Bot.*, **25**, 199–207.

SHELDRAKE, A. R. (1973). Auxin transport in secondary tissues. *J. exp. Bot.*, **24**, 87–96.

STOUT, P. R. and HOAGLAND, D. R. (1939). Upward and lateral movement of salt in certain plants as indicated by radioactive isotopes of potassium, sodium and phosphorus absorbed by roots. *Am. J. Bot.*, **26**, 320–4.

THAINE, R. (1969). Movement of sugars through plants by cytoplasmic streaming. *Nature, Lond.*, **222**, 873–5.

THAINE, R., DE MARIA, M. E. and SARISALO, H. I. M. (1975). Evidence of trans-cellular strands in transverse cryostat sections of *Cucurbita pepo* sieve tubes. *J. exp. Bot.*, **26**, 91–101.

WARK, M. C. (1965). Fine structure of the phloem of *Pisum sativum*. II. The companion cell and phloem parenchyma. *Aust. J. Bot.*, **13**, 185–93.

WARK, M. C. and CHAMBERS, T. C. (1965). Fine structure of the phloem of *Pisum sativum*. I. The sieve element ontogeny. *Aust. J. Bot.*, **13**, 171–83.

7

Resistance to Desiccation and Frost

We are concerned here with two aspects of plant physiology of considerable economic importance. Low temperatures and lack of water are frequently the limiting factors for plant growth and survival. To aid agricultural development the plant physiologist requires to establish satisfactory experimental criteria of resistance and to understand how far modified cultural practices can assist subsequent survival under conditions of high water stress or freezing temperatures. These problems are also of great scientific interest for their study exposes dramatically major gaps in our understanding of the regulation of the vital activities of living cells.

RESISTANCE TO DESICCATION (DROUGHT HARDINESS)

Under conditions of acute water shortage some plants can reduce their rate of water loss to a very low level by means of morphological features and physiological mechanisms so that a survival water content is maintained in their internal tissues. Such plants possess resistance due to *avoidance* of water deficit. In other cases resistance to drought results from an ability to survive considerable reduction of the water content of the living cells. Here the term ***drought hardiness*** is used to describe this capacity of living tissues to endure an exceptional degree of dehydration, rather than used in a more general sense to refer to the capacity of the plant to survive in a xeric habitat. The term *tolerance* is also used for this capacity for endurance.

Measuring desiccation: defining criteria of hardiness

The extent of desiccation can be expressed as a percentage reduction

of the full (saturating) water content, or as the percentage of water present
in the partially dehydrated tissue, or by reference to the relative humidity
of the atmosphere (water vapour pressure) with which the material is in
equilibrium. The highest water deficit (lowest water content) at which
the plant can survive has been used as a criterion of hardiness. The
adoption of this criterion faces certain difficulties. It has been stressed
that 'between the cell which is alive and that which is dead there are
numerous intermediate transitions' (Alexandrov, 1964). This comment
is particularly relevant in studies involving isolated cells or tissues, where
the possibility of testing for long-term survival is precluded. Thus an
ability by cells to accumulate a 'vital' stain such as neutral red (used
as the criterion for viability), may persist for a time after other vital
activities have been critically impaired. In view of this criticism other
workers have used as a criterion of hardiness some measure of cellular
injury. This requires careful standardization of the measure of damage
and a recognition that the extent of injury may depend upon the time
that has elapsed after the establishment of desiccation and before damage
is assessed. Injury symptoms may take hours, days or weeks to become
manifest, plants may apparently recover and then die some days later.
Irrespective of the criterion of injury or survival it has proved important
to standardize the desiccation treatment to which the plant or tissue is
submitted. The ability to withstand a given degree of dehydration is
profoundly influenced by the speed of desiccation and of reimbibition
and by the time spent in the desiccated state.

Critical Water Saturation Deficit (CSD)

A value which has been widely used to compare drought hardiness
between species and which seems to have a limited but real usefulness is
the **critical** (lethal) **water saturation deficit** or CSD. This is defined as
the water loss (expressed as a percentage of the water content at full
saturation) which results in death of the organism.

$$\text{CSD} = \frac{(\text{saturation water content}) - (\text{lethal water content})}{\text{saturation water content}} \times 100$$

Since water contents are determined from differences in the fresh and
dry weights, the equation can also be expressed:

$$\text{CSD} = \frac{(\text{saturation fresh weight}) - (\text{lethal fresh weight})}{(\text{saturation fresh weight}) - (\text{dry weight})} \times 100$$

A classification of plants on the basis of their CSD results in the following general scheme:

	CSD
True mesophytes	< 25
Xerophytic mesophytes	25–50
Mesophytic xerophytes	50–75
True xerophytes	> 75

As with all such classifications it is to be regarded as only a general guide to desiccation resistance. Some xerophytes have lower CSDs than mesophytes, but survive drying conditions by virtue of their ability to cut down water loss. As CSD is simply a measure of the capacity of the tissues to endure dehydration, a factor which gives a better indication of survival in the field is the ratio between the CSD and cuticular transpiration, i.e. water loss per unit area when stomata are closed (see Chapter 4, p. 68). This ratio is high for xerophytes since not only is their CSD generally high, but their cuticular transpiration is low. Specimen values for this ratio are:

Impatiens noli-tangere (a hydrophyte)	4
Stachys recta (a xerophyte)	16
Rhododendron ferrugineum (a xerophyte)	59
Sedum telephium ssp. *maximum* (a xerophyte)	90
Opuntia (desert xerophyte)	4000

Developmental changes in desiccation resistance

The CSD values quoted above refer to plants in the vegetative condition. Desiccation resistance however varies greatly not only from species to species, but in the same plant at different developmental stages. Most angiosperms pass through a stage of very low water content as mature seeds. In fleshy fruits, the water content of the mature seeds is much lower than that of the surrounding tissues. Ripening tomato seeds with a water content of as high as 80% will lose water even when placed in distilled water suggesting that in fleshy fruits at least part of the water loss from the seeds must be by an active excretion of water. When fruits are ripe the water content of the seeds ranges from about 25% to over 50% and, except where seeds are enclosed in a fleshy fruit, they continue to dry until their water content is in equilibrium with atmospheric humidity, at which stage they contain 5 to 20% water. The water content of some seeds can be experimentally reduced still further without loss of viability (either by storage in vacuum or by brief heating to above 100°C). Reduction of the water contents of seeds of *Raphanus sativus*, *Brassica napus* and *Nigella damascena* to 1·4–1·8%, by brief heating at 120–137°C, retarded their subsequent germination, and delayed flowering in the resulting plants. These effects could be partially reversed by application of the growth-regulating substances, gibberellic acid and kinetin. Seeds of birch (*Betula* spp.) have been stored for $1\frac{1}{2}$ years with water contents of 0·01–0·4%, without loss of ability to germinate. Not all seeds, however, are so highly resistant towards desiccation. Seeds of silver maple (*Acer saccharinum*) are shed from the parent plant with a water content of 58% and die if this falls below 30–34%; similarly the seeds of several citrus fruits and wild rice (*Zizania aquatica*) also are very sensitive to desiccation. The desiccation resistance of seeds is lost gradually during their germination. In germinating dwarf French bean seeds the early stages of hydration are completely reversible; the seeds can be allowed to imbibe until they contain 40–50% water and then be dried back to the air-dry condition and this can be repeated several times without impairing subsequent growth. Up to 98% of the water can be removed from wheat seedlings up to the stage when the coleoptile is 3–4 mm long without lethal effect; the emerged radicles are killed by this treatment but new roots can still be formed from initials in the embryo. After this stage wheat seedlings become progressively more sensitive to desiccation. Similar results have been obtained with seedlings of other species.

After germination, most flowering plants can never again endure desiccation to really low water contents. There are, however, some very interesting exceptions. The 'resurrection plants' such as *Myrothamnus flabellifolia* and *Chamaegigas intrepidus*, both from the hot dry regions of South Africa, can dry right down to contain as little as 7% water and revive quickly when wetted. The aquatic plant *Ramondia nathaliae* from Macedonia can endure reaching an air-dry condition when its pool dries up. Such an ability to endure desiccation is much more common among bryophytes, lichens and algae than among flowering plants.

In many instances it has been reported that the younger parts of plants and seedlings can survive a given degree of desiccation for a longer time than the mature parts, and meristematic cells have therefore been regarded as hardier than mature tissue cells. The validity of such a generalization is however doubtful for during removal of water from whole plants there is a redistribution of water from the mature parts and towards the growth regions. Further, in evergreens, mature leaves are hardier than young or ageing ones. In perennials of temperate and arctic climates, desiccation resistance in stems and leaves shows a regular seasonal change, being greatest during the winter months, at which time the water content of the tissues falls due to diminished water uptake by the roots (Fig. 7.1). In deciduous species, resistance to desiccation is increased by removal of the most susceptible organs by leaf abscission. It seems generally true that long-term cultivation with a low water supply induces xeromorphism and that short periods of moderate desiccation can confer on plants the ability to endure subsequently more severe desiccation. However the claims made by various Russian workers, that partial drying of imbibed grains hardens cereals against drought for the rest of their life, cannot be regarded as established.

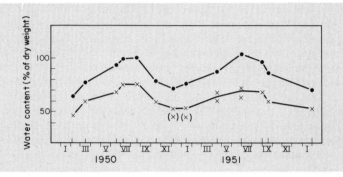

Fig. 7.1 Yearly variation in desiccation resistance of needles of stone pine (*Pinus cembra*) measured as water content at which injury occurs. Upper curve : incipient injury, 1–2% of leaf area injured ; lower curve : one third of leaves dead. Injury was judged by the loss of semipermeability, resulting in the outward leakage of fluorescent vacuolar compounds. (Adapted from Pisek and Larcher, 1954, *Protoplasma*, **44**, 30–48.)

Physical and chemical effects of desiccation

The most satisfactory explanation for death from desiccation is that this is a direct consequence of structural disorganization resulting from water removal. The drying protoplast is subjected to stress (tension) due to its contraction in volume and its adherence to the cell wall; this tension could lead to cytoplasmic rupture in the drying cells. In agreement with this concept of the nature of desiccation injury it has been found that gradual desiccation can be endured much better than sudden drying and that gradual remoistening is also beneficial since, if the dried tissue is rapidly flooded with water, stresses are again produced as the walls and outer cytoplasmic layers are rapidly hydrated. By very careful desiccation in graded sucrose solutions, or exposure to gradually decreasing humidity, followed by equally gradual remoistening, Iljin (1935) was apparently able to bring epidermal cells of numerous species, usually considered non-resistant, to the air-dry state and to revive them. This led him to conclude that all protoplasm can be desiccated completely if this is done with sufficient care. This conclusion must at present be accepted with reserve as his recognition of survival was based entirely upon the ability of the cells to take up neutral red. Nevertheless such experiments emphasize the protective value of slow changes in water content. At the molecular level structural damage may be expressed by denaturation of macromolecules, mainly proteins and particularly membrane proteins. The plasmalemma, being attached to the wall, would be particularly subject to strain. Rupture of membranes at the submicroscopic level may occur without gross rupture of cytoplasm and indeed many authors now think this fine level damage, rather than rupture on a coarser level, to be the most common cause of death. Reactions of protein sulphydryl (SH) groups may be important. Many proteins contain a certain number of SH groups, and disulphide (SS) bridges derived from oxidation of two closely approaching SH groups may maintain the native configuration of the protein. It is postulated that, during desiccation, proteins are unfolded by mechanical stress, bringing SH groups previously masked within the molecule to the surface, while at the same time the withdrawal of water brings the molecules close together. The SH groups of adjacent molecules then could form SS bridges, binding the molecules into irreversibly denatured aggregates. Furthermore the increased concentration of ions which follows dehydration could play a part in the denaturation of proteins for surface ionic charges are involved in the maintenance of protein structure.

Metabolic changes also occur on desiccation. Growth slows down and stops as turgidity is lost. Photosynthesis rapidly declines in rate and eventually ceases with decreasing water content (Fig. 7.2). In leaves this is partly due to the exclusion of carbon dioxide by stomatal closure but a direct effect on the photosynthetic apparatus is also involved, for the rate of photosynthesis falls quickly when submerged aquatics are dehydrated in sugar solutions. Decreases in protein content (due to enhanced protein breakdown) and losses of mineral ions to the external medium also take place during desiccation of tissues. In contrast to other metabolic activities respiration rate frequently rises considerably during the early stages of desiccation (Fig. 7.2), falling only as this continues to a more extreme level. The initial rise in respiration rate has been regarded as caused by an increased sugar concentration (see below), or by uncoupling from the normally linked synthesis of ATP. If respiration is uncoupled it represents a wasteful exhaustion of the plants' nutrient reserves. Some authors, however, have interpreted the rise in the respiration rate as a mechanism for providing additional energy for the repair of structural damage caused by desiccation (and also as providing some water as an end product!). On this latter view, the metabolic changes that occur on desiccation fall into two phases: early in desiccation aspects of metabolism are enhanced, tending to combat injury, but, as dehydration continues, this gives place to a phase of falling metabolic activity, symptomatic of injury. During and after rehydration, the rates of photo-synthesis and respiration gradually return to their normal levels provided that there has been no irreparable injury but this occurs the more slowly the more severe the desiccation. Desiccation can thus bring about two very different types of injury: rapid direct structural damage to protoplasm, and slower indirect damage consequent upon metabolic disturbance.

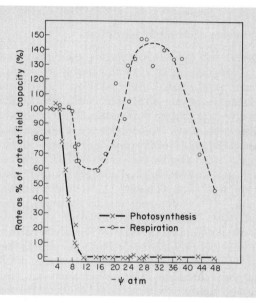

Fig. 7.2   The effect of water stress on the rates of photosynthesis and respiration in loblolly pine (*Pinus taeda*) seedlings. Water stress is expressed as the leaf ψ in atmospheres. Rates of photosynthesis and respiration are given as a percentage of the rates with the soil moisture at field capacity. (Adapted from Brix, 1962, *Physiologia Pl.*, **15**, 10–20.)

The extent of injury is clearly determined not only by the degree of desiccation reached, but the duration of time over which a subnormal water content persists. If the water content remains high enough to permit the continuance of metabolic activity, the persistence of the disturbed metabolism will result in a progressive increase in injury. A time factor is, however, involved even when the water content is extremely low; presumably adverse changes continue in the tissues even though metabolism may be reduced below the detectable level. Provided the critical water saturation deficit is not reached, leaves have, in some instances, been observed to endure a greater water loss better than a lesser one, and some epidermal strips have survived extreme better than less severe desiccation. Seeds must be stored at a low water content, otherwise they lose their viability more rapidly. Where tissues are very sensitive to structural injury moderate dehydration will be less injurious than extreme dehydration; where tissues are less sensitive towards structural injury a really low water content will have the beneficial effect of inhibiting the progress of metabolic disturbance.

Physiological basis of drought hardiness

Both structural and biochemical factors are involved in hardiness. Many hardy plants have small cells and it may be predicted that the smaller the volume dehydrated, the weaker are the mechanical stresses created. Resistant tissues are often characterized by flexible cell walls which readily cave in or fold up during dehydration thus minimizing the tension on their protoplasts. However, many hardy plants do not have particularly small cells and clearly seasonal changes in resistance proceed without changes in cell size or wall flexibility. It therefore seems that certain physiological and biochemical changes are more important than cell size and wall flexibility. The most clear-cut of these is a decrease in osmotic potential (OP) of the cells due to an increased sugar content resulting from starch hydrolysis. The decreased OP will reduce water removal by lowering vapour pressure but, probably more important, sugar serves to stabilize protoplasmic colloids, preventing their denaturation by replacing water molecules from the hydration shells. Artificial application of sugar solutions during desiccation has been shown to reduce desiccation injury. There is some evidence for the protection of SH groups against oxidation to SS bridges in hardy tissues. This would not only prevent protein aggregation, but would also maintain in an active state enzymes depending on free SH groups for their activity. Other changes whose biochemical nature cannot be clearly specified also lead during the induction of hardiness to an increase in the resistance of protoplasmic proteins to denaturation, an increase in the amount of water strongly bound to colloids and an increase in the viscosity and elasticity of cytoplasm.

Recently, attention has been drawn to nucleic acid metabolism as a factor in drought resistance. In a study of the effects of desiccation on two members of the Oleaceae, the desiccation-resistant olive (*Olea europaea*) and the non-resistant *Ligustrum sinensis*, it was found that, on dehydration, the leaves of olive showed a striking increase in both DNA and RNA, whereas in *Ligustrum* leaf DNA content fell and there was only a slight increase in RNA (Fig. 7.3). Furthermore it was found that the average base composition of the RNA in olive changed, the ratio of

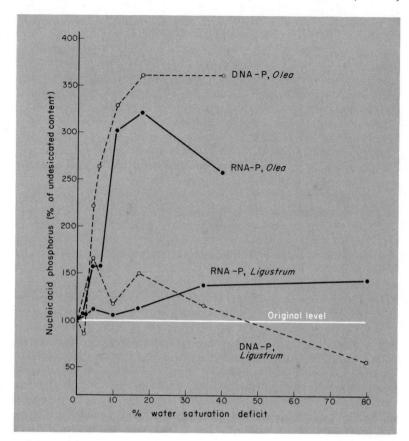

Fig. 7.3 The effect of desiccation on nucleic acid contents of leaves of the desiccation-resistant olive and the sensitive *Ligustrum*. (From Kessler and Frank-Tishel, 1962, *Nature, Lond.*, **196**, 542–3.)

guanine plus cytosine to adenine plus uracil increasing from 1·07 to 1·38; this may be significant because the guanine-cytosine base pairs are more stable, being more strongly hydrogen-bonded. An increase in total RNA and in the proportion of guanine plus cytosine has been observed also in maize seedlings during desiccation. These changes have been interpreted as indicative either of the formation of a more resistant protoplasmic structure, or of an increased metabolic capacity, enhancing the ability of the plant to recover from injury. RNA mediates in protein synthesis; an increased RNA content could therefore speed up synthesis of protein to replace that which is denatured.

RESISTANCE TO COLD (FROST HARDINESS)

Frost hardiness and cold damage

Plants do not possess any specific system of temperature regulation. Occasionally where heat loss is slow, as in the centres of tree trunks, temperatures as much as $10°C$ above the ambient have been recorded. Generally, even inside bulky plant organs, the temperature is only slightly above mean air temperature. Under conditions of rising air temperature, plant organs are usually clearly below ambient temperature. Avoidance of temperature shift is not possible and hardiness or tolerance is the sole means of resistance.

Difficulties similar to those encountered in defining and assessing desiccation resistance apply also to cold resistance. The effects of cold depend not only on the lowest temperature reached but upon rates of cooling and warming, the time for which the minimum temperature persists and the subsequent treatment after warming.

Examples of minimum temperatures which can be endured by flowering plants are given in Table 7.1. Since the lowest temperature recorded in regions of the earth where plants grow is -60 to $-70°C$, it is clear from this Table that certain plants and plant structures can endure at least for short periods temperatures below those they will ever encounter in nature—indeed very close to absolute zero ($-273°C$). Plant species native to climates with a cold winter are more resistant than the species of warm climates. The cold resistance of perennials of temperate and arctic zones undergoes striking seasonal changes (Figs. 7.4, 7.5), being very much higher in the winter months than in summer; without the winter increase in resistance plants of these zones would be unable to survive the rigours of winter. The increase in hardiness occurs in the autumn as a consequence of the falling temperature and shortening day length and is associated with the onset of winter dormancy. The loss of hardiness follows from the relatively rapid rise in temperature in the following spring. Artificially, hardening can be induced at any season by chilling, and resistance destroyed in mid-winter by warming. In the field, cold injury is most frequent in spring when late frosts act on the non-hardy tissues. In severe winters, greater resistance is developed than in mild ones.

Resistance varies greatly between the organs of a plant. Underground structures are much less resistant than aerial parts, and their resistance is much more uniform over the year, because soil temperatures never fall as low as air temperatures and show less annual temperature variation. In a study of 43 species from a mid-European deciduous woodland, the minimum temperature endured by any underground organ was found to be $-13 \cdot 5°$C, and the annual amplitude of variation, i.e. difference between the highest and lowest minimum temperature, varied according to species from $4 \cdot 5$ to $8 \cdot 5°$C. Aerial parts from the same woodland plants could survive in temperatures below $-40°$C, and annual variation between highest and lowest minimum temperatures varied from 9 to 36°C. Buds increased in resistance with distance from the ground. These differences in resistance showed a clear correspondence with the temperatures that the organs could be called upon to endure in their environment.

Some tropical species are killed on being cooled to between 0 and $+5°$C, but in the majority of plants injury or death from cold occurs only when ice forms in the tissues. The estimated freezing points of plants

Table 7.1   Some examples of low temperature resistance of flowering plants and plant organs.
Where the time endured is given, it specifies the particular experimental conditions without implying that this is the longest time that can be endured. In the examples marked *, the temperature given shows the limit of resistance; in the other cases, temperatures lower than those shown were not tested. ? indicates that time endured or criterion of survival is not clearly indicated in the reference source.

Plant material	Temperature, °C	Time endured	Criterion of survival
Pollen grains	c. -273	2 hours	Germination.
Seeds, vacuum dehydrated	c. -273	10 hours	Germination.
	-253	77 hours	Germination.
	-190	6 weeks	Germination.
Winter leaves, *Pinus strobus*	-196	5 minutes	Tetrazolium test for dehydrogenases; appearance for 4 weeks.
Bark cells, *Morus* twig	-196	160 days	Plasmolysis tests.
Germinating seedlings, *Pisum sativum*	-183	1 minute	Subsequent growth.
Bark cells, *Robinia pseudacacia*	< -59	?	Vital staining; cell permeability tests.
*Winter buds, temperate zone deciduous trees	-21 to < -40	2 hours	Absence of visible damage often up to 5 weeks.
*January leaves, *Hedera helix*	-25	Varied; cooling rate kept constant	Appearance; tetrazolium test for dehydrogenases.
*Winter leaves, *Quercus ilex*	-13	?	?
*Summer leaves, *Quercus ilex*	-6	?	?

(strictly, of their liquid phases) vary from just below zero to lower than $-5°C$ (see Levitt, 1972), but plants do not always show a definite freezing point, the amount of ice increasing with falling temperature over a considerable temperature range. Many plant protoplasts and cell walls can be supercooled considerably, and it is clear that supercooling is less injurious than ice formation. Because different species start to freeze at different temperatures it has been suggested that the frost hardiness of a plant should be measured not in terms of the actual temperature that it can withstand, but by the difference between its own 'freezing point' and the lethal temperature. Any plant that is killed as soon as it freezes would on such a scale have a frost hardiness of zero. This criterion is, however, of little practical use because of the difficulty of defining the freezing procedure and recognizing the freezing point.

Physical and chemical effects of frost

Frost injury could arise from one or more of the following: mechanical damage by ice crystals; dehydration tensions due to water withdrawal into the growing ice crystals; structural damage due to shrinkage on dehydration and to excessive rapid flooding with water when the ice melts; protein denaturation due to dehydration and the increased concentration of electrolytes produced by freezing. Except for mechanical damage from ice crystals similar changes are implicated in desiccation injury. Metabolic disturbances are less likely to be important in frost injury because at freezing and sub-freezing temperatures metabolic reactions are often lowered below the limit of detection. Metabolic disturbances cannot however be ruled out in species that die of low temperature shock (rapid cooling to temperatures above their freezing point), since some chemical reactions still proceed in a frozen medium; indeed some enzymatic reactions are actually accelerated in ice.

Freezing can be intracellular, ice crystals forming inside the cells, or extracellular, with the ice confined to extracellular (intercellular) spaces. Intracellular ice can form when cooling is sufficiently rapid, and is fatal unless the cooling rate is so fast that the cell contents 'vitrify', the ice crystals then being of submicroscopic dimensions. Such cooling rates can however be achieved only under laboratory conditions. With slow cooling, ice formation always begins outside the cells, and the water passes out from the cells to the growing crystals; the lipid nature of the plasmalemma offers a high resistance to seeding crystals of ice entering the protoplast. Such slow cooling is therefore endured better than rapid cooling, and parallels what happens in plants frozen naturally in the field where only extracellular ice has been recorded. Frost hardiness therefore normally means resistance to *extracellular* freezing, since no tissues can endure intracellular freezing and the mechanical damage by ice crystals which is the cause of death on intracellular freezing is not involved. Though extracellular ice can greatly compress and distort cells, and may, for example, separate the epidermis widely from the palisade tissue in some leaves, no cell rupture occurs. The presence of extracellular

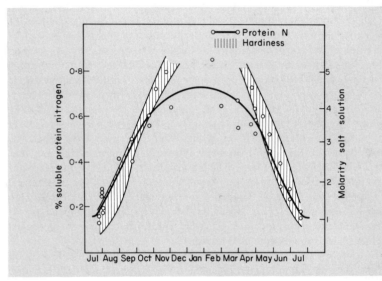

Fig. 7.4 Changes during the year in hardiness and water-soluble protein nitrogen in the living bark cells of the black locust (*Robinia pseudacacia*). Hardiness is shown as the range of molarities of balanced salt solution whose dehydrating action the cells can survive. (From Siminovitch and Chater, 1958, in *The Physiology of Forest Trees*, ed. Thimann, K. V., 219–50. Copyright 1958. The Ronald Press Co., New York.)

ice therefore does not in itself inflict any irreversible injury. Just as slow cooling is endured better than fast cooling, so with slow thawing, tissues can survive freezing treatments that are fatal if followed by sudden thawing.

The present view is therefore that frost damage is caused primarily by the withdrawal of water into ice crystals and that frost injury is a form of desiccation damage. In support of this it has proved possible to measure indirectly the frost resistance of tree bark by measuring its resistance towards dehydration by plasmolysing solutions (Fig. 7.4) or by drying out in air. As in the case of desiccation at higher temperatures, the moment of injury can be during dehydration (freezing) or rehydration (thawing), or develop gradually in the dehydrated (frozen) state, depending on the time course followed. If then frost damage is primarily due to dehydration it can be postulated that the injury is due to the development of mechanical stresses and the denaturation of macromolecules.

Freezing has been shown to impair the activities of some enzymes, but many enzymes can withstand freezing and the most important effect is again thought to be damage to cellular membranes through denaturation and aggregation of membrane proteins. Involvement of the plasmalemma is shown by the fact that loss of semipermeability and outward leakage of cell contents are usually among the first signs of freezing injury. Aggregates of denatured protein (bound by SS bridges) could interrupt the normal structure of the bimolecular lipid layer (which is highly impermeable to hydrophilic compounds) and create in effect 'holes' through which water-soluble compounds can leak. The aggregation of proteins would be favoured by breaks in the lipid layer, caused by the mechanical stresses set up in the membrane by water withdrawal. The lipid layer would be susceptible to breaking, for the hydrophobic forces of attraction between the lipid molecules become weak at low temperatures. Protection can sometimes be afforded by application of compounds which do not penetrate the plasma membrane. In isolated chloroplasts and mitochondria freezing destroys the capacity for phosphorylation, an activity dependent on membrane integrity, and fine structural studies have shown chloroplast membrane disorganization at freezing.

In spite of the fundamental equivalence of freezing and desiccation injury, the removal of a given quantity of water by freezing does not have precisely the same effect as the removal of an identical amount by drying at a higher temperature. One obvious reason for this difference is that at freezing temperatures metabolic disturbances are largely inhibited. Freezing resistance often parallels desiccation resistance closely, i.e. the more resistant a tissue is towards freezing, the more resistant is it also towards desiccation. Nevertheless the fatal degree of dehydration has a different value when achieved by freezing than when reached by drying. The effect on the protoplasts is related not only to the total amount of water removed, but to the conditions under which it is removed.

The physiological basis of frost hardiness

From the above discussion it would be expected that the frost resistance of a tissue will depend on both the amount and state of water in its cells. The greatest cold resistance is encountered in dry seeds. Before subjection to the very low temperatures shown in Table 7.1, the seeds were dried as completely as possible in a vacuum; the minute traces of water left were in a bound state inaccessible to freezing. During the period of frost hardening of perennials, there is a tendency for a decrease in the total water content in the tissues, and an increase in the proportion of bound water, associated with an increased hydration capacity of cell colloids. In many species there is also an increase in soluble carbohydrates (Fig. 7.5), most commonly sucrose, but also (in certain cases) of other sugars, and of polyhydric alcohols. These soluble carbohydrates apparently stabilize protoplasmic colloids and by increasing the osmotic value lower the freezing point of the cell contents, in some instances by as much as several degrees. Increases of up to 20% in cytoplasmic contents during development of frost hardiness have been reported. In the bark of the black locust tree, and in ivy leaves, soluble protein content increases on hardening and falls in the spring parallel to the loss of hardiness (Figs. 7.4, 7.5). Although during the winter no new protein species were detectable in the black locust bark by electrophoresis of bark extracts, one protein increased greatly in proportion to the others. If the synthesis of protein is inhibited in lengths of the stems by interrupting their nitrogen supply by ringing, then hardening fails to occur. The autumnal increase in protein in the bark of many tree species is accompanied by an increase in RNA content (compare the increases in RNA occurring during induction of desiccation resistance). Increases in bark lipids have been reported from some species and the degree of unsaturation of the lipids increases. The more fluid nature of unsaturated lipids might permit coalescence on thawing and repair of 'membrane holes' formed on freezing. Protein sulphydryl groups are said to become less susceptible to oxidation to SS bridges during hardening. There is also a suggestion that the chains of proteins synthesized during the hardening period may fold into frost-stable configurations. The tertiary structure of a protein molecule is maintained by a combination of hydrophilic and hydrophobic bonds between amino acids in the polypeptide chain and the same chain can fold into several configurations according to conditions. The hydrophilic bonds remain strong at low temperatures, when the hydrophobic bonds are weakened. If proteins synthesized during hardening fold with their hydrophilic groups concentrated in the interior of the molecule, the hydrophilic bonds formed there could keep the chain from unfolding and denaturing as cellular water is lost on freezing. The protoplasm as a whole becomes more hydrophilic and colloid hydration increases. Although most workers agree that the protoplasts withdraw more easily from the walls when frost resistance has been induced, agreed data on changes in protoplasmic viscosity and elasticity are lacking. Frost resistant cells are more permeable to water making it easier for water to leave the cells and lessening the risk of intracellular freezing. Hardy cells supercool more readily than non-hardy cells but the reason for this is not known.

The courses of the annual changes in frost and desiccation resistance of plants of temperate zones run parallel; hardening against frost by low temperature treatment hardens also against desiccation and *vice versa*.

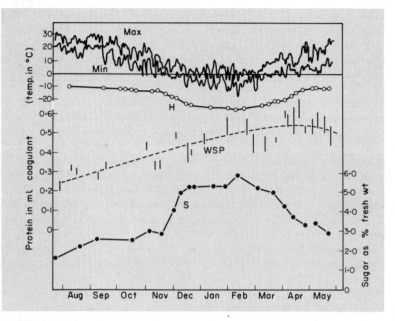

Fig. 7.5 Annual changes in frost hardiness 'H' (measured as temperature endured), water-soluble protein content 'WSP' and soluble sugars 'S' in the leaves of ivy, *Hedera helix*; the actual temperature maxima and minima are given in the top curves. Viability in the hardiness test was judged by a tetrazolium test for activity of dehydrogenases. Protein is measured as ml coagulated by ethanol precipitation from leaf extract. (Adapted from Parker, 1962, *Pl. Physiol., Lancaster*, **37**, 809–13.)

Further during the time of greatest resistance towards frost and desiccation, plants show high resistance towards other injurious agents such as high temperature, certain chemicals, lack of oxygen and high hydrostatic pressures. This has led some authors to the concept of a 'general resistance', a protoplasmic condition in which protoplasm shows hardiness against all injurious influences. Although resistance to a number of injurious influences may have a common basis, it is an oversimplification to deny the existence of more than one mechanism of resistance. The resistance to high temperature of a number of temperate zone evergreens shows two annual maxima. One coincides with the winter maximum of cold and drought resistance, and can therefore be regarded as an aspect of the 'general resistance'; the second maximum however occurs in mid-summer when the frost resistance is at a minimum, and is clearly a separate phenomenon related to the high summer temperatures. Cold hardening increases heat resistance, but the reverse is not true. Furthermore when we talk of a 'general resistance' we are thinking only of resistance at the cellular level and ignoring other factors characteristic of the particular species which are superimposed on cellular resistance. Thus resistance in the field is modified by plant habit and organ anatomy.

The ability of any plant to develop drought and frost resistance is limited by its genetic constitution and such potentialities are under polygenic control. Species, varieties and ecotypes show differing capacities to develop hardiness. Successful breeding of varieties resistant to drought and frost would result in greater productivity and provide more varied crops over large areas of the earth's surface. In 1966, India was being threatened with famine because drought had caused widespread failure of the rice harvest. Such problems have faced Man on this planet throughout history. Nevertheless within a relatively short time the resistance of plants to adverse conditions may be exploited and increased by the development of varieties designed for growth at a space station on the moon or even some remote planet. Intensive research into these problems carried out in the interests of the conquest of space may yet benefit those of us who remain earthbound.

FURTHER READING

ALDEN, J. and HERMANN, R. K. (1971). Aspects of the cold-hardiness mechanism in plants. *Bot. Rev.*, **37**, 37–142.

ALEXANDROV, V. Y. (1964). Cytophysiological and cytoecological investigations of heat resistance of plant cells toward the action of high and low temperature. *Q. Rev. Biol.*, **39**, 35–77.

HENCKEL, P. A. (1964). Physiology of plants under drought. *A. Rev. Pl. Physiol.*, **15**, 363–86.

LEVITT, J. (1972). *Responses of Plants to Environmental Stresses*. Academic Press, New York and London.

SELECTED REFERENCES

KESSLER, B. and FRANK-TISHEL, J. (1962). Dehydration-induced synthesis of nucleic acids and changing of composition of ribonucleic acid: a possible protective reaction in drought-resistant plants. *Nature, Lond.*, **196**, 542–3.

LEVITT, J. (1969). Growth and survival of plants at extremes of temperature—unified concept. *Symp. Soc. exp. Biol.*, **23**, 395–448.

MAZUR, P. (1965). Causes of injury in frozen and thawed cells. *Fedn Proc. Fedn Am. Socs exp. Biol.*, **24**, 2 (III), Suppl. **15**, S 175–82.

SIEGEL, S. M., HALPERN, L. A., GIUMARRO, C., RENWICK, G. and DAVIS, G. (1963). Martian biology: the experimentalist's approach. *Nature, Lond.*, **197**, 329–31.

SIMINOVITCH, D. (1963). Evidence from increase in RNA and protein synthesis in autumn for increase in protoplasm during the frost hardening of black locust bark cells. *Can. J. Bot.*, **41**, 1301–8.

SIMINOVITCH, D. and CHATER, A. P. J. (1958). Biochemical processes in the living bark of the black locust tree in relation to frost hardiness and the seasonal cycle. In *The Physiology of Forest Trees*, ed. THIMANN, K. V., 219–50. Ronald Press, New York.

8

Growth: Progress and Pattern

THE DEFINITION AND MEASUREMENT OF GROWTH

Growth is one of the most fundamental and conspicuous characteristics of living organisms being the consequence of increase in the amount of living protoplasm. Externally this is usually manifested by the growing system getting bigger and growth is therefore often defined as an irreversible increase in the mass, weight or volume of a living organism, organ or cell. The size increase must be permanent; the swelling of a cell in water is not growth, being easily reversed by returning the cell to a sufficiently concentrated solution. It is, however, possible to consider as growth, changes not immediately involving increase in size. An amphibian embryo, or a *Selaginella* female gametophyte, for a long time utilizes the nutrient store with which it was released from the parent, to produce many new cells, without any size increase yet growing in the sense that protoplasm is increasing at the expense of stored nutrients.

Growth can be measured in a variety of ways. Since increase in the amount of protoplasm is difficult to measure directly, one generally measures some quantity which is more or less proportional to it, such as:

1. *Fresh weight.* This measurement is usually easy and may be possible without injury to the growing system. However, a plant organ must be detached from the plant to be weighed, and an entire plant which has been removed from its growth surroundings for weighing can hardly be replaced undisturbed. Thus growth measurements by weighing usually necessitate the taking of successive samples from a series of plants.
2. *Dry weight.* This is sometimes considered more meaningful than fresh weight, because the increase in fresh weight may be largely the

result of water uptake, and fluctuations in fresh weight may occur as a result of fluctuations in the plant's water content. In a germinating seedling, the dry weight decreases while the seedling is growing, and in such a case the fresh weight increase is a better indication of growth.

3. *Length.* A suitable measure in the case of an organ growing in one direction with uniform diameter, such as a young root tip or a pollen tube.

4. *Area.* Used to assess growth in a system growing mainly in two dimensions, such as an expanding leaf.

Length and area measurements have the attraction that they can be carried out on the same organ over a period of time without destroying it.

These are the chief criteria applied in assessing the growth of a multicellular organism like a flowering plant. For microscopic unicellular organisms, or tissue cultures, other measurements are possible and indeed more suitable. *Volume* of a cell mass can be determined by centrifuging the cells in a graduated centrifuge tube, and for single cells volume can be calculated from measurements made under the microscope. Increase in the *turbidity* of a cell suspension is related to increase in the *number of cells* present. Cell number can also be estimated by direct counting using a special slide (haemocytometer) originally designed for counting blood cells. Other special criteria are estimates of *protein nitrogen* or *respiration rate* per unit of cell mass. The units in which growth is expressed are as diverse as the methods of measurement (increase in weight, area, length, cell number, protein nitrogen, per hour, day, week), and growth rates can be expressed in absolute or relative terms (see p. 138, *et seq.*).

Growth is always accompanied by change in form and physiological activity, by **differentiation**. The identical cells produced by cell division in an apical shoot meristem enlarge and at the same time become different from the meristematic cells, and from each other, forming for instance parenchyma or xylem or phloem. In their mature form these tissue cells are of very different structure and function. Nevertheless certain growth processes are common to all cells and, during the initial stages of a cell's development, these common processes predominate. In the meristem, the newly formed cells grow first by **plasmatic growth**, a synthesis of protoplasm. In cells destined to remain meristematic, a doubling of cell mass is followed by division; in those destined to undergo further growth there follows a phase of **expansion** (elongation) **growth**, characterized by rapid volume increase, water uptake accompanied by vacuolation, and cell wall synthesis. Then, as expansion slows down, divergences in cell development become dominant. While basic protoplasmic components, such as enzyme proteins and nucleic acids, increase in quantity in all cells during growth, the proportional increases in particular enzymes differ so that cells of varied metabolism are formed. Cell wall growth occurs in all cells, but as differentiation proceeds characteristic differences in the pattern, extent and chemical composition of the new wall material become apparent. The completion of differentiation leads to the formation of the mature living tissue cell or dead cell element. The mature tissue cells ultimately age and die. Such a sequence of changes, constituting the overall process of **development**, unfolds during the life history of every cell and is represented diagrammatically in Fig. 8.1. Similar developmental stages may be distinguishable in the life history of an organ or organism. Although developmental stages overlap in time it is still possible to separate growth from differentiation experimentally and conceptually. Thus it is possible to suppress differentiation by applying appropriate inhibitory chemicals while permitting growth to continue. Further these two aspects of development seem in many

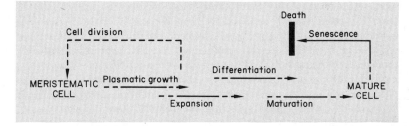

Fig. 8.1 Diagrammatic representation of the sequence of processes which constitute the development of a cell of a higher plant.

developing systems to be mutually competitive: conditions which favour rapid growth often suppress differentiation, and *vice versa*. For instance, plants whose growth is retarded by a deficient water supply may show an enhanced degree of cellular differentiation (see also Chapter 9).

In the light of the above discussion, it is possible to advance a definition of growth as follows: 'Growth is a synthesis of protoplasm, usually accompanied by a change in form and an increase in mass of the growing system. The total mass increase may be many times that of the increase in the mass of the protoplasmic components proper.' Again, from the above it is clear that growth can be considered at several levels. In order of increasing complexity, one can distinguish growth at the level of the cell, the tissue, the organ and the organism. The growth of a system above the cell level is brought about by a combination of *cell multiplication* and *cell growth*. One single maize root tip can give rise to 17 500 new cells per hour, or 420 000 per day. During the development of a root tip meristem cell into a root parenchyma cell it expands by about 30 times; volume increases of several hundred-fold are not uncommon; in the water melon (*Citrullus vulgaris*) the volume of the initial cells increases by 350 000 times and, in extreme cases, development of water-storage cells may involve expansions of a million-fold.

LOCALIZATION OF GROWTH IN SPACE AND TIME

Flowering plants continue growth throughout their life history by virtue of persistent localized growth centres or meristems. Elongation growth and the formation of organs result from the activities of meristems at the root and shoot apices and, in monocotyledons, also of additional intercalary meristems at internodes and leaf bases. Increases in the diameters of plant axes are brought about by the activities of vascular and cork cambia. New cells are formed in these meristems and the development of mature tissue cells by growth and differentiation takes place in close proximity to the meristems. Whilst still in the seedling stage the plant already contains cells at all stages of development—meristematic, expanding, mature, senescent and dead. The age of a plant and the age of its cells are quite different. Trees live for hundreds or even thousands of years, but their tissue cells have a much more limited life, rarely more than one or two years, exceptionally up to 100 years in tree pith. The life history of an entire plant of indeterminate growth cannot therefore be divided into stages corresponding to those depicted in Fig. 8.1. Frequently, however, during the development of organs of determinate growth, a phase of cell division comes first, with no or slight cell expansion and this is then followed by cell expansion growth not associated with increase in cell number. This growth pattern has been shown in the *Arum* spadix (Fig. 8.2) and in cucurbit fruits, tomato fruits and ripening bean cotyledons. In apical meristems a region of cell division is separate from a region of expansion; cells in the dividing region do not expand appreciably, and cells in the expanding region divide very infrequently. In fruits, separation of cell division and expansion is temporal rather than spatial. But this rule is not universal; in potato tubers, cell division and expansion proceed concurrently at least while the tuber grows from a weight of c. 40 mg to 200 g; during this time cell number increases 500 times, divisions continuing at a uniform rate throughout the period, while the average cell volume increases tenfold. Full size has not been reached in the tuber at 200 g, so that a later phase involving only expansion growth may be involved.

For leaves, it used to be thought that cell division was completed in the primordium stage, and then expansion followed. More recent work has

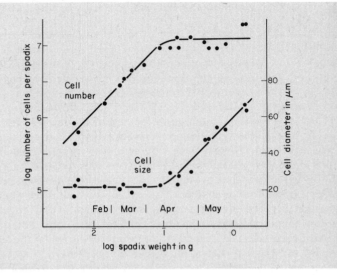

Fig. 8.2 Development of *Arum maculatum* spadix. The stages of cell division and cell expansion are distinctly separate. (From Simon and Chapman, 1961, *J. exp. Bot.*, **12**, 414–20. By permission of the Clarendon Press, Oxford.)

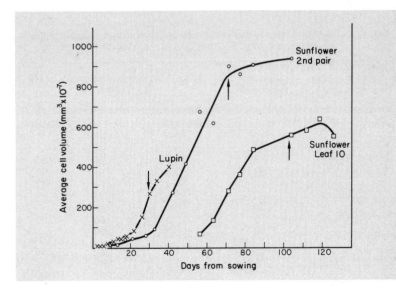

Fig. 8.3 Development of sunflower and lupin leaves. Arrows denote the cessation of cell division; the phases of cell division and cell expansion overlap. (From Sunderland, 1960, *J. exp. Bot.*, **11**, 68–85. By permission of the Clarendon Press, Oxford.)

shown that to be incorrect, at least in several species which have been investigated in detail. In the lupin (*Lupinus albus*) and sunflower (*Helianthus annuus*), cell division continues during 50–75% of the entire lifespan of the leaf, and most of the divisions take place after leaf emergence (Fig. 8.3). In the cucumber (*Cucumis sativus*) leaf, 70–98% of the cells are formed after unfolding. In marrowstem kale (*Brassica oleracea* var. *acephala*), cell divisions continue to the end of the life of a leaf. It is, however, true that the cell division rate is much higher in the primordium, as reflected by the observation that the ratio of number of cells dividing to total number of cells falls as leaf growth proceeds and, in the cucumber leaf, this fall in ratio occurs quite sharply, suggesting a change from one developmental phase to another. The earlier view that there was a clear distinction between division and expansion phases in leaf growth was based on counts and measurements of epidermal cells only, and it is now clear that these cells may cease dividing before all the rest of the leaf cells as in the tobacco leaf. Again, all species do not behave in an identical manner and, in the leaves of strawberry (*Fragaria vesca*), the cell division and expansion stages are much more distinct than in lupin, sunflower and cucumber.

Size differences between organs of similar basic anatomy may be traceable to differences in cell volume or cell number or both. Table 8.1

Table 8.1 The relationship between cell size and fruit size in cucurbit fruits. (After Sinnott, E. W., 1939, *Am. J. Bot.*, **26**, 179–89.)

Species	Diameter of mature fruit, mm	Average diameter of inner cells of the fruit wall in μm		
		When fruit diameter = 2 mm	At time of last cell division	At maturity
Cucurbita pepo	39	14·5	27·0	80
(7 varieties)	45	15·5	26·8	98
	62	17·1	25·8	142
	120	17·5	30·7	125
	300	16·8	38·0	—
	315	12·4	27·8	200
	360	15·8	36·0	—
Lagenaria	105	14·5	34·0	140
vulgaris (3 varieties)	170	13·2	26·2	165
	100	15·5	29·0	300
Cucumis anguria	31	17·7	18·5	150
Citrullus vulgaris	310	15·2	29·6	700

presents a selection of data from an investigation of fruit growth in 12 varieties of cucurbits drawn from 4 genera and in which the largest fruits had a volume more than a thousand times that of the smallest. The final fruit size was determined by a combination of three factors: cell number, the degree of cell expansion during the period of cell division, and the amount of expansion after cell division had stopped. On the whole, the larger-fruited races had a more extended period of cell division, thus producing more cells, and a greater amount of expansion both during the division and expansion phases. However, the same fruit size could be reached by different balances between cell division and expansion. Several authors have concluded that in leaves of any one species, size differences are due to differences in cell number rather than cell size; in the sunflower and the morning glory (*Ipomoea hederacea*) the larger leaves actually have the smaller cells.

CONDITIONS NECESSARY FOR GROWTH

A number of conditions are necessary for plant growth. The plant system must be in a potentially growing state: a mature tissue is no longer capable of growth except in response to special stimuli such as result from wounding. It must also receive or be able to synthesize the growth hormones which control cell development (see Chapter 9).

Its environment must provide a supply of water, oxygen and nutrients, and a suitable temperature. Plants can grow only when their cells are turgid and, in nature, water supply often limits growth. Most flowering plants require oxygen for growth, although the seedlings of some aquatic plants can pass through the stages of germination and early seedling growth under anaerobic conditions, examples being rice (*Oryza sativa*) and the water plantain (*Alisma plantago-aquatica*). In their natural environment these plants normally germinate under water or in mud, where there is very little oxygen.

The flowering plant is characteristically autotrophic, obtaining the mineral nutrients for its growth from soil or water and manufacturing all its essential organic constituents from carbon dioxide, water and inorganic ions. However its separate organs are not self-sufficient with respect to organic nutrients; even young leaves that already are photosynthesizing continue to require to import organic nutrients or particular growth hormones. The dividing and growing cells of a plant are nurtured by metabolites and growth hormones (or their precursors) synthesized in the specialized tissues of the organism.

The temperature range compatible with plant growth varies from species to species (Table 8.2). Within this range there is an optimum temperature whose value will depend also upon the other conditions controlling growth. Plants native to warm habitats require higher temperatures for growth than those of cooler regions. The optimum growth temperature for winter wheat, a cereal of cool temperate climate, is 20–25°C; for maize, a cereal from warmer climate, it is 30–35°C. Higher plants are less tolerant of extreme temperatures than some micro-organisms (Table 8.2). The effect of temperature on growth is complex.

Table 8.2 Temperature limits for the growth of some flowering plants and microorganisms. (Data from Pfeffer, W., 1903, *The Physiology of Plants*, II. Clarendon Press, Oxford; Ingraham, J. L. and Stokes, J. L., 1959, *Bact. Rev.*, **23**, 97–108; Stiles, W., 1950, *An Introduction to the Principles of Plant Physiology*. Methuen, London.)

Species	Minimum °C	Maximum °C
Flowering plants:		
Pisum sativum (roots)	−2	44·5
Sinapis alba	0	>37
Triticum vulgare	0–5	42
Lepidium sativum	2	28
Acer platanoides	7–8	26
Zea mays	9	46
Cucurbita pepo	14	46
Cucumis sativus	15–18	44–50
Psychrophilic bacteria	−10	Up to 45
Thermophilic micro-organisms:		
Aspergillus	15	60
Bacteria	38–45	75
Blue-green algae	?	85–89

An alternation of a lower temperature at night and a higher temperature during the day is frequently better for growth than any one constant temperature. The optimum growth temperature varies between organs of a plant and changes as a plant ages; what emerges as the optimum depends also on whether one considers the total growth over a long time period or the growth rate during a short interval. The temperature limits for growth of a plant are generally narrower than the temperature limits for individual physiological processes. Respiration for instance continues at a temperature at which growth is inhibited (Fig. 8.4). Growth follows from a harmonious interaction of all physiological processes and the required balance is disturbed at temperatures not inhibitory to the component processes, or immediately damaging to the cells.

Light was not listed above as a growth requirement because although flowering plants normally need light for photosynthesis, and hence for growth, they can grow in the dark if a supply of organic nutrient is available and may be able to complete their life history in darkness. Maize has been grown from seed to seed setting in the dark on an artificial sugar supply and *Arisaema triphyllum* (Araceae) has been raised in the dark from its large corm for four successive seasons. If light is thus not absolutely necessary for growth, it nevertheless profoundly influences growth and development (see Chapters 11 and 12). The phenomenon of etiolation indicates that light tends to suppress elongation growth, to promote leaf expansion (particularly in dicotyledons), and to enhance differentiation.

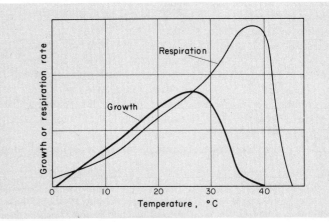

Fig. 8.4 The effect of temperature on growth and respiration in the bean, *Phaseolus vulgaris*. At extreme temperatures, growth ceases before respiration stops. (From Bünning, 1953, *Entwicklungs- und Bewegungsphysiologie der Pflanze,* Springer-Verlag, Berlin.)

The effect that light has on growth depends on the species, its age, previous growth conditions, and on the light intensity and wave-length. Young plants are more sensitive to light inhibition of their elongation than older ones. The inhibition of elongation by light is thought to act through an effect on the supply of growth hormones and on the sensitivity of the cells to these hormones.

Under natural conditions, plants often grow more in height during the night than during the day provided that the temperature at night is not too low. The growth of the date palm is stopped completely by direct sunlight. Bamboos in various tropical regions have been shown to grow in total height 1·8–2·8 times more during the night than during the day.

However in this instance the controlling factor seems to be water supply rather than light. In general, the water contents of plants are higher by night than by day (Fig. 4.1, p. 47) due to the development of a water deficit from transpiration. Many studies indicate that growth is greater by day if temperature is the limiting factor and greater by night if water is limiting. The highest growth rates therefore often occur in the early morning (temperature rising, and water content still high) and early evening (temperature still high, and water content beginning to increase).

GROWTH RATES

Quantitative comparisons between the growth of living systems can be made from two viewpoints. One can measure and compare their **absolute growth rates**, i.e. the total growth of each per unit time; or one can compare their **relative growth rates**, the growth of each per unit time expressed on a common basis, e.g. per unit initial weight. To estimate plant yields the absolute amounts of growth are required; to compare the growth activities of two systems their relative growth rates must be measured. If two leaves with initial areas of 5 and 50 cm² respectively both expand by a further 2 cm² in a day, then the absolute growth of each leaf is the same, but the smaller leaf has a ten times higher relative growth rate than the larger.

The relative rates of linear elongation growth of a number of plant

Table 8.3 Rates of linear elongation growth of some higher plant organs and fungal hyphae expressed as percentage increase per minute per unit length of the growing zone. (After Pfeffer, W., 1903, *The Physiology of Plants*. II. Clarendon Press, Oxford; and Stiles, W., 1950, *An Introduction to the Principles of Plant Physiology*. Methuen, London.)

Organ	Species	Growth rate
Pollen tubes	*Impatiens Hawkerii*	220
	Impatiens balsamia	100
Staminal filaments	*Triticum* and *Secale*	37·5
Shoot growing zones	*Bambusa*	1·27
	Bryonia	0·58
Root, fastest zone	*Vicia faba*	0·36
Fungal hyphae	*Botrytis cinerea*	83–200
	Mucor (Rhizopus) stolonifer	118

organs are compared in Table 8.3. The values are given as percentage increases per minute, i.e.

$$\frac{\text{Length increase per min, in mm}}{\text{Length of the growing zone, in mm}} \times 100$$

This table is compiled from results obtained under varied experimental conditions, but the differences in growth rates recorded are far greater than accounted for by differences in external conditions. However favourable the conditions of growth, the growing zone of a *Vicia* root will not double its length in a minute, as will the growing zone of some fungi. Very high steady rates are maintained by fungal hyphae; similar but only short-lived rates are developed by pollen tubes and staminal filaments. The elongation of the latter is completed in a matter of minutes and results from a very rapid expansion of the constituent cells, during which wall extension greatly outstrips synthesis of new cell wall material.

Bacteria are frequently described as having the highest growth rates of all living organisms; bacterial cells can double their mass and divide to form daughter cells in 20–30 minutes. The duration of the cell cycle in the meristems of higher plants is much longer than this. In pea root tips, the duration of mitosis is 3 hours at 15°C and about 1 hour at 30°C, while the average interval between two successive cell divisions is about 22 hours (see Chapter 9 for further discussion of the cell cycle). The high growth rates of microorganisms, and their high rates of physiological activity in general, are believed to be related to their small size, which allows rapid diffusion of metabolites and gases into and out of the cells.

Table 8.3 depicts the relative growth rates per unit growing zone. The absolute growth rates will depend on these values, and on the sizes of the growing zones. In the hyphae of *Botrytis*, the growing zone is only 0·018 mm long, so that even with a 200% increase in length per minute, the total extension growth made in 24 hours (the daily absolute growth rate) is about 5 cm. In the bamboo shoot, with a relative growth rate of only 1·27% per minute, the growing zone is 5 cm long, and hence the daily absolute growth rate is about 90 cm. Differences in absolute growth rates of plants are thus largely the result of differences in the length or volume of the growing zones.

The extent of total growth achieved during a given time period varies enormously between plants. A marrow plant (*Cucurbita*) or a hop (*Humulus*) grows from seed to a length of 12 metres in a summer; an oak seedling will grow to 12 cm in this time; since mass varies as (length)³, the differences in mass are much greater still. Marrow and hop are annual plants, with large growing zones, and produce much soft, thin-walled tissue; the oak, a perennial, has a small growing zone and quickly becomes woody. The oak plant can be regarded as showing a higher degree of differentiation and, as already indicated, growth and differentiation are often mutually antagonistic.

Mathematical analysis of growth

Growth lends itself to mathematical analysis, and formulae have been devised to express various types of growth. The simplest case is that of **constant linear** or **arithmetic growth** shown by a root elongating at a constant rate. Then:

$$L_t = L_0 + rt \qquad (8.1)$$

where
$$L_0 = \text{length at zero time}$$
$$L_t = \text{length at time } t$$
$$r = \text{growth rate, or elongation per unit time.}$$

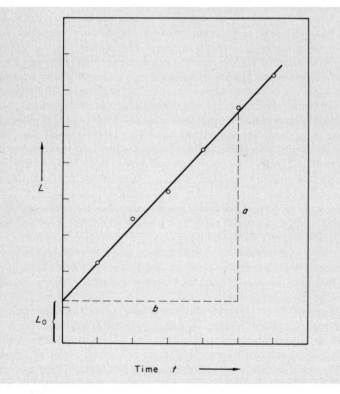

Fig. 8.5   Constant linear growth in length (diagrammatic): a plot of total length, L, against time, t, gives a straight line. See text for further explanation.

If L is plotted against time we obtain a straight line (Fig. 8.5); the intercept of the graph gives L_0, and the slope, a/b, gives the growth rate r. If r is known, the length L_t can be obtained from the formula for any value of t, the time; or alternatively, the value of r can be obtained from successive measurements of L_t.

Constant linear growth is observed only in relatively few growing systems. More frequently, the growth rate does not remain constant. In an entire root system any one tip may be elongating at a steady linear rate; but more and more new tips are continually formed; hence the rate of

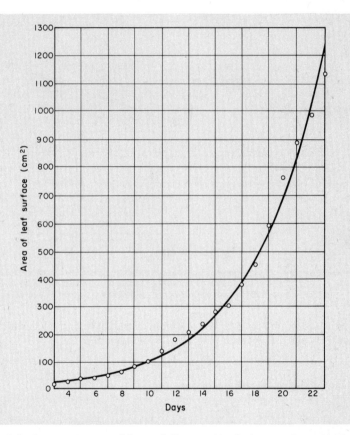

Fig. 8.6 Constant exponential growth illustrated by the increase in total leaf area of a cucumber (*Cucumis sativus*) plant; a plot of the leaf area (equivalent to *L* of equation *8.2*) against time gives a curve of ever-increasing steepness. (From Gregory, 1921, *Ann. Bot.*, **35**, 93–123. By permission of the Clarendon Press, Oxford.)

elongation of the root system as a whole keeps increasing. What may still remain constant is the relative growth rate per unit growing mass and, in that case, we have **constant exponential** or **constant logarithmic growth**. Denoting the relative growth rate by r', for constant exponential growth we have:

$$L_t = L_0 e^{r't} \qquad (8.2)$$

where e is the base of natural logarithms. This is the formula for continuous compound interest. In this case a plot of L against time will give a

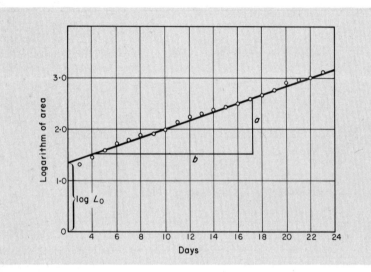

Fig. 8.7   A plot of the logarithm of cucumber leaf area (data of Fig. 8.6) against time: a straight line is now obtained. See text for further explanation.

curve as shown in Fig. 8.6; and to obtain a straight line, the logarithm of L must be plotted against t (Fig. 8.7). From equation 8.2

$$lnL_t = lnL_0 + r't \qquad (8.3)$$

or, converting to logarithms of base 10,

$$\log L_t = \log L_0 + \log e^{r't} \qquad (8.4)$$

In Fig. 8.7, the intercept gives $\log L_0$ and the slope a/b gives $\log e^{r'} = 0.43\ r'$.

A period of such exponential growth is found in the development of many living systems but, since it implies growth at an ever-increasing rate, it can proceed only for a limited period in the development of an organism. If mass increase of the plant is plotted against time from the commencement to the cessation of growth we obtain an S-shaped or *sigmoid curve* as illustrated in Fig. 8.8. This curve shows that growth is slow initially but it then speeds up and for a time approximates to exponential, later slowing down and finally stopping; with the onset of

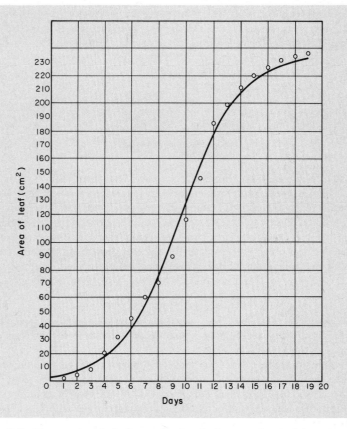

Fig. 8.8 The grand period of growth of a single cucumber leaf (source as for Fig. 8.6). Curve for a whole plant would be similar.

senescence there may occur an actual loss of mass. This sequence covers what is often called the ***grand period*** or ***grand curve*** of growth of the organism. It is not difficult to see why the period of high relative growth rate is limited. In the very young plant, mass increase means an increase in growing points and in photosynthetic area, the growth potential expands as the mass expands and growth is exponential. However not all the new tissue remains growing nor does it all add to the synthetic capacity of the plant. Thus the proportion of non-growing and non-photosynthetic tissue soon increases, and leads to a decline in relative growth rate. The loss of mass during senescence results from an excess of respiration over photosynthesis and from abscission of organs.

There is one formula which in some cases (though by no means universally) can be used to describe the grand curve of growth; this corresponds to the formula for an autocatalytic monomolecular reaction:

$$\frac{dx}{dt} = kx(a-x) \tag{8.5}$$

which on integration gives:

$$\log \frac{x}{a-x} = k(t-t_1) \tag{8.6}$$

where a is the final maximum size, x is the size at any time t, t_1 is the time when half the growth is completed (i.e. when $x = a/2$), and k is a constant. This relationship holds for growth when the curve for the grand period of growth is quite symmetrical, the decrease from exponential growth occurring at exactly the same rate as the increase to exponential growth. It can be applied to describe the leaf growth illustrated in Fig. 8.8 by substituting the following numerical values in the formula:

$$\log \frac{x}{236-x} = 0 \cdot 200 \, (t-9 \cdot 46) \tag{8.7}$$

the maximum leaf area being 236 cm^2, and the time for half growth being 9·46 days.

Though in some cases equation 8.6 describes the growth sequence almost perfectly, no particular conclusions can be drawn from the mathematical fit. Growth is not governed by one master reaction, but involves directly or indirectly all the metabolic reactions of cells. Growth and a monomolecular autocatalytic reaction are expressed by the same formula for different reasons. In the chemical reaction, rate initially increases because the more product is formed, the more catalyst there is; subsequently the rate decreases because the substrate of the reaction is exhausted. The initial increase in growth rate, in so far as it is due to an increase in the enzymes and templates that catalyse the growth reactions, can be considered as an autocatalytic process. The fall-off in rate is, however, brought about by a complex of factors not comparable with those involved in the chemical reaction.

The progress of growth during development: Growth rhythms

Smooth growth curves as shown in Figs. 8.6 and 8.7 are obtained only when the experimental material is grown under uniform conditions, and measurements are taken at fairly long time intervals. In nature, irregular fluctuations are superimposed on the growth curve by chance fluctuations of environmental factors such as temperature, light intensity and water supply. Figure 8.9 shows the course of maize growth in the field; the

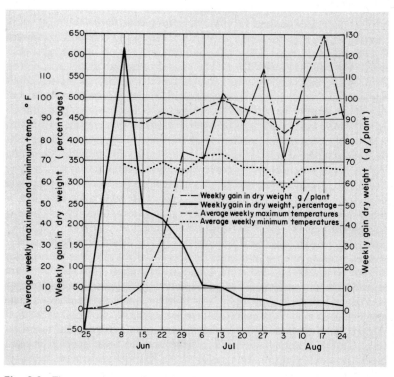

Fig. 8.9 The growth rate of maize (*Zea mays*), expressed as the weekly dry weight gain, under natural conditions. (From Miller, *Plant Physiology*, Copyright 1931, McGraw-Hill Book Co. Used by permission of McGraw-Hill Book Co., New York and Maidenhead.)

weekly growth rate is seen to fluctuate considerably and temperature is apparently one factor responsible for this. But the general shape of the grand period curve is still recognizable, and a smooth curve could be obtained by putting the line of best fit through the points.

If measurements are made at short time intervals such as hourly, then rhythmic changes in growth rate become apparent. Growth has a *diurnal rhythm*, with maxima and minima occurring at definite times of day. This is only to be expected under natural conditions, because of the regular diurnal alternation of day and night conditions, in particular the alternation of light and darkness. A plant grown from seed under constant conditions and in darkness does not show a diurnal growth rhythm. But once a rhythm has been initiated, and a single period of illumination may suffice for this, the rhythm will persist in continuous darkness for 2–3 days, or even longer. Thus growth conforms to the general pattern of diurnal rhythms in metabolic activity shown by many physiological processes which are partly controlled by the diurnal changes in external conditions and partly endogenously by a 'biological clock' mechanism of unknown nature. The growth of tomato plants is inhibited if the plants are subjected to light:dark cycles of 6:6 or 24:24 hours and this has been explained on the basis that the endogenous rhythm of the plants cannot be adjusted to these light:dark cycles. The diurnal growth cycle may show one or several maxima and minima of growth rate. In the roots of a number of species, 2 to 4 maxima of elongation occur in a 24-hour period, the maxima of elongation growth coinciding with minima of cell division activity (see also Chapter 12, p. 243).

Growth rhythms not related to the 24-hour period are also known. Growing shoot tips rotate in a circle (as viewed from above). This movement or *nutation (circumnutation)* is most pronounced in climbers, in which it aids the plant to twine round a support. Nutation is brought about by a wave of growth moving round the axis tip; at any instant, growth is most intense in one limited region of the tip, and the wave of activity completes a cycle round the tip in anything from 1·25 to 24 hours according to species and environmental conditions. The nutational rhythm is not dependent upon any rhythm in the external conditions, and will continue in a constant environment, though the speed of rotation is affected by changes in the environmental conditions, such as temperature. The direction of nutation is fixed and, in most species, is anti-clockwise as viewed from on top.

The grand curve of growth represents the life history of ephemerals and annuals and the course of growth during one growing season in perennials. In temperate habitats, most of the shoot growth of perennials is completed within a short period in the spring and early summer; some trees for example complete 90% of a year's growth in a 30-day period, starting 7–14 days after the commencement of growth, these first days representing the slow phase of the grand period. Such an early cessation of growth must be the result of some internal control mechanism and sometimes there does occur a second brief flush of growth later in the season. Root growth continues longer into the summer. In wet tropical habitats, growth in a plant community as a whole continues all the year round and with equal intensity, but in individual plants periods of high and low growth activity alternate, with a periodicity measured in months. Perennials therefore appear to show an endogenous growth rhythm in which each cycle may extend to several months. In habitats where climatic conditions vary over the year, such growth rhythms have become synchronized with the climatic rhythms, but in the more constant tropical climate where the environment does not exert a synchronizing influence, each plant or even separate branch of a plant grows according to its own innate rhythm.

Normally a phase of vegetative growth is followed by one of reproductive growth, and this transition is usually marked by the shoot apex changing quite abruptly from the production of vegetative organs to the production of flowers. This is usually reflected in the growth curve of the plant as a new surge of growth after the grand period curve of vegetative growth has levelled off. This transition is discussed more fully in Chapter 12.

MORPHOGENESIS

Plant development involves increase in size (growth) and the emergence of its organs and their arrangement in space (morphogenesis). The process of morphogenesis is inseparable from growth; the location of the apical meristems determines the branching and overall shape; a lobed leaf is produced by unequal growth along different radii; a fruit that grows equally in all directions becomes round, one which elongates preferentially along one axis becomes oblong. Shaping of organs by a morphogenetic movement of cells, which plays an important part in animal morphogenesis, is not possible in a flowering plant, where the cells are immobile. Thus, in plants, shape results from differential growth, in different regions and in different directions.

In morphogenesis we are concerned with the primary initiation of organs, and their subsequent development. Organ initiation establishes the basic pattern, the branching of shoot and root, the positioning of leaves and so on. Each organ is then moulded by its pattern of growth and differentiation.

Leaves and axillary buds are initiated close to the shoot apex. Commonly the primordia arise singly on the apical dome of the stem and the position of initiation moves in a circle round the apex. Since the apex elongates between the formation of every two successive primordia, the leaves get pulled out into a spiral round the stem. The precise positioning of the leaves, their *phyllotaxis*, is characteristic of the species. A very common arrangement is a 2/5 spiral, in which the sixth leaf lies directly above the first, and the spiral joining the leaves in order passes twice round the axis in moving from the first leaf to the sixth. Sometimes leaves arise in pairs or in whorls. Buds are initiated a little below the shoot apical meristem in most leaf axils.

The branching of the shoot could therefore potentially reflect the phyllotaxis, but in fact many of the buds initiated never grow out, being inhibited by the apical bud (***apical dominance***). The inhibition is usually thought to be mediated by growth regulators secreted by the apex, but monopolization by the apical bud of growth factors transported upwards from the roots has also been suggested as a causative factor. Branch angles are also under apical control. Apical dominance is much more marked in some species than in others. When the apical meristem is cut off, laterals below it often grow out in profusion; this reaction is utilized when pruning is applied to encourage bushiness in a shrub or tree (see also Chapter 11).

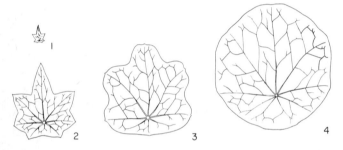

Fig. 8.10 Morphogenesis in leaves of three strains of *Tropaeolum*. The juvenile leaf shape is identical for all (1), but through differences in the relative growth rates in the main vein and intervein directions, the adult shapes come to differ. (From Whaley and Whaley, 1942, *Am. J. Bot.*, **29**, 195–200.)

In roots, laterals are formed some distance back from the tip meristem, in a region where the primary tissues are mature. Initiation takes place in the pericycle, opposite or lateral to the protoxylem points, so that root branching is related to vascular anatomy. Roots do differ in the extent of lateral initiation and in the duration of growth of individual root axes but nevertheless exhibit less range of form than do shoot systems.

After organ initiation and outgrowth have mapped out the overall growth pattern, each organ is moulded by its own pattern of growth and differentiation. As an example of how leaf shapes result from differential growth, leaves of three strains of *Tropaeolum* are illustrated in Fig. 8.10. At an early developmental stage, the leaves have identical shapes in all three strains (leaf 1). Shape differences in the mature leaves are brought about by different amounts of growth along the main veins relative to growth in the intervenal areas. In leaf 2, approximately equal growth along both directions has preserved the outline of the young leaf; in the others, greater relative growth in the intervenal regions has served to obliterate the lobing, partly in leaf 3 and completely in leaf 4.

It is frequently observed that a constant ratio is maintained between the growth rates of different parts of a plant. This type of relationship is known as **allometric** (heterogonic) growth, and the relationship can be expressed mathematically by the allometry formula. If x and y represent the sizes of two parts growing allometrically, and k equals the ratio of their growth rates, then

$$y = bx^k \tag{8.8}$$

where b is a constant ($b=$ the value of y when x is taken as unity). Taking logarithms,

$$\log y = \log b + k \log x \tag{8.9}$$

A plot of $\log x$ against $\log y$ gives a straight line and the slope of the graph gives k. If both parts are growing at equal rates, the slope of the graph is at $45°$ and $k=1$. Fig. 8.11 shows allometric growth exhibited by the stems and roots of some cultivated plants. An allometric relationship has also been observed in many cases between growth rates of leaf parts, and between the growth rates of the organs in a developing flower. Allometric growth plays an important part in the morphogenesis of all organisms.

Primary organ initiation results from cell divisions oriented so as to produce a tissue mass standing out from the initiating tissue. Subsequent differential growth involves both directional and localized cell divisions and directional cell elongation. In the *Tropaeolum* leaves shown in Fig. 8.10, the growth differences in the intervenal regions of the three types are effected through cell divisions, more cells being produced in these regions in leaves 3 and 4 than in leaf 2. Fruit shape in the Cucurbitaceae similarly depends on the direction of cell divisions. In round-fruited species, cell divisions in the fruit occur at random in all directions; the more elongate the fruit is to be, the more strictly are the planes of cell divisions orientated so as to produce new cells mainly along the axis of elongation. On the other hand, leaf shape in the aquatic plant *Callitriche intermedia* is determined both by the direction of cell division and cell expansion. This plant produces linear submerged leaves and ovate aerial leaves. Orientated cell divisions even while the leaf primordia are small produce shape differences for the two types and, when elongation commences, cells of the linear leaves expand primarily in the direction of leaf elongation whereas the cells of the ovate leaves expand isodiametrically.

Certain aspects of morphogenesis are discussed in more detail in Chapters 11 and 12.

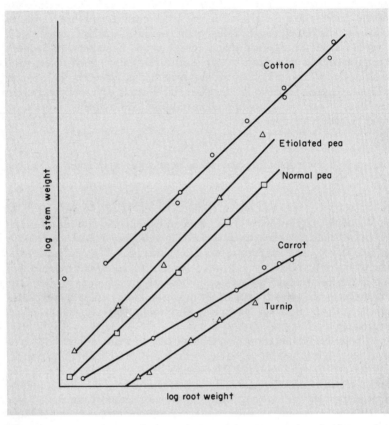

Fig. 8.11 Allometric growth shown between the stems and roots of a number of species. The vertical scale is reduced to one-half in the case of etiolated peas. (From Pearsall, 1927, *Ann. Bot.*, **41**, 549–56. By permission of the Clarendon Press, Oxford.)

Heteroblastic development

In many plants, a juvenile stage can be distinguished from a mature stage by differences in external form such as leaf shape, leaf anatomy, degree of thorniness and stem growth habit. Physiologically the juvenile stage is distinguished by greater ease of rooting and taking of grafts, and by low or no capacity for flower formation. Species with a distinct juvenile form are said to show *heteroblastic* development; if a juvenile form is not apparent, the development is *homoblastic*. Division into these categories is not absolutely clearcut for all plants show some change of form and activity in passing from the seedling to the mature condition. The term heteroblastic is applied where different forms are clearly distinguishable during development after the early seedling stages. Some authors regard species with homoblastic development as either showing the mature form precociously, passing through the juvenile stage so quickly that this is not noticeable, or else as persisting in a permanent juvenile stage.

The change from juvenile to mature form is more or less gradual, and in trees may take a long time: 10–15 years in *Citrus* species and up to 60 years in oak and beech. In perennials the plant's basal part, formed during the juvenile phase, retains its juvenile properties after the growing tops have passed into the mature state and cuttings taken from the basal part behave as juvenile. Reversion to the juvenile condition occurs when adventitious shoots are formed, and the first leaves of shoots growing out from buds on mature parts tend to show a juvenile character. Hedge plants can be kept in a permanently juvenile state by continued pruning, so that new buds are continually induced to grow out.

The most thorough studies in the field of heteroblastic development have been carried out on changes in leaf shape, these changes being among the most conspicuous aspects of heteroblastic development capable of quantitative expression by measurements of ratios between leaf length and width, or by counts of leaf lobe numbers. Often the first-formed leaves are of simpler shape than the mature, as in the bean, and the morning glory (*Ipomoea hederacea*) (Fig. 8.12). In the ivy (*Hedera helix*) it is the juvenile leaves that are lobed, the mature leaves being entire, and the entire plant habit changes from prostrate or climbing to upright when the mature stage is reached. Anatomically, mature leaves show a higher degree of cellular differentiation and xeromorphy than juvenile leaves. Trees which in their mature stage produce sun and shade leaves produce exclusively shade leaves on the juvenile parts. In several plants such as larkspur (*Delphinium*) and cotton (*Gossypium*), the shapes of juvenile leaves can be interpreted as arising from arrested development, for all leaves start on the same course of development but, in progressively younger leaves, the development stops at progressively earlier stages. A series of full-grown leaves along a plant represents the change from juvenile to mature and also represents the developmental stages of one single *mature* leaf.

There is good evidence that the nutritional status of the plant is one of the controlling factors in heteroblastic growth. Low carbohydrate status favours retention of the juvenile form. In a low light intensity (below 0·23 full sunlight) *Ipomoea hederacea* never produces leaves of adult morphology, and plants bearing mature leaves can be made to revert to the production of juvenile leaves by shading. Changes in the internal carbohydrate status may effect the changes in morphology by acting both on the initiating apex and on the later development of the

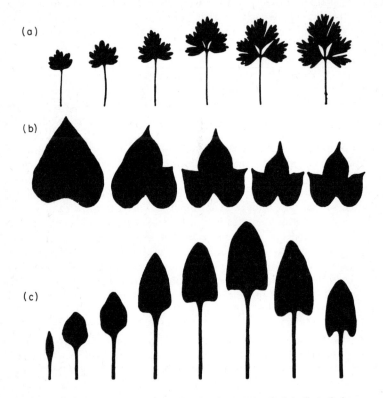

Fig. 8.12 Examples of heteroblastic development of (a) first 6 leaves of *Delphinium ajacis*; (b) first 5 leaves of *Ipomoea hederacea*; (c) first 8 leaves of sugar-beet (data from Belskaya, 1940). (From Ashby, 1948, *New Phytol.*, **47**, 153–76.)

leaves. Carbohydrate supply is limited in a young plant, but, as its photosynthetic capacity increases, the carbohydrate level in the plant rises, and the change from juvenile to adult form takes place. An effect of photoperiod (see Chapter 12) on heteroblastic development has been claimed in some instances. A general physiological ageing of the plant, particularly of its meristems, has also been invoked as an explanation for heteroblastic development. Reversion to the juvenile form has been obtained in adult ivy shoots by grafting them to juvenile plants and even by growing them in the same culture solution along with juvenile cuttings, suggesting that the growth regulating substances present, or their specific levels, characterize the juvenile plant. In the ivy, the juvenile form has been found to contain higher levels of gibberellins and of phenolic compounds that act as co-factors in promoting rooting in conjunction with auxin.

Heteroblastic development has been regarded as representing a recapitulation of the phylogeny of the species and in some cases this view may be justified. In *Acacia* species, the juvenile form has pinnate leaves whereas in the adult plant these are replaced by phyllodes (flattened petioles). Pinnate leaves are typical of the family Leguminosae to which *Acacia* belongs, and the phyllodes of *Acacia* are highly specialized structures. It can therefore be postulated that the ancestors of *Acacia* had pinnate leaves similar to those now borne on its juvenile plants. In many other cases there is however no convincing evidence for the appearance of ancestral characters in the juvenile phase and the demonstration that environmental and nutritional factors can determine the change from juvenile to adult form also argues against the hypothesis of phylogenetic recapitulation. It has even been postulated by some authors that juvenile forms, far from being evolutionary relics, are special adaptations to the conditions in which the young plant develops.

Aquatic plants commonly exhibit **heterophylly**, producing submerged and aerial leaves of very different structure. Typically, the submerged leaves are long and ribbon-like in monocotyledons, finely divided in dicotyledons, whereas the aerial leaves are not uniform in shape in this way. A third type of leaf, floating on the water surface, is present in some species. The submerged leaves are usually formed first while the plant is growing up through water, and the aerial leaves are formed when it surfaces. These leaf types are produced as a response to changing external conditions and, if an aerial shoot is submerged, it begins to form the submerged type of leaf again. The heterophylly of aquatics is not directly related to the maturity or physiological age of the plant.

FURTHER READING

ALLSOPP, A. (1965). Heteroblastic development in cormophytes. In *Encyclopedia of Plant Physiology*, ed. RUHLAND, W., **15/1**, 1172–221. Springer-Verlag, Berlin.

BONNER, J. T. (1963). *Morphogenesis*. Athenaeum, New York.

CUTTER, E. G. (1971). *Plant Anatomy: Experiment and Interpretation. Part 2, Organs*. Contemporary Biology Series, Edward Arnold, London.

DORMER, K. J. (1972). *Shoot Organization in Vascular Plants*. Chapman & Hall, London.

EVANS, G. C. (1972). *The Quantitative Analysis of Plant Growth.* Studies in Ecology, Vol. 1, Blackwell Scientific Publications, Oxford.

KRAMER, P. J. and KOZLOWSKI, T. T. (1960). *The Physiology of Trees.* McGraw-Hill, New York and Maidenhead.

MOREY, P. R. (1973). *How Trees Grow.* Studies in Biology, no. 39, Edward Arnold, London.

WHALEY, W. G. (1961). Growth as a general process. In *Encyclopedia of Plant Physiology*, ed. RUHLAND, W., **14**, 71–112. Springer-Verlag, Berlin.

SELECTED REFERENCES

ASHBY, E. (1948). Studies in the morphogenesis of leaves. *New Phytol.*, **47**, 153–76.

BROWN, R. and BROADBENT, D. (1950). The development of cells in the growing zones of the root. *J. exp. Bot.*, **1**, 249–63.

SINNOTT, E. W. (1939). A developmental analysis of the relation between cell size and fruit size in cucurbits. *Am. J. Bot.*, **26**, 179–89.

SUNDERLAND, N. (1960). Cell division and expansion in the growth of the leaf. *J. exp. Bot.*, **11**, 68–85.

9

Cell Growth and Differentiation

Consideration of the problems of growth and differentiation at the cellular level clearly centres around aspects of cell physiology and biochemistry and as such would take us right outside the central theme of this text, the physiology of the whole plant. However the position of cells within the multicellular plant body is one of the critical factors determining their behaviour; cells become what they are because of where they are. When we pose the question of why primary plant meristems are restricted to the root and shoot apex and when we enquire into how, from such meristems, cellular differentiation proceeds to give the patterns of tissue distribution characteristic of roots, stems and leaves, we must inevitably seek to describe the internal environment of the plant. At present such descriptions are clearly incomplete and probably very crude. Such an internal environment must have as important components the distributions within the developing plant organ of gaseous, inorganic and organic nutrients and of growth-regulating substances. Thus the study, by the techniques of cell physiology and biochemistry, of the factors which initiate and maintain cell division, of those which initiate and limit cell expansion and of those which determine the pathways of differentiation will help us to identify the crucial physico-chemical factors of the internal environment which delineate the visual patterns of tissue and organ development.

Such micro-environmental controls operate to regulate cell physiology. It is therefore essential to have an appreciation of the biochemical events involved in cell division, cell expansion and differentiation.

CELL DIVISION

Cells undergoing repeated division go through a repeating cell cycle during which there occurs an increase in cell mass, a replication of the genetic material and division of the cell mass and of the duplicated genetic material to give rise to daughter cells. The sequence can be represented thus:

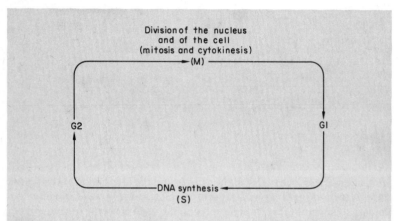

The two periods of interphase which respectively precede (G1, the first gap) and follow (G2, the second gap) the S phase are periods during which events essential to the initiation of chromosome replication and mitosis occur. Cell growth proceeds throughout interphase. In plant cells this cycle can be completed in 16–24 hours but can take much longer due to extensions of interphase (particularly of G1). Both the whole cycle and mitosis itself are sensitive to temperature (Fig. 9.1). Two examples of the duration of stages in the cell cycle of root cells are shown in Fig. 9.2. At near optimum temperatures mitosis takes from 30 minutes to 3 hours depending upon species and cell size. Usually metaphase and anaphase are short relative to prophase and telophase. Thus in pea endosperm in which $M = 3$ hours the following values (minutes) were recorded: prophase, 40; metaphase, 20; anaphase, 10; telophase, 110.

In a discussion on the cell cycle we must draw upon cytological descriptions, autoradiography and knowledge of DNA structure and of the enzymes and intermediates involved in nucleic acid metabolism. Unfortunately the nature of chromosome structure which is central to an understanding of chromosome reproduction, contraction and movement remains speculative.

The recognition of DNA as a constituent of plant nuclei dates from the introduction of the Feulgen staining technique (1924). Techniques for isolating chromosomes show that most of the nuclear DNA is located in these structures. Many workers have been able to demonstrate that the DNA content of nuclei from different types of cells within the same

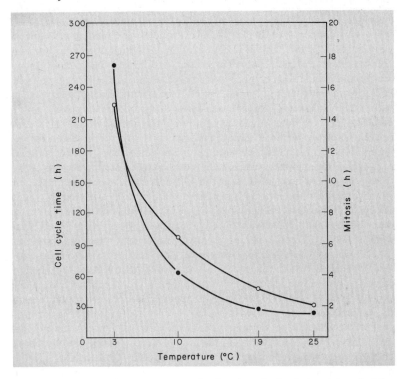

Fig. 9.1 Influence of temperature on the duration of mitosis (—o—) and of the cell cycle (—•—) in cells of the root tip meristem of seedlings of *Vicia faba*. (Data from Evans and Savage, 1959, *Expl Cell Res.*, **18**, 51–61.)

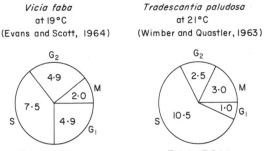

Fig. 9.2 Duration of separated stages of the cell cycle in root tip cells of *Vicia faba* at 19°C (data of Evans and Scott, *Genetics*, 1964, **49**, 17–38) and of *Tradescantia paludosa* at 21°C (data of Wimber and Quastler, *Expl Cell Res.*, 1963, **30**, 8–22). For key to labelling of the separate stages see text, p. 156.

organism is proportional to the number of chromosomes (haploid sex cell nuclei contain half the DNA of the nuclei of diploid meristematic body cells, and these half the DNA of cell nuclei which during differentiation become tetraploid). More important, prophase nuclei contain twice the diploid DNA content (4C) and telophase nuclei the diploid content (2C); a doubling of nuclear DNA content occurs during a particular period (the S phase) of interphase. The duration of the S phase and its initiation can be determined by studying the incorporation of radioactive phosphorus (^{32}P) or tritium (^{3}H)-labelled thymidine into chromosomal DNA. This phase in which duplication of the genetic material of the chromosomes takes place is therefore a critical step in the cell cycle. Autoradiography has shown that the DNA is the conserved component which remains intact during chromosome duplication and that in this it differs from the chromosomal protein and RNA. The conservation is described as 'semi-conservative', best explained by outlining the classical work of Taylor, Wood and Hughes (1957) on chromosome duplication in root tip cells of *Vicia faba* following a pulse of (i.e. feeding for a short time with) ^{3}H-labelled thymidine. The β-particles of tritium have low energy, travelling only a fraction of one μm from their point of emission. Thus the silver grains whose development in the photographic emulsion results from the β-particles are very close to the labelled structure. It is therefore possible to determine if only one or both of the sister chromatids are labelled and how uniform the labelling is along a chromatid. It was found that all chromatids were equally labelled in the first division after the short period of ^{3}H-thymidine treatment. However after the second division the predominant situation was that the chromosomes had one labelled and one unlabelled chromatid; after the third division half the chromosomes were entirely unlabelled and the other half had one labelled chromatid. This result would accord with the theory that each strand of the double stranded DNA molecule persisted during chromosome duplication and acted as a 'template' for the formation of a complementary strand from precursor units in the nucleus (one such precursor, thymidine, carrying during the first division a detectable level of label). The expression 'the predominant situation' was used above because during the second division certain chromatids, otherwise labelled, contained an unlabelled segment and the otherwise unlabelled sister chromatid contained at the corresponding locus a labelled segment. The experiments not only showed the persistence of the DNA strands but that reciprocal exchange of segments can occur between sister chromatids (crossing over).

These considerations naturally lead us to ask what initiates the S phase of the cell cycle and determines its duration. There are many cases where nuclei within the same cytoplasm show very high synchrony in their division, suggesting the operation of a control mediated via the cytoplasm.

Even cases of apparent asynchrony may also imply an involvement of the cytoplasm in controlling nuclear DNA synthesis. Thus in the protozoan *Euplotes*, DNA synthesis starts in the micronucleus at the close of the previous cell division and is completed in 3 hours. Only when the DNA content of the micronucleus has doubled does DNA replication commence in the macronucleus.

During interphase there occurs not only replication of DNA, but the synthesis of the other chromosome components, and of material involved in the mitotic spindle, increase in the number of mitochondria and other organelles, and increase in cell mass. While DNA synthesis is confined to the S phase, the synthesis of other cytoplasmic and nuclear constituents occurs over a longer time (in G1 and G2). Thus RNA is synthesized from late telophase, through the entire interphase and up to the mid-prophase of mitosis. Synthesis of histones (basic nuclear proteins), begins in G1 and continues through G2. It is also during interphase that the energy source is built up for the contraction, condensation and movement of chromosomes and for the reconstruction of the interphase nucleus during mitosis. Studies with plant cell cultures (see Chapter 12), synchronized in cell division, have shown that the rates of physiological processes and the syntheses of individual enzymes and metabolites during interphase follow a sequential and repeating pattern during successive cell cycles.

Mitosis does not proceed without prior DNA replication but DNA replication alone is not sufficient to ensure that mitosis will follow as evidenced by the development of polytene (many-stranded) chromosomes. The nature of the signal which terminates G2 and initiates mitosis is not known. The hypothesis that the achievement of a critical cell mass by cell growth during interphase precipitates mitosis cannot be upheld. It is true that mean cell size is often very stable in active meristems and that the growth phase can be prolonged and mitosis prevented by repeated amputation of the cytoplasm (for example in *Amoeba*). However in contrast to this there are many instances where cells go through a succession of divisions without further growth so that daughter cells become smaller with successive divisions; this is seen during plant embryology, in the behaviour of cultured plant cells and in the growth, under appropriate conditions, of certain unicellular algae. In such cases interphase is usually shorter than where cell mass is being maintained by interphase growth but it still occupies a high proportion of the cell cycle and exceeds in duration the S phase.

This description of the cell cycle has been developed to emphasize the many points at which inter- and intra-cellular controls could operate. To talk of some experimental treatment promoting cell division is only the very first step; to understand its mechanism of action it is necessary to be able to describe its specific impact on some component process in a very complex sequence of integrated biochemical events.

We now know that higher plants contain hormones called *cytokinins*. These have been defined as compounds that induce cell division in plant cells in association with a second group of hormones, the auxins. The discovery of the unique properties of coconut milk (the liquid endosperm of *Cocos nucifera*) in stimulating cell division in isolated tissue fragments raised the question of the natural occurrence in plants of specific cell-division factors. Thus pieces of the stem pith of tobacco (*Nicotiana tabacum* var. Wisconsin 38) when placed on a medium supplying sugar, inorganic salts, various vitamins and an auxin such as indol-3yl acetic acid (IAA), naphthalene acetic acid (NAA) or 2,4-dichlorophenoxyacetic acid (2,4-D), remained alive for some time but failed to grow. Increasing the auxin concentration in the culture medium induced swelling of the cells but did not initiate cell division in the explanted tissue. If some vascular tissue was left attached to the isolated pith some cell division occurred, particularly in the vicinity of the vascular tissue, suggesting the presence in the vascular tissue of an essential cell division factor. However addition of coconut milk to the medium led to continuing cell division throughout the explant and to the development of a growing callus tissue irrespective of the presence of any vascular tissue. The coconut milk could be replaced by an appropriate concentration of an extract of yeast or of aged or autoclaved herring sperm DNA. Further examination of the extract of autoclaved DNA led to the isolation of its active principle and its chemical identification as 6-furfurylaminopurine. This compound was termed *kinetin* because of its activity in promoting cell division (cyto-kinesis). Subsequently it has been shown that compounds similar in physiological activity and chemical composition to kinetin occur univer-sally in higher plants. The compound 6-(4-hydroxy-3-methyl-2-butenyl)-aminopurine has been isolated in pure form from immature corn kernels and termed zeatin (Fig. 9.3). N^6-(Δ^2-isopentenyl)adenine (IPA), another very active cytokinin, also occurs in corn kernels. The natural cytokinins occur free, bound to a pentose sugar (nucleosides), or bound to sugar and phosphate (nucleotides). Kinetin, though often used in experiments, is not a natural plant hormone.

Any consideration of how these cytokinins promote cell division must have regard to their other physiological activities. Thus in a number of experimental systems kinetin has been shown to promote cell expan-sion. It also in some cases has very striking effects on morphogenesis as discussed in Chapter 11. When applied to the excised leaves of many plants it prevents yellowing (a complex series of changes equivalent to those which take place during the senescence of leaves prior to leaf fall). The application of kinetin stabilizes chlorophyll content and chloroplast

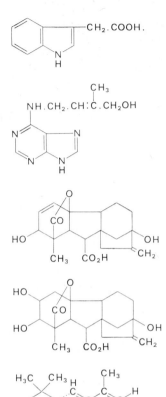

Auxins

Indol-3yl acetic acid (IAA); also indolylacetonitrile, indole aldehyde and other indole derivatives, some of which have still to be chemically characterized.

Cytokinins

Zeatin [6-(4-hydroxy-3-methyl-2-butenyl)aminopurine] occurs also as zeatin nucleoside and zeatin nucleotide; also other 6-substituted and aminopurines and related compounds yet to be identified. The synthetic substance, kinetin, is 6-furfurylaminopurine.

Gibberellins

Gibberellic acid (gibberellin A_3) found in seeds of barley and *Echinocystis* and in *Festuca pratensis*.

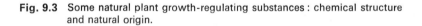

Gibberellin A_8 found in immature seeds of *Phaseolus multiflorus* and *Phaseolus vulgaris*.

Many other gibberellins (A_1, A_4, A_5, A_6, A_7, A_8, A_{17}, A_{19}, A_{20}), some not yet fully identified, occur in higher plants.

Abscisins

Abscisic acid (abscisin II, dormin) isolated from cotton fruits and sycamore leaves.

Fig. 9.3 Some natural plant growth-regulating substances : chemical structure and natural origin.

structure and stabilizes or even increases leaf protein content (see also Chapter 11, p. 226). In a number of plants kinetin is active in breaking the dormancy of seeds and buds, including lateral buds normally inhibited by the main growing apex (apical dominance) (see Chapter 8, p. 148). In certain instances kinetin application has been shown to promote flowering of plants maintained under unfavourable photoperiods (see Photoperiodism in Chapter 12, p. 235), and in plants otherwise requiring a cold treatment for flower induction. This broad spectrum of kinetin activity is paralleled by the diverse physiological effects of the other groups of plant hormones, the auxins and the gibberellins. At the level of *mechanism of action* such diversity could follow either from the regulation of some single process central to plant growth and development or from the active substance influencing independently a number of aspects of cell metabolism. The concept that plant hormones control single master reactions is usually favoured on the grounds that key molecules in metabolism must presumably have been subjected to natural selection and that this would operate in favour of compounds of high specific activity.

In considering the possibility that cytokinins act through some 'master reaction' two findings must be borne in mind: (i) that the effects of cytokinins are dependent upon both the absolute concentration of cytokinin and the concentration of cytokinin relative to that of other known plant hormones and (ii) that applications of cytokinins, auxins and gibberellins have been shown to cause rapid changes (changes within 1 hour of application of the hormones) in nucleic acid metabolism and enzyme synthesis, the direction of these changes and the ensuing physiological expression altering with change in the concentration of the applied hormone. When to this we add recognition of the overlapping diversity of action of the known plant hormones it is tempting to suggest that they are all concerned with controlling gene expression and that they interact at this level. In the language of genetics, the plant hormones are repressors or derepressors of genes.

To understand recent work on how cytokinins may act it is necessary to remind ourselves of the main kinds of nucleic acid, of their intracellular localization and of their function. Nucleic acids isolated from plant cells can be separated into: DNA (both nuclear and cytoplasmic); ribosomal RNAs (r-RNA) concerned in ribosome construction and, within the nucleus, concentrated in the nucleoli; messenger RNAs (m-RNA) whose synthesis and export to the cytoplasm carries the genetic information from the chromosomal DNA to the sites of protein synthesis; and transfer RNAs (s-RNA) which are of relatively low molecular weight and are responsible for the activation of the free amino acids so that they can become attached to the m-RNA 'templates' during protein synthesis. When protein synthesis is proceeding the ribosomes can be seen organized into groups (polyribosomes) and from electron microscope studies it seems that the several ribosomes of each polyribosome are attached to a single long strand of m-RNA which keeps the ribosome cluster together.

Under certain conditions the cells of a tissue culture derived from pea roots show doubling of the chromosomes without division of the nucleus (endomitosis). Mitosis and cytokinesis in such cells can be initiated by supplying kinetin and its effect appears to be quite specific. This and other observations indicate that kinetin is not implicated in the DNA duplication occurring during the S-phase of the cell cycle.

A number of workers have shown that applications of kinetin or of other active cytokinins are quickly followed by changes in the content of cellular RNA and in certain such studies evidence has been obtained by simultaneous feeding of radioactive phosphorus (^{32}P) and orotic acid labelled with ^{14}C that the cytokinin either changes the rate of RNA synthesis or its rate of turnover (synthesis versus degradation). In a number of cases where cytokinin application has raised the RNA level this has been shown to be accompanied by enhanced protein synthesis. Indirect evidence that cytokinins can promote m-RNA synthesis comes from experiments involving the use of inhibitors such as actinomycin-D which inhibit this DNA-dependent RNA synthesis and from the observation that kinetin can preserve polyribosomes under conditions otherwise leading to their breakdown. Other studies point to cytokinins promoting nucleolar activity and increasing or maintaining the number of ribosomes per cell (promoting r-RNA synthesis). Although increased synthesis of some enzymes (for instance the enzyme, tyramine methyl-pherase, in seedling barley roots) has been reported to follow kinetin application, in other cases cytokinin-mediated repression of enzyme synthesis has been observed (for example repression of the nucleic acid degrading enzymes, ribonuclease and deoxyribonuclease). The present position is that the physiological activity of cytokinins appears to arise from their controlling influence in RNA metabolism, but we cannot yet define how they exert this control nor how the changed RNA metabolism leads to the observed physiological responses.

The definition of cytokinins as substances that induce cell division in association with auxins implies that auxins must also exert a controlling influence at some point(s) in the cell cycle of meristematic cells. Attention will be directed to the intervention of auxins in RNA metabolism when discussing their essential role in cell expansion. However from the detailed studies with cultured tobacco tissue which led to the discovery of kinetin and from other similar work on the induction of division in tissue explants evidence has been obtained pointing to the necessity of auxin for DNA doubling (S phase), mitosis (M phase) and new wall formation (cytokinesis). Auxins induce cell division in association with endogenous or externally applied cytokinins. However here again the mechanism of action at particular points in the cell cycle has yet to be elucidated.

CELL EXPANSION

The transition of the cells of plant meristems into differentiated cells almost invariably involves increase in cell size, often a many hundred-fold increase and this cell expansion is the first visible sign of differentiation. Accompanying this expansion process there is a massive uptake of water and associated with this the appearance of liquid vacuoles and their coalescence into a central vacuole. As earlier indicated (Chapter 8, p. 130) the cell wall does not thin out as it increases in area; synthesis of new cell wall material takes place continuously throughout the period of increase in cell volume. Further although cells remain turgid during cell expansion, the uptake of water is not the consequence of an increased solute content in the vacuoles but arises through changes in the plasticity of the cell wall and the maintenance of an effective (although sometimes

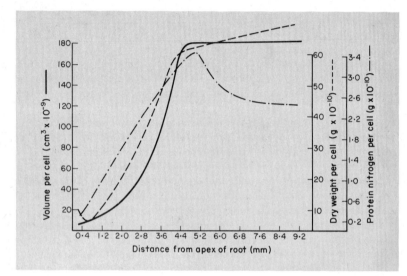

Fig. 9.4 Changes occurring during cell expansion in seedling pea roots. The progress of cell expansion parallels the scale of distance from the apex of the root (i.e. cells examined at different distances from the apex are equivalent to stages in the expansion process though which each cell passes). Cell expansion is completed at c. 4·8 mm from the apex. As the cells expand in volume there is a parallel increase in the dry weight per cell and the protein content per cell. (Data from Brown and Broadbent, 1950, *J. exp. Bot.*, 1, 249–63.)

decreasing) solute concentration within the protoplast. Again although much of the increase in protoplast volume is accounted for by the growth of vacuoles there is during cell expansion an increase in the volume of cytoplasm and often in the number of cytoplasmic organelles per cell. Thus either permanently or transiently (according to the subsequent course of differentiation) the expanding cell has a higher protein, lipid and RNA content than the meristematic cell from which it is derived (Fig. 9.4). The period of cell expansion is one characterized by active metabolism and net biosynthesis.

The process of cell expansion which occurs in the zone of elongation of roots has been studied by both microscopic and biochemical techniques. Microscopic studies have shown that there are changes in staining reactions and optical properties of the cell walls (probably indicative of changes in the relative contents of pectins, hemicelluloses, and cellulose), increases in the number of mitochondria with well developed cristae (correlated with a rise in O_2 uptake per cell), increases in the extent of the endoplasmic reticulum and of Golgi vesicles, and increase in the proportion of ribosomes bound to the endoplasmic reticulum membranes and organized in polyribosomes. Biochemical studies have shown that during cell expansion there are, associated with the increase in protein content, marked changes in the absolute and relative activity of enzymes. Although the pattern of change in RNA content is not identical in the roots of different species, or in the different cell lineages within the root, there is general agreement that significant changes take place in rate of RNA turnover as estimated from the speed at which radioactive atoms enter and leave the RNA and in the relative amounts of the different fractions into which the total RNA can be split by modern methods of chromatography. Current theories of the role of the RNAs as the agents translating genetic information into cytoplasmic activity inevitably suggest that these RNA changes may be critical in initiating, processing and terminating the phase of cell expansion.

The plant growth hormones termed *auxins* are usually defined by their physiological activity at very low concentrations and their essentiality for cell expansion. This definition is in accord with their discovery in studies on the growth and tropisms (see Chapter 10) of the grass coleoptile. In grass seedlings the emergent plumule is protected during its passage through the soil by a hollow, cylindrical, apically closed sheath or coleoptile (Fig. 9.5). The elongation of this coleoptile (from a length of 10 mm or less) to its final length (of 80 mm or more) is a consequence of the expansion, and predominantly elongation, of its constituent cells. This elongation can be prevented by removal of the apical 2 mm of the coleoptile and restored by replacing the coleoptile tip back in position or replacing the excised tip by a block of agar jelly which has previously collected diffusible material from the surface of an excised tip (Fig. 9.6A). The substance essential for the expansion of the coleoptile cells and which is supplied to them by the apex of the coleoptile is the auxin, indol-3yl acetic acid (IAA) (Fig. 9.3). The uniform basal movement of this auxin from the apex to the regions of cell expansion is disturbed by the unilateral action of gravity or light so that more auxin reaches the side respectively nearest to the centre of the earth or remote from the source of light. Then as a consequence of unequal cell expansion on the two sides of the organ a tropic curvature results (for a more detailed discussion see Chapter 10). The classical Went curvature assay for auxin activity (Fig. 9.7) involves measuring, under standardized conditions, the curvature induced in the etiolated decapitated oat coleoptile by supplying auxin to one side only of the apical cut surface from an agar block.

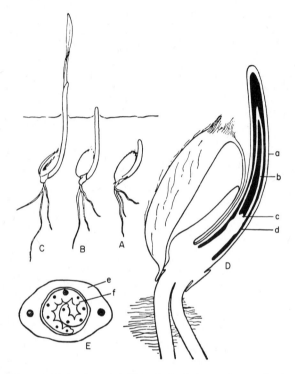

Fig. 9.5 Structure of the grass seedling, A, B, C; stages in germination; stage C shows emergence of first leaf from apex of the coleoptile. D: section taken at stage A; a, coleoptile; b, first leaf; c, stem apex; d, node; the region below d, mesocotyl. E: transverse section through coleoptile; e, coleoptile; f, first leaf; vascular strands in coleoptile and first leaf shown shaded. (From James, 1943, *An Introduction to Plant Physiology*. Clarendon Press, Oxford.)

IAA is referred to as '*diffusible*' auxin in the sense that it can be collected by diffusion from a cut surface into an agar block. Its movement through the coleoptile or other plant organ is however not by diffusion through the cell walls or through the symplast (continuity of cytoplasm from cell to cell). Its movement is polarized; it moves preferentially or exclusively in one direction in the living tissues of an organ and this

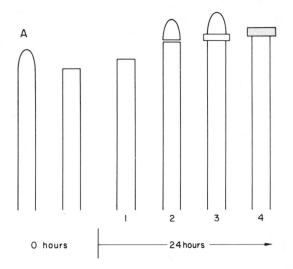

Fig. 9.6(A)   Diagram showing the effects on growth of an etiolated coleoptile of (1) decapitation (growth ceases then slowly resumes); (2) placing the tip back in position; (3) placing the tip back in position but with a thin sheet of agar or gelatin between tip and stump; (4) replacing the tip with a block of agar which has previously been enriched with auxin by diffusion from an excised tip.

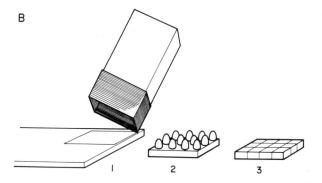

Fig. 9.6(B)   Technique of collecting diffusible auxin from excised coleoptile tips and of preparing blocks suitable for seating on decapitated coleoptiles. (1) Cutting the sheets of agar; (2) coleoptile tips placed cut surface downwards on the agar; (3) showing how agar sheet is cut up into blocks.

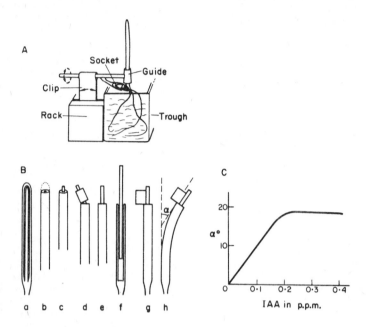

Fig. 9.7 The Went Curvature Test.
(**A**) *Avena* seedling holder which enables the coleoptile to be orientated strictly
vertical before decapitation.
(**B**)   Diagrammatic representation of steps in the test: (a) intact coleoptile; (b)
first decapitation; (c) first decapitation with first leaf pulled upwards and hence
detached at its base; (d) second decapitation performed within several hours of (c)
to bring linear extension to zero; (e) coleoptiles after second decapitation; (f)
longitudinal section showing the detachment of the cylindrical first leaf; (g)
application of the agar block containing either a known amount of IAA or of an
auxin whose activity is to be assayed; (h) curvature (α) produced in 2 hours under
standardized conditions. All the above operations are conducted in dim red light,
at constant temperature and at a relative humidity of close to but not above 90%.
(**C**)   Dose response curve relating $\alpha°$ to concentration of IAA in the agar block
(expressed as parts per million). Note the very limited concentration range over
which α is proportional to concentration.

polarized movement can occur against a concentration gradient (Fig. 9.8)
(see also Chapter 6, p. 107).

Although the transported auxin of the oat coleoptile and probably of
many other plant organs is IAA, the transportable auxin is only part of
the total extractable auxin (auxin extracted by ethyl ether or other
similar solvent). This has led to the concept that the auxin directly
involved in cell metabolism is chemically modified and probably linked

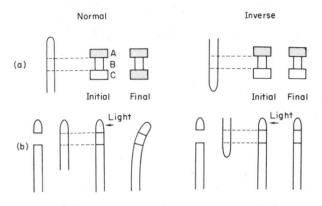

Fig. 9.8 Diagrams illustrating the polarity of auxin transport in the *Avena* coleoptile. **(a)** A, agar block containing auxin; B, segment of coleoptile cut out from coleoptile as shown; C, plain agar block. Degree of shading indicates auxin content of agar. Left side, normal transport, right side section inverted—no transport (after Went, 1935, *Bot. Rev.*, **1**, 162–82). **(b)** Transmission of photo-tropic stimulus through an introduced segment of coleoptile. *Left side*, stimulus passes normally orientated segment; *right side*, stimulus does not pass an inverted segment (after Beyer, 1928, *Z. Bot.*, **20**, 321–417). (Both via Went and Thimann, 1937, *Phytohormones*. Macmillan, New York.)

to some high molecular weight cell constituent. This concept is expressed by the term '*bound*' auxin. Further although IAA is the transported auxin in many plant organs, there is convincing evidence for the wide-spread natural occurrence of other indole compounds with auxin activity and it is very doubtful whether the activity of more than a few of these is to be accounted for on the basis that they act as precursors of IAA. It is also important to bear in mind that a wide range of synthetic com-pounds have properties which justify their classification as auxins by their effects on growth and development and often also by their polar transport within the plants. Examples of such compounds are the substituted phenoxyacetic acids (such as $2,4\text{-}D = 2,4$-dichlorophenoxy-acetic acid), the naphthalene and naphthoxyacetic acids, and the phenyl-aliphatic acids (such as phenylacetic and phenylpropionic acid). From a consideration of the auxin activity of a wide range of synthetic and natural substances certain features of chemical structure might be recog-nized as essential and the formulation of such 'rules' relating structure to activity has been attempted by various workers. Thus it was postu-lated that auxin activity depended primarily on three essential units of structure: an unsaturated ring-system, a carboxyl group and at least one α-hydrogen atom, all having a definite spatial relationship with each other, so that the auxin molecules can 'fit on' at the centre of its action in the cell. However, with the further progress of research, compounds are continuously being found which appear to break such rules. Perhaps too little attention has been paid to the importance of physical properties (e.g. surface tension effects, lipid solubility, etc.) in relation to auxin activity. Furthermore attempts to relate chemical structure to auxin activity are handicapped by our ignorance regarding the nature of the 'bound' forms of auxins in which they probably intervene in metabolism.

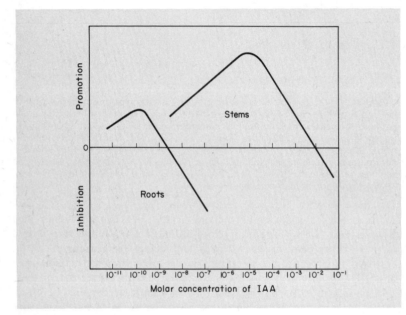

Fig. 9.9 Generalized representation of the influence of indol-3yl acetic acid (IAA) on the linear growth of roots and stems. Note the log. scale of molarity of IAA. (After Thimann, 1938, *Am. J. Bot.*, **24**, 407–12.)

In studying the influence of auxin on cell expansion in the oat coleoptile it was found that there was an optimum auxin concentration and that less cell expansion occurred at higher and lower auxin levels. The dose response curve to auxin of stems (hypocotyls and coleoptiles are similar) and roots is shown diagrammatically in Fig. 9.9. This indicates that there is a linear relationship between extension growth and the logarithm of the applied auxin concentration. Figure 9.9 also indicates that the optimum auxin concentration differs very greatly according to the kind of plant organ under investigation.

Almost contemporary with the discovery of the controlling influence of auxin upon coleoptile elongation, it was shown that auxin is released into agar by excised root tips. However this auxin appeared to restrict cell expansion in the root and the positive geotropic response of roots (in contrast to the negative geotropism of shoots—see Chapter 10) was formerly explained on the basis that the enhanced auxin level in the lower half of the organ inhibited cell expansion in roots (but enhanced it in stems). These observations could be explained if the auxin supply in the region of cell elongation in the root was above the optimum value, and studies with excised root segments (allowed to deplete their cells of their natural auxin) and with cultured excised roots receiving a restricted supply of sugar have shown that, at an appropriate low concentration, certain auxins (particularly the naphthalene acetic and naphthoxyacetic acids) can greatly enhance cell expansion in root cells and that an auxin is probably essential for this process. From studies on the changing response to external auxin of the seedling radicle from the beginning of germination, it seems that very young roots have a sub-optimal endogenous level of auxin but that this rises as root growth proceeds to become in due course supra-optimal, further rise in activity being then controlled by rise in the activity of auxin-destroying enzyme(s). The problem of the role of auxin in the control of root growth is an intriguing one particularly in view of recent evidence that one important aspect of the shoot-root relationship is mediated by the transport of auxin, via the vascular tissue, from the shoot to the root. This raises the possibility that cell division and expansion in roots may be controlled by interaction between auxin of shoot origin and cytokinin and gibberellin synthesized within the root.

The mechanism of action of auxins cannot be considered in isolation; their interaction with other plant growth regulators suggests that they all impinge on some central aspect of metabolism. The association of cell expansion with a net gain in protein and with changes in the relative activities of a number of enzymes would suggest prior changes in cytoplasmic RNA. In line with this, and as indicated above, studies with seedling roots of a number of species have shown that significant RNA synthesis takes place as the small cells of the root meristem embark upon the phase of cell expansion. That *total* RNA may be little changed or decrease or increase as the expansion process proceeds does not conflict with the evidence that maintenance or increase of particular RNAs in the cytoplasm is essential to the continuation of cell expansion. Evidence that auxins may initiate and control cell expansion by influencing RNA synthesis comes from work with isolated pea epicotyl segments where IAA-induced cell expansion is associated with the appearance of the enzyme indoleacetyl aspartate synthetase and with hypocotyl segments of soybean where elongation is enhanced by application of 2,4-D. In these segments auxin-induced elongation and enzyme synthesis were blocked by the antibiotics actinomycin-D (which blocks DNA-dependent RNA synthesis) and puromycin (which prevents growth of the polypeptide chains at the ribosomes) and by 8-azaguanine (which becomes incorporated into m-RNA and makes it a 'nonsense' RNA).

As earlier indicated, during cell expansion the turgor pressure remains constant or declines and there is an increase in the cell wall materials so that wall thickness is maintained or increased as cell surface area rises. During cell expansion there occur, particularly early in the process, changes in the physical properties of the wall and middle lamella which permit increase in cell area without increase in turgor pressure and irrespective of simultaneous synthesis of wall material. Some time after cell expansion is initiated, there however also occurs a continuing synthesis of the cell wall polysaccharides including cellulose. Heyn in 1931 first reported values for the elasticity and plasticity of the plasmolysed etiolated oat coleoptile calculated from measuring the bending of the horizontal coleoptile under applied weights and its recovery on removal of the weights (Fig. 9.10) and obtained evidence that immediate pretreatment with auxin increased the value of both properties and particularly of the plastic component. Such softening of the cell wall by auxin has been confirmed by subsequent studies and probably involves a loosening or dissolution of structural chemical bonds. The way in which auxin does this is not known but one way in which wall structure could be loosened would be by esterification (methylation) of the free carboxyl groups of pectins. It has been shown that auxin promotes incorporation into the pectins of the cell wall of the methyl group of the amino acid methionine and that auxin enhances the activity of certain esterase enzymes and, in particular, of pectin methylesterase. During cell expansion not only is there increase in dry weight per cell (largely accounted for by increased cell wall material) but it can be demonstrated that ^{14}C from sugars and organic acids is rapidly incorporated into cell wall constituents during expansion. Whether auxins specifically intervene in the synthesis of cell wall constituents is even more controversial. Of course in auxin-stimulated cell expansion there is enhanced wall synthesis but certain workers have obtained evidence that auxin promotes the wall structure dissolution which initiates expansion and that the phase of wall synthesis is promoted by calcium and inhibited by auxin. If this is so one of the factors operating to terminate the phase of cell expansion may be a rising level of intracellular auxin.

Although in the above discussion we have discussed the role of auxins in cell expansion it must be emphasized that auxins, like the cytokinins and gibberellins, have a wide range of physiological effects. Thus auxins

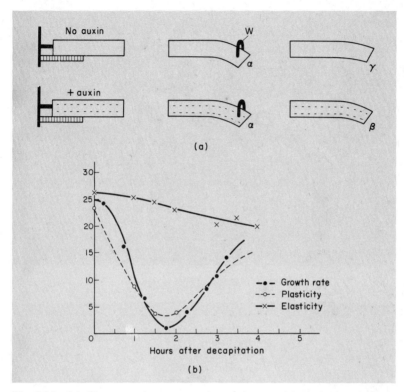

Fig. 9.10   (a) Diagrammatic representation of the experiment of A. N. J. Heyn (*Recl Trav. bot. néerl.*, 1931, **28**, 113–244). Coleoptiles removed from seedlings and held horizontally are submitted to a weight (250 mg) as shown (labelled W) for 60 minutes. The bending (angle α) is measured (and is independent of whether the coleoptile is treated or not with auxin). The weights are removed and the angle is measured again. The angle decreases much more in the untreated than the treated coleoptile; so that α > β > γ. The reduced 'regain' in the auxin-treated coleoptile is due to the IAA increasing the plasticity of the cell walls. (b) When coleoptiles are decapitated their growth declines (although after about 2 hours it rises again due to 'physiological regeneration of the tip', a process resulting in renewed auxin synthesis at the apex). The plasticity of the cell walls (not their elasticity) closely follows growth rate (and auxin content). (Data from Heyn, 1932, *C. r. hebd. Séanc. Acad. Sci., Paris*, **194**, 1848–50.)

promote adventitious root initiation in cuttings (Fig. 9.11), and are involved in fruit development, in the abscission (falling) of leaves and fruits, in the control of cambial activity, flower initiation and in sex determination in plants with unisexual flowers (see also Chapter 12). Study of these various physiological responses shows that, at the cellular

Fig. 9.11 Rooting of lemon cuttings. Treatments: *upper row*, basal end of cuttings in tap water for 8 hours; *lower row* in indol-3yl acetic acid (500 p.p.m.) for similar period. Cuttings photographed 17 days after treatment. (From Cooper, 1935, *Pl. Physiol., Lancaster*, **10**, 789–94.)

level, auxin is involved not only in the control of cell expansion but also of cell division and cell differentiation. When discussing the discovery of kinetin it was emphasized that the promotion of active cell division in the tobacco callus depends upon an appropriate external supply of *both* a cytokinin and an auxin. Prior to the discovery of kinetin it was known that auxin was essential to cell division in the wound callus of many plants; many excised plant tissues apparently synthesize adequately the cytokinin essential for their continuing growth but are dependent upon an external supply of auxin.

CELL DIFFERENTIATION

Cellular differentiation occurs in multicellular organisms and is the process leading to the development of the specialized structures and functions which characterize mature tissue cells. These cells are derived in higher plants from cells initiated by division at the primary and secondary meristems.

Cell expansion is an aspect of differentiation involving not only change in shape and volume but in physiological function (as evidenced by the changing activity of enzymes). Further some measure of cell expansion is involved in the differentiation of all tissue cells.

Differentiation into incipient shoot and root poles occurs prior to division in the fertilized ovum of flowering plants, gymnosperms and pteridophytes. Following the establishment of this polarity, the walls which effect cell cleavage are appropriately orientated as development of the embryonic sporophyte or gametophyte is initiated. Such polarity can be regarded as a spatial differentiation within the cytoplasm of a single cell. However tissues derived from such polarized cells themselves appear to show polarity and often for some particular physiological activity it is, in consequence, possible to demonstrate polarity in the whole organ concerned. One example of such polarity has already been given in describing auxin transport (Fig. 9.8, also see Chapter 6, p. 107). Morphogenic effects resulting from such polar transport of growth-regulating substances have long been known. Thus Vöchting in 1878 described how willow shoots form roots at their physiologically basal ends and buds at their apical ends irrespective of their orientation during the rooting period. A similar phenomenon can be readily demonstrated with segments of *Taraxacum* roots (Fig. 9.12). The establishment of such polarity in cell aggregates and growing organs appears to be involved in the normal differentiation of cells to give the tissue patterns characteristic of plant organs. Longitudinal and lateral gradients of major nutrients and metabolites, of dissolved gases and of growth-regulating substances are characteristic of growing organs and may be visualized as a three-dimen-

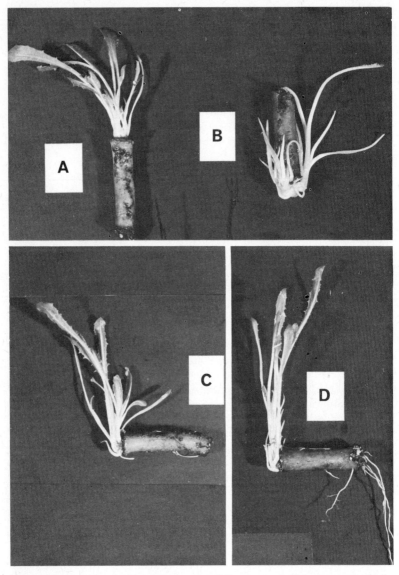

Fig. 9.12 Polarity of segments of roots of *Taraxacum officinale*, as shown by the development of shoots at their apical ends (ends adjacent to junction of root and shoot) irrespective of orientation during the sprouting period. A: upright; B: inverted; C and D: horizontal. Lateral root development is enhanced by application of a lanoline paste containing IAA to the basal end of the segment (D). Application of IAA to the apical ends of the segments will suppress shoot bud initiation, causing roots to develop at both ends of the segments. (Photo. by G. Asquith.)

sional physico-chemical pattern established or modified by tissue polarity. The forces operating on each cell are determined by its position (albeit changing with time), in this micro-environment pattern; cells are what they are because of where they are within the plant.

Tissue cells can always in theory (and sometimes in practice) be traced back to a daughter cell arising within the group of permanently meristematic cells and subsequently displaced from this group into a region of cell expansion and differentiation. However cell division is not restricted to the apical or lateral groups of meristematic cells; there are transition zones adjacent to the meristems in which cells may undergo a limited number of divisions prior to their maturation. Therefore in the lineage connecting a given tissue cell with its point of origin at the apex there may occur a number of cell divisions; these and the initiating division in the meristem may exert a determinative influence on differentiation. Cells are what they are not only because of where they are but because of where they originated within the region where cells are being initiated. This can be illustrated by drawing upon studies on the differentiation of epidermal (piliferous layer) cells in roots such as those of *Phleum pratense*. The seedling roots of this grass are transparent and have a rudimentary root cap. This has enabled growth and differentiation to be followed in continuous files of epidermal cells by a photomicrographic technique. The epidermis shows two kinds of cells; short cells (trichoblasts) which produce root hairs and long cells which remain hairless. Ultimate, or occasionally penultimate, divisions in the epidermis differentiate the trichoblasts from the hairless cells. About one-third of these cell divisions are equal and both daughter cells of the division become hairless cells. The remaining two-thirds of the divisions are very unequal and, of the pair of cells, the short more apical ones develop into trichoblasts and the longer basal ones develop into hairless cells. The initiation of a trichoblast occurs as a result of an asymmetric mitosis (for further discussion of this aspect of differentiation the reader is referred to the volume in this series by Professor Elizabeth Cutter entitled *Plant Anatomy: Experiment and Interpretation, Part 1*). Similar unequal divisions are involved in the differentiation of the sieve tube unit cell and the companion cell from a common mother cell and in the differentiation of stomatal guard cells and supporting cells in the leaf epidermis.

Studies on the giant chromosomes of insect cells and nuclear transplantation experiments in amphibians can be quoted as evidence that as cells differentiate more or less permanent changes take place in their nuclei. Examination of nuclei isolated from seedling pea roots has revealed differences in nuclear volume and in DNA, RNA and protein contents according as to whether the nuclei were from meristematic, expanding or mature cells. Such differences would however be expected between nuclei from different cytoplasmic environments. Further the capacity of certain mature plant tissue cells to return, under the influence of appropriate stimuli such as wounding or treatment with growth-regulating substances, to the meristematic state and subsequently to display their capacity to function like the fertilized egg (see Chapter 12, p. 259) or to embark upon new lines of differentiation argues that the nuclear changes associated with differentiation in plants are reversible. Cells with very different phenotypes may be of identical genotype. The term *totipotency* is used to describe this capacity of plant cells to display at different times and under appropriate stimuli different aspects of their genetic potentialities, including their potentiality to initiate a new multicellular individual. Nevertheless it is important to recognize that it has not been demonstrated that *all* plant tissue cells, whilst still alive, retain this totipotency.

Doubt regarding the universal retention of totipotency during the differentiation of plant cells seems to be justified on various grounds. Callus cultures derived from a number of plants will, when first isolated, give rise to shoot buds and roots either spontaneously or in response to the incorporation into or omission from their culture media of appropriate concentrations of growth-regulators, like auxin and cytokinins (see Chapter 11). In most cases, the callus if maintained in culture loses this capacity for organogenesis. This could be due to progressive depletion of some unknown growth-regulator carried over in the initial explant and in certain cases this may prove to be the explanation. However in some instances a correlation has been observed between loss of the capacity to initiate organs and the development of polyploidy (both euploidy and aneuploidy) and of chromosomal aberrations. Such cytological changes could be regarded as resulting from the abnormal conditions of *in vitro* culture. However it has been observed: (i) that separate callus isolates from the same plant may differ markedly in their initial capacities to give rise to organs and (ii) that polyploidy is a widespread concomitant of normal cellular differentiation. Thus in roots it has been found that certain tissues are characterized by a predominant level of polyploidy. Cortical cells are frequently tetraploid, vessel unit cells in the metaxylem are tetraploid or octoploid or of even higher ploidy and endodermal cells are frequently tetraploid. A close correlation has been found between the presence of tetraploid cells and the origin of root nodules in leguminous plants. However the cells of such tissues are rarely if ever *all* at the predominant level of ploidy suggesting that polyploidy arises during differentiation and is not essential to its initiation and normal progress. The physiological consequences of this development of polyploidy in tissue cells are uncertain although studies on volumes reached by metaxylem vessel unit cells and polyploidy of the vessel unit cells suggest that each increase in ploidy of the nucleus permits a further increment of cell expansion (Fig. 9.13); nuclear volume (which is related to DNA content) and cell volume at maturity are related. That a given amount of nuclear material may be able to support a given extent of cell expansion is also suggested by studies on the development of fibres. Thus often the long primary phloem fibres become multinucleate in plants whereas the shorter secondary phloem fibres remain uninucleate. In explaining what happens in the cell expansion phase of differentiation we have to account not only for its initiation and orderly continuation but for its limitation.

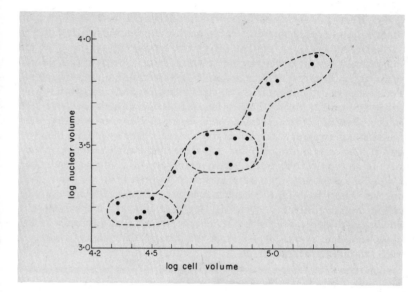

Fig. 9.13 Plot of log. nuclear volume against log. cell volume for developing metaxylem unit cells in *Arisaema triphyllum*. The clustering of the groups (indicated by enclosure in the broken lines) indicates a periodicity in the growth of cell and nucleus. (From List, Jr., 1963, *Am. J. Bot.*, **50**, 320–9.)

Reference to fibres serves to remind us that during the differentiation of certain cells there occur profound changes in cell shape and also changes in wall thickness and chemical composition. Changes in cell shape imply localized growth of the cell wall; during the differentiation of fibres their apices grow and intrude among the associated cells. Similarly highly localized depositions of cell wall material occur resulting in wall thickening which is uneven and often takes the form of an organized pattern. The obvious examples of such patterns are the annular, spiral and reticulate thickenings of the longitudinal walls of proto- and metaxylem vessels. Microscopists working in the second half of the nineteenth century, including the botanist Strasburger, observed an aggregation of cytoplasm, more dense and granular than the rest, which was streaming in a definite pattern and in a topographical relation to the wall thickenings such as rings and reticulations. A cytoplasmic organization preceded the appearance of a pattern in the secondary cell wall. More recent studies on the submicroscopic structure of cell walls has revealed that the framework of the cell wall is made up of orientated cellulose microfibrils and that these are normally laid down in the inner face of the wall with a uniform parallel orientation during cell expansion. When cell expansion is complete each successive layer of secondary wall is characterized by uniformly orientated microfibrils although the orientation may differ in successive layers. The mechanism and exact site of synthesis of the microfibrils remain uncertain, but there is evidence that a cytoplasmic organization internal to the external cell membrane (plasmalemma) determines the alignment of the microfibrils. One particularly interesting observation made during the electron microscopic study of growing cells in the roots of *Phleum pratense* and *Juniperus chinensis* was that their peripheral cytoplasm contained numerous microtubules (25 nm diameter and at least several μm long) and that these microtubules were orientated parallel to the microfibrils at the inner surface of the adjacent wall (Fig. 9.14). Similar observations have subsequently been made on many other species. There is also evidence that such orientation of the microtubules cannot be accounted for by the development of stress in the cytoplasm consequent upon cell growth but reflects an orientating capacity of the cytoplasm, and is thus an aspect of the intracellular polarity associated with cell differentiation.

PATTERNS OF DIFFERENTIATION

The arrangement of the various tissues of roots and stems is not only characteristic of the organ but in its details is characteristic of each species. The view has been advanced that this pattern is determined by the pre-existing pattern, that the formative influences are transmitted from the mature to the young cells. This hypothesis however faces the immediate difficulty that the original development of the characteristic tissue patterns, both in the embryo and whenever new shoot or root meristems arise, must be explained. The alternative hypothesis that the pattern is determined by the apical meristem itself is supported by many lines of evidence. Thus by the technique of culturing isolated root tips it can be shown that the very small root tips (in certain species tips of only 0·5 mm) which do not include any cells showing visible differentiation will give rise to roots having the anatomy typical of the radicle of the species. Again using the same technique, decapitated roots (apex removed) can be induced to form a new apical meristem. The vascular pattern in the new growth then does not line up with that in the root stump. Seedling and cultured pea roots are triarch. When cultured pea roots initiate a new apex following decapitation, the number of proto-xylem groups in the new growth can be increased to six if the new apex

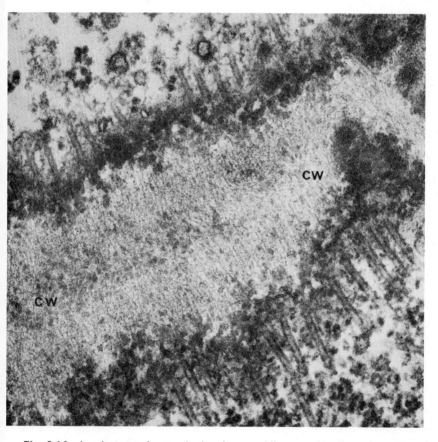

Fig. 9.14 An electron micrograph showing an oblique section through a cell wall (cw) separating two cells of the root tip of *Juniperus chinensis*. The micro-fibrillar structure of the cell wall is visible and the fibrils are parallel to the tubules in the adjacent cytoplasm. The apparent ending of the microtubules in the wall and in the cytoplasm is an illusion caused by the plane of sectioning; the micro-tubules are in fact many μm long. (From Ledbetter and Porter, 1963, *J. Cell Biol.*, **19**, 239–50.)

is developed in presence of 10^{-5} M IAA (Fig. 9.15). The hexarch condition persists when growth is continued in this auxin medium, but on transfer to auxin-free medium linear growth is accelerated and the xylem becomes triarch. In the auxin-free medium not only is growth accelerated but the root apex decreases in diameter. Size and growth rate of the root apex determine the pattern of vascular tissues differentiated below the apex.

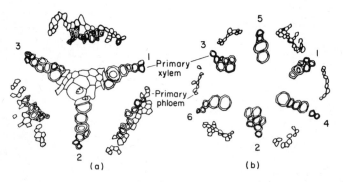

Fig. 9.15 Vascular pattern in cultured pea roots as seen in transverse section. (**a**): triarch root normally observed (protoxylem points numbered); (**b**) hexarch pattern arising during culture in a medium containing 10^{-5}M indol-3yl acetic acid. (From Torrey, in *Cell, Organism and Milieu*, ed. Rudnick, 1959, 189. Ronald Press, New York.)

The concept that a distribution pattern of growth regulators emanating from the apical meristem may predetermine the differentiation pattern is supported by some interesting recent work with callus cultures. Under appropriate conditions of culture such callus masses are free of vascular tissues or contain only a few scattered tracheid-like cells. Experimental induction of vascular tissue development in such callus masses has been achieved by making a V-shaped incision in the upper surface of the callus and inserting into this incision either a shoot bud or a supply of an auxin and a sugar (Fig. 9.16a), which must be either sucrose or one of a few other α-glycosyldisaccharides. In these experiments both xylem and phloem were differentiated and the balance between them could be controlled by the concentration of sugar applied. When the callus masses were sectioned, transversely to their vertical orientation during the experiment, the vascular strands were seen to be arranged in a roughly circular pattern and to be linked by an 'interfascicular cambium' giving rise to additional vascular tissue (Fig. 9.16b). The diameter of the circle and distance below the incision at which differentiation was initiated

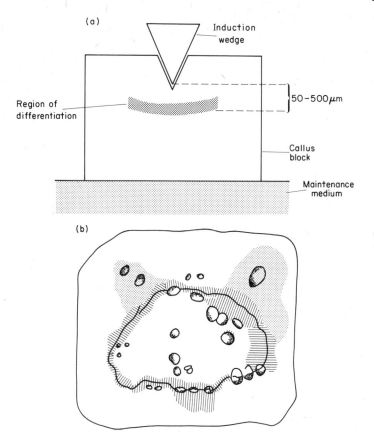

Fig. 9.16 (a) Diagrammatic section drawn through a cylindrical block of callus with an induction incision cut in the centre of the upper surface. Introduction of auxin and sucrose via this induction wedge resulted in differentiation of vascular tissue in the region indicated. (From Jeffs and Northcote, 1967, *J. Cell Sci.*, **2**, 77–88.) (b) Diagrammatic transverse section through a callus cylinder of *Syringa vulgaris* taken 450 μm below the surface 54 days after insertion of an induction wedge (see diagram **a**) containing 4% sucrose and 0·5 p.p.m. of the synthetic auxin, naphthalene acetic acid. Note the ring-like distribution of vascular nodules and the formation of a cambium (continuous line) involving the nodules and becoming more or less continuous across the interfascicular regions. Cellular regions laid down by cambial activity are shown by radial parallel lines. (From Wetmore and Rier, 1963, *Am. J. Bot.*, **50**, 418–30.)

were influenced by the auxin concentration applied; the circle was inflated and the region of differentiation lowered at high auxin concentrations. The incision is acting as an artificial apex from which substances exerting a controlling influence on cambial initiation and cell differentiation are diffusing.

Studies on vascular cambium initiation and the development of secondary vascular tissues in cultured roots give further support to the concept enunciated above but indicate that, within the organ, distribution patterns of substances additional to auxin and sugar may be important. As normally cultured, excised roots show little or no secondary thickening. Professor Torrey and his co-workers at Harvard noted that excised pea or radish roots showed very limited secondary thickening during the first culture passage following initiation of the root cultures from seedling root tips. No secondary thickening was observed on further subculture.

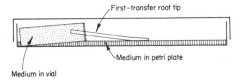

Fig. 9.17 Technique to enable sucrose and growth regulators to be fed to a growing excised root tip via the basal cut end. (From Torrey, 1963, *Symp. Soc. exp. Biol.*, **17**, 285–314.)

Attempts to enhance the secondary thickening in the first culture passage by introducing growth-regulating substances (auxin was tested exhaustively) or enhancing the sucrose concentration of the medium were unsuccessful. It is however possible to supply all or part of the nutrients to the excised root tip via its basal cut end (Fig. 9.17). Torrey used this technique to supply sucrose and auxin via the base to excised seedling root tips of pea and then found that there was enhanced cambial activity and development of secondary xylem well beyond the confines of the vial in which the IAA and sucrose were contained. On subculture, after growth for 14 days the root tip continued growth but no cambium was initiated. More recently the same workers have induced a high level of vascular cambium activity and good differentiation of secondary xylem and phloem in first passage radish (*Raphanus sativus*) roots supplied via their basal ends with sucrose, auxin (IAA, α-naphthalene acetic acid and 2,4-D were all effective), a cytokinin (kinetin and a number of other substituted aminopurines were effective) and *myo*-inositol (Fig. 9.18). However here as with the pea roots the above treatment did not induce cambial activity when the root tips were taken into a second culture passage. There is presumably critical depletion of some unidentified factor(s) as the roots grow in culture. It was concluded that the induction of secondary thickening in roots depends upon the root apex receiving sucrose and an appropriate mixture of growth-regulating substances by transport from the shoot systems. The early (1920) observation by Garner and Allard that radish forms thickened roots when the shoot is under short day conditions, but only fibrous roots if the shoot is in long days seems to support Torrey's hypothesis. However the extent to which growth regulators synthesized in the root may be involved in the promotion of secondary thickenings may vary from species to species. Roots are known to synthesize auxins, cytokinins and gibberellins. The fact that gibberellic acid had no promotive effect on cambial activity in the radish root cultures described above may be because this regulator was synthesized in adequate amount in the roots. In experiments on the

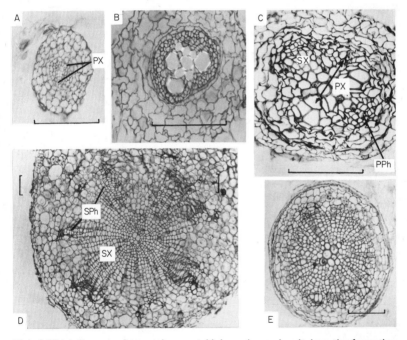

Fig. 9.18 Influence of an auxin, a cytokinin and *myo*-inositol on the formation and functioning of vascular cambium in cultured radish roots (*Raphanus sativus*). Sections cut in the region of maximum root diameter. All scales equal 100 μm. PX, primary xylem; SX, secondary xylem; PPh, primary phloem; SPh, secondary phloem. A: No growth factors supplied via the vial (see Fig. 19.17); B: No cytokinin supplied; C: No auxin supplied; E: No *myo*-inositol supplied; D: All three growth factors supplied. (Photograph supplied by J. G. Torrey, Biological Laboratories, Harvard University.)

induction of cambial activity in woody twigs both auxin and gibberellic acid have been found to be necessary to reproduce the stimulus to cambial activity normally released by opening buds in the spring. Further, in experiments on cultured tomato roots applications of auxin, cytokinin, gibberellin and other factors via the basal end of the root tip have been ineffective but introduction of *meso*-inositol into the medium bathing the tip has enhanced linear growth and cambial activity. In cultured tomato roots some secondary thickening takes place in medium containing *meso*-inositol when the roots are maintained in continuous culture, although the cells derived from the cambium show only very limited cell expansion and imperfect differentiation of the secondary vascular tissues. Clearly these results taken together emphasize that cambium initiation and activation and the differentiation of the new cells into xylem and phloem cells are under multifactor control and that we cannot yet specify all the factors involved. It can be postulated that the root tip meristem is the centre from which these factors move in a basipetal manner to create the necessary concentration patterns and that the root tip receives these factors or their precursors by transport (possibly via the phloem and procambial cells) from mature root tissue cells or from the shoot system or from both simultaneously.

If a growth-regulator causes cells to exhibit some aspect of their genetic potentialities which can be interpreted as a specialized function it can be regarded as implicated in differentiation. Further, if differentiation is under multifactor control we might expect that for a cell to respond in a particular way to a hormonal stimulus it must be 'ripe' to do so and this may imply that the cell must have undergone a partial differentiation. Just such a situation has been referred to in Chapter 2 dealing with control of the embryo on mobilization of food reserves within the seed. The particular instance is that of the role of a gibberellin released by the barley embryo in the induction, specifically in the aleurone layer, particularly of α-amylase but also of the activity of proteinases and other enzymes.

The **gibberellins** were first isolated from the culture medium used to grow the fungus *Gibberella fujikuroi* (the conidial stage of *Fusarium moniliforme*), which is the pathogen responsible for the foot rot ('foolish seedling' or 'Bakanae') disease of rice. The main compound responsible for the ability of the culture filtrate to induce excessive stem and leaf elongation in rice seedlings and to stimulate internode elongation in genetic dwarf plants of pea (Fig. 9.19) was isolated in 1954 and named gibberellic acid (gibberellin A_3, Fig. 9.3). This gibberellin was subsequently shown to occur in immature seeds of barley, *Echinocystis* and *Festuca pratensis* and further study has shown that gibberellins are very widely and probably universally distributed in higher plants. The known number of these naturally occurring gibberellins (designated A_1, A_2, A_3,

$A_4, \ldots$) is now quite large (over 30 and still growing); all have the same basic gibbane carbon skeleton but differ in the substituent groups in the ring system. This multiplicity of physiologically active gibberellins is in contrast with the single well authenticated natural auxin (IAA) and the few natural cytokinins. This could mean that particular gibberellins intervene in more limited aspects of the control of gene activity, that is to say, are more specific in their action than can be visualized with regard to auxin and the cytokinins.

Fig. 9.19 The influence of gibberellic acid (GA) on the growth of variety 'Meteor' dwarf pea. The plant on the left received no GA and shows the typical dwarf habit. The remaining plants treated with GA; the dose per plant in micro-grams is shown. With doses up to 5 micrograms there is increased linear growth of the stems with increase in GA dosage. This is the principle of the dwarf pea assay for gibberellins. (Photograph from Marshall Cavendish *Encyclopedia of Gardening*, 1968. By Dr. L. C. Luckwill, Long Ashton Research Station.)

There is strong evidence that at least in part the enzyme activity induced by the natural gibberellin of the barley embryo is due to its initiation of the *de novo* synthesis of the enzymes. Studies supporting this conclusion have involved the use of chloramphenicol (which in many systems acts as an inhibitor of protein synthesis) and of certain metabolic inhibitors such as ethionine (a homologue of methionine) and studies of the incorporation of ^{14}C-labelled amino acids into protein. As in other instances where we have considered the mechanism of action of such plant hormones, there is here again evidence that gibberellic acid modifies DNA-dependent RNA synthesis, causing change in amount and in the chemical nature (purine: pyrimidine base ratios) of that fraction of the RNA which seems to correspond to m-RNA. Do gibberellins act in this way in their other physiological effects both already mentioned and those to be discussed in Chapters 11 and 12? This is still uncertain but studies of the action of gibberellins on stem segments of dwarf pea indicate that those gibberellins active in the dwarf pea assay (Fig. 9.19) and only those cause characteristic changes in the pattern of RNA synthesis. It must however not be overlooked that gibberellins (and there is some evidence that this may also be the case with auxins) have very rapid effects on the permeability and structural stability of cell membranes (mitochondrial membranes, aleurone grain membranes and possibly also the plasmalemma and tonoplast) and that the hypothesis that plant hormones are themselves repressors and/or derepressors of genes or the immediate precursors of these regulators of gene activity awaits experimental demonstration.

FURTHER READING

AUDUS, L. J. (1972). *Plant Growth Substances. I. Chemistry and Physiology.* Leonard Hill, London.
STREET, H. E. (1969). *The Repertoire of Plant Cells.* Leicester University Press.
STREET, H. E. (1969). Growth in organised and unorganised systems: knowledge gained by culture of organs and tissue explants. In *Plant Physiology*, ed. STEWARD, F. C. Vol. 5B, 3–224. Academic Press, New York and London.
STREET, H. E. and COCKBURN, W. (1972). Growth and differentiation. Chap. 9 in *Plant Metabolism*, 2nd edition. Pergamon Press, Oxford.
TORREY, J. G. (1967). *Development in Flowering Plants.* Macmillan, New York.
WILKINS, M. B. (ed.) (1969). *The Physiology of Plant Growth and Development.* McGraw-Hill, London.

SELECTED REFERENCES

EVANS, M. L. (1974). Rapid responses to plant hormones. *A. Rev. Pl. Physiol.*, **25**, 195–223.
HESLOP-HARRISON, J. (1967). Differentiation. *A. Rev. Pl. Physiol.*, **18**, 325–48.
KENDE, H. (1971). The cytokinins. *Int. Rev. Cytol.* **31**, 301–38.
LANG, A. (1970). Gibberellins; structure and metabolism. *A. Rev. Pl. Physiol.*, **21**, 537–70.
ROELOFSEN, P. A. (1965). Ultrastructure of the wall in growing cells and its relation to the direction of the growth. *Adv. bot. Res.*, **2**, 69–145.
SCOTT, T. K. (1972). Auxins and roots. *A. Rev. Pl. Physiol.*, **23**, 235–58.
STREET, H. E. (1966). The physiology of root growth. *A. Rev. Pl. Physiol.*, **17**, 315–44.
STREET, H. E. (1968). Factors influencing the initiation and activity of meristems in roots. In *Root Growth*, Proc. 15th Easter School, Univ. Nottingham, ed. WHITTINGTON, W. J., pp. 20–41. Butterworths, London.

IO

Growth Movements

TROPISMS

Introduction

In flowering plants, growth not only results in mass increase and morphogenesis, but is involved in various responses to external stimuli. Plants alter the orientation of their parts in space in relation to external stimuli through either growth movements, or localized turgor changes. Growth movements, which occur in response to unidirectional stimuli and result in the positioning of the plant part in a direction related to the direction of the stimulus, are termed *tropisms*. If the growth movement is directly towards the source of the stimulus, the reaction is described as *positively orthotropic*; if directly away from it, as *negatively orthotropic*. If the organ becomes orientated at an angle to the stimulus we speak of a *plagiotropic* response and, if this angle is a right angle, of a *diatropic* response.

Pioneer studies on the orthotropic reactions towards light and gravity, phototropism and geotropism, led to the discovery of plant hormones. Charles Darwin, in 1880, reported upon his studies of the positive phototropic curvature of grass coleoptiles and of the hypocotyls of dicotyledonous seedlings and, finding that the bending failed to occur when extreme tips of the organs were shaded by metal foil 'hats', concluded that some stimulus must be transmitted from the tip to the curving region. Rothert (1894) extended these observations to a wider range of plant material. Then came the studies of Fitting (1907), Boysen Jensen (1910–1911) and Páal (1914–1919), which established that when the tip of a coleoptile is cut off and placed back in position the stimulus is not interrupted but passes across a moist cut surface or a gelatin layer. The stimulus failed to be transmitted when a thin sheet of mica, platinum foil or cocoa butter was placed between the tip and the responding part of the organ. Such observations made a chemical nature of the stimulus probable (Páal), though explanations in terms of 'induced polarity' were also advanced (Fitting). Appropriate transverse incisions indicated that the conduction of the stimulus occurred along the shaded side of an illuminated organ, and replacing the coleoptile tips asymmetrically on their stumps by itself produced curvatures without unilateral

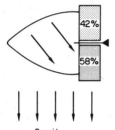

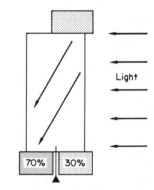

Fig. 10.1   1. Diversion of diffusible auxin to the lower side when a coleoptile tip is placed horizontally, demonstrated by collecting the auxin released from the cut surface in two agar blocks (stippled) separated by a razor blade. The total amount of auxin leaving the coleoptile tip is not significantly altered by submitting the tip to the geotropic stimulus, but now 58% of the total is released from the lower half. (Experiment by Dolk, 1929.) 2. Diversion of diffusible auxin to the shaded side when a coleoptile tip is unilaterally illuminated. Technique as in 1 above. Again the total amount of auxin collected is not significantly altered by the phototropic stimulus but 65% of the total is released from the half furthest from the light source. (Experiment by Went, 1928.) 3. An agar block containing auxin is placed upon the upper cut surface of a segment of hypocotyl from a radish (*Raphanus*) seedling. The segment is correctly orientated (upper part uppermost). The hypocotyl is subjected to unilateral illumination. The auxin as it is transported through the hypocotyl is diverted to the shaded side as shown by the two-block technique described above. (Experiment by van Overbeek, 1933.)

The amount of auxin collected in the agar blocks can be estimated by Went's curvature test (see Fig. 9.7, p. 168).

illumination (Páal, 1918). The straight growth of *Avena* coleoptiles decreased severely or stopped when they were decapitated and could be restored by placing the tips back in position (Söding, 1925; Went, 1928) (Fig. 9.6A, p. 167). The stimulus involved in the phototropic reaction was thus apparently also active in controlling normal growth. Parallel observations were made in the study of geotropism, viz, that the tip of a stimulated organ produced a growth-controlling stimulus which under the influence of gravity was transmitted along the lower side.

Clear demonstration of the chemical nature of the stimulus was achieved in 1928 by Went. He demonstrated that the chemical agent could be collected in agar blocks by diffusion from the cut surfaces of coleoptile tips (Fig. 9.6B), and that in consequence when these blocks were placed unilaterally on decapitated coleoptiles, they caused a curvature away from the side receiving the chemical messenger (the growth hormone) by diffusion from the block. Went used this technique to develop an assay of the hormones or auxin based upon measuring the degree of growth curvature occurring under standard conditions and in standard time in the etiolated *Avena* coleoptile (see Chapter 9, Fig. 9.7). Further, by means of collecting the hormone from the lighted and shaded sides of an illuminated coleoptile tip into separate agar blocks, Went was able to prove that the total amount of hormone released from the tip was not altered significantly, but more hormone passed to the shaded than the lighted side (Fig. 10.1). Between the years 1926 and 1928, Went and Cholodny independently put forward a hormonal theory of geotropism and phototropism, which in its essentials has stood the test of time and will presently be discussed. The discovery of auxin in these studies led on to the recognition that plant growth in general is regulated by plant hormones (see Chapters 9, 11 and 12). For excellent and more detailed accounts of these classical investigations reference should be made to Went and Thimann (1937).

Survey of tropisms

The most important tropisms manifested by flowering plants are *geotropism* in response to gravity, ***phototropism*** in response to light and ***haptotropism*** (thigmotropism) in response to touch. In addition to these, some plant organs can also show tropic responses towards chemicals (chemotropism), temperature gradients (thermotropism), presence of water (hydrotropism), flowing water (rheotropism), oxygen (aerotropism) and even towards electric fields (galvanotropism), but these reactions are of more limited occurrence and will not be considered further here.

The capacity to react to certain stimuli can be lost by mutation. Mutants of rice and maize are known which have lost the ability to react to gravity, i.e. are ageotropic (non-geotropic), and the maize mutant is also aphototropic. These tropic responses of plant organs resemble the tactic movements of motile unicells (phototaxis, chemotaxis and thermotaxis) in so far as similar unidirectional stimuli are involved and in that the motile organisms move in a direction related to the direction of the environmental stimulus. Plants moreover show the phenomenon of autotropism, in that the orientation of organs can be fixed positionally in relation to other organs. Leaf positions with respect to the stem, the angles of lateral roots (higher than first order) in relation to the axis that bears them, and the angles between axillary branches and the main stem, are autotropically determined. In reacting to a unidirectional stimulus a plant organ may overshoot the equilibrium position and return to it by an autotropic counter-reaction; a plant in which an over-curvature is produced by gravity will straighten this out on a klinostat (p. 194) in the absence of any further gravitational stimulus.

All tropisms are effected by differential growth rates on opposite sides of the reacting organ. A vertically orientated main root grows equally on all sides and therefore grows straight; when placed at right angles to the field direction of gravity by being laid horizontally, the upper side in the region of curvature grows faster than the lower and a curvature is produced, directing the root again along the field direction of gravity. The curvature results from an enhanced growth rate on one side, or a reduced growth rate on one side, or a combination of both, and hence only a growing organ can show a tropic growth reaction. During development, the sensitivity of an organ towards a particular stimulus increases to a maximum, then decreases and finally is lost when the organ reaches maturity and ceases to grow. Mature nodes of grasses and some other jointed plants, e.g. *Tradescantia* and *Dianthus*, react geotropically while mature nodes of the Commelinaceae also react phototropically but, in such nodes, growth is resumed as a result of stimulation. The differential growth rates involved in tropisms are very largely confined to regions where growth is by cell expansion, the cells on the convex side expanding faster and becoming longer and thinner-walled than on the concave side; cell division has been implicated in only a few cases.

Tropisms are of supreme importance in establishing and maintaining the correct orientation (the liminal direction) of plant organs (Fig. 10.2). Rice mutants which have lost geotropic reactivity through x-ray treatment collapse flat on the ground and become lodged. Interactions between different tropisms occur: leaf orientation, for instance, is determined by a combination of tropic (or nastic, see p. 210) responses towards light and gravity, in conjunction with autonomous tendencies for unequal growth on the upper and lower sides. Light modifies the reactivity of plants towards gravity; the orthogeotropic sensitivity of shoots is lowered by light, but etiolated shoots of *Sinapis alba* show a poor geotropic reaction. The plagiogeotropic runners of *Circaea* and *Fragaria*, which normally grow along the soil surface, turn upwards as if negatively geotropic when the plants are kept in the dark; plagiogeotropic rosette leaves and shoots may turn upwards even in weak light. Some

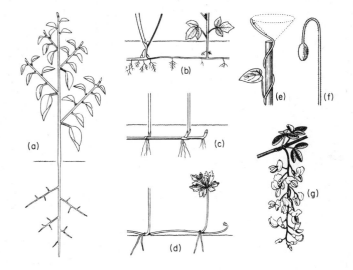

Fig. 10.2 Various types of growth habit controlled by geotropic responses. Schematic. a: dicotyledonous plant with orthotropic main root (positively geotropic), main stem (negatively geotropic), secondary roots and side shoots (plagiotropic) and tertiary roots (non-geotropic). b: diageotropic root of *Rubus idaeus*, raspberry. c: diageotropic rhizome of *Eleocharis*. d: diageotropic runners of *Ranunculus repens*, creeping buttercup. e: twining shoot of *Ipomoea purpurea* showing strong circumnutation and lateral geotropism. f: young peduncle of *Papaver*, poppy, showing positive geotropism. g: inflorescence of *Laburnum anagyroides*; the axis is non-geotropic, and the inflorescence hangs down under its own weight. (From Larsen, 1962, in *Encyclopedia of Plant Physiology*, ed. Ruhland, **17**/2, 34–73. Springer-Verlag, Berlin.)

plagiogeotropic subterranean organs, on the other hand, behave as if positively geotropic on illumination (see p. 209).

The sign (positive or negative) of the tropic response of an organ may change during its growth; this happens frequently in reproductive organs, where the flower bud, the open flower and the fruit may each have a characteristic orientation due to a different geotropic response of the pedicel (see also Chapter 12 and Fig. 12.6, p. 246). The flower stalk of the peanut (*Arachis hypogaea*) is at first negatively geotropic, but after fertilization it becomes positively geotropic and buries the fruit in the soil. The phototropic reaction of the flower stalk of the ivy-leaved toadflax (*Cymbalaria muralis*) changes from positive to negative after fertilization; this results in the fruits being pushed into crevices of the rocks or walls on which the plant grows.

The zygomorphic form of some flowers, e.g. *Asphodeline lutea* (Fig. 10.3) is produced in response to gravity and regular flowers form on a plant rotated during floral development on a klinostat (an instrument designed to allow a plant to be exposed equally to gravity on all sides by means of continuous rotation at a controllable speed). Here gravity acts as a morphogenetic factor. Torsions in some organs, e.g. the twisting of orchid flowers which makes the labellum point downwards, are gravity-induced.

Fig. 10.3   The flower of *Asphodeline lutea*, formed under the influence of natural gravity (*left*) and on a klinostat (*right*). (From Bünning, 1953, *Entwicklungs- und Bewegungsphysiologie der Pflanze*. Springer-Verlag, Berlin.)

GEOTROPISM

Suitable experimental material for the investigation of geotropism is provided by primary seedling roots (positive response), and by young seedling shoots and cereal coleoptiles (negative response). The tropic curvature in a seedling root laid horizontal becomes visible after 30–60 minutes and the apex becomes directed downwards; the bending is produced in the region of most rapid growth. Geotropic root curvature usually results from a strong inhibition of growth on the lower side, accompanied by either no change or slight stimulation or even some weak inhibition on the upper. Hence during curvature the root growth as a whole slows down. In shoots, inhibition of growth on one side is usually associated with stimulation on the other, so that the overall growth rate remains unchanged, though even in shoots there may be an overall inhibition of growth. Continuous stimulation is not necessary; and after a period of stimulation curvature will occur if the test object is subsequently rotated on a klinostat (slowly, to avoid development of any appreciable centrifugal force). The minimum time during which the stimulus must be allowed to act to lead to subsequent curvature is the *presentation time*; the time required for an observable response to appear is the **latent time** or **reaction time**, and this is usually measured from the end of presentation time, so that the time for the response to appear is presentation time + latent time. In the organs of flowering plants, the minimum presentation time with natural gravity and at room temperature varies from 30 seconds or less to 25 minutes, and the latent time from 35 to 120 minutes. The duration of presentation time and reaction time is increased by lowering the temperature, and availability of oxygen is needed for completion of both processes.

The intensity of geotropic stimulation can be varied in two ways. One is to place the material at different angles to the vertical; the force acting on it is then **g** sin α, where α is the angle with the vertical and **g** is the force of gravity. The other method depends on the fact that a centrifugal force has the same effect on plants as natural gravity, and involves rotation at various speeds on a klinostat or centrifuge, thereby subjecting the plant to a centrifugal force which can be expressed as a fraction or multiple of **g**. It has been found that a certain minimum or threshold stimulation is needed to produce a geotropic curvature; a long presentation time is needed with a weak force, and vice versa. The product of presentation time and force required to produce the first perceptible curvature remains constant over a wide range of force. In a series of experiments with the oat coleoptile, this held true for forces of 58·4 to 0·08 **g**, with corresponding presentation times from 5 seconds to over an hour. The threshold for the oat colcoptile was thus about 300 **g**-seconds, at 16–17°C. Under continuous stimulation, maize roots have responded to a force as low as 0·0005–0·001 **g**. Several periods of sub-threshold stimulation can be additive and result in curvature, provided the intervals between the periods of stimulation do not exceed a value which depends on the organ investigated. With short intervals the value of the threshold may actually be reduced when stimulation is applied intermittently rather than given continuously. This indicates that the primary stages in geotropic perception can be saturated at a very low level of stimulation and that some system must revert to the original (unstimulated) state before it can again be affected by the stimulus.

As the amount of stimulus is raised above threshold value, the response becomes stronger, the latent time decreasing and the curvature increasing. When a physiological response is directly proportional to the amount of stimulus which produces it, it is said to obey the **stimulus-quantity** *law.* For geotropism, the law holds within a limited range of stimulus quantities; the response rises to a maximum with increased stimulation; then further increases in the stimulus give no further increase in reaction, which now must be limited by internal factors, and very strong stimulation becomes inhibitory; in one series of experiments with pea roots, inhibition was found to result from forces in excess of 111 **g.**

Geotropic curvature occurs in the region of cell elongation, always some distance back from the shoot or root apex. However, the chief region of perception of the gravitational stimulus is at the tip of roots and of coleoptiles and following stimulation a message is transmitted thence to the reacting region. In the stems of dicotyledon seedlings sensitivity is greatest at the tip but also extends for some distance back from the apical meristem. A decapitation of an organ, which leaves the elongation zone intact, often abolishes its reactivity towards gravity, or at least strikingly diminishes it, raising the threshold of stimulation. In roots, the root cap has been found to be the site of perception in a number of species, e.g. *Zea mays, Pisum sativum, Lepidium sativum* and *Lens culinaris*, though in some cases—e.g. *Vicia faba*—it has been claimed that the cap can be removed without abolishing sensitivity.

It might be argued that decapitation causes loss of the capacity to react through the shock effect of wounding, but in a number of instances it has been shown that growth is not inhibited, indeed removal of the root cap while abolishing geosensitivity may give a transient increase in growth rate. Further, if decapitation is delayed for some period after presentation time but carried out before reaction is complete, a normal curvature develops, and deliberate wounding of root tips without removal of the cap does not prevent the development of curvatures. In some maize varieties the cap can be teased off without any cutting but there is complete loss of geotropic reaction. Again curvatures usually, although admittedly not always, take place when the excised tip is replaced. Curvature is produced when a stimulated tip is placed on an unstimulated stump, and the two need not be of the same species, nor from the same organ: a root stump can, for instance, be induced to curve by a stimulated coleoptile tip. Evidence for the importance of the tip in the perception of gravity can also be obtained in experiments not involving its excision. By suitable orientation on a klinostat, the root tip and the elongating region can be subjected to centrifugal forces in opposite directions (Fig. 10.4). The resulting curvature is then determined by the direction of the force acting on the tip, even when this is considerably weaker than that applied further back.

The geotropic response thus consists of the following stages separable in space and time. (1) *Perception* of the external stimulus (gravity), resulting in (2) the *induction* of a metabolic change in the sensitive region, (3) *conduction* of a physiological influence or stimulus inside

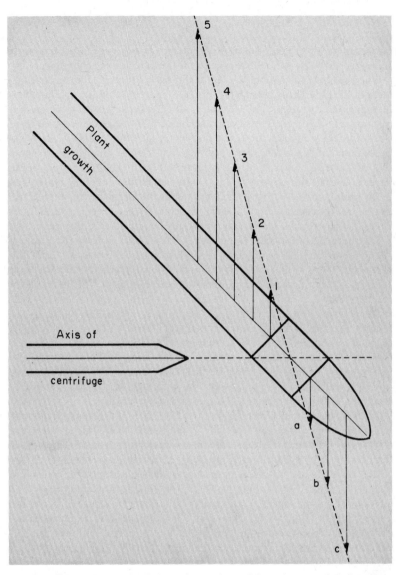

Fig. 10.4 Centrifugal stimulation of root tip and base in opposite directions. The arrows a, b, c, show the direction of forces acting on the tip which projects beyond the centrifuge axis; the arrows 1 to 5 represent the forces acting on the basal part; the lengths of the arrows are proportional to the forces. If 1·5 to 2 mm of the tip is allowed to project beyond the axis, the root behaves as if the tip alone were stimulated, though the forces acting on the base in the opposite direction are much stronger. (From Larsen, 1962, in *Encyclopedia of Plant Physiology*, ed. Ruhland, **17**/2, 34–73, Springer-Verlag, Berlin.)

the organ to the region where it produces (4) the *geotropic reaction* expressed through differential growth on the two sides of the organ.

The classical explanation (the 'Cholodny–Went theory') for the development of the differential growth rate has been in terms of induced differences in auxin concentration. The elongation of cells in the growing region of a plant organ is controlled to an important extent by the auxin received from sites of auxin synthesis. In a root or a shoot growing vertically, the concentration of auxin reaching the growing cells is equal on all sides. When a root or shoot is, however, placed horizontally, more auxin is found on the lower side than the upper (Fig. 10.1). In shoots, the auxin is synthesized in the apical meristem, transported basipetally to the elongating region and the auxin concentration difference is achieved by a redistribution, or lateral transport; the lower side gains at the expense of the upper. In roots, there is controversy about sites of synthesis: at least some of the auxin found in roots is thought to be transported acropetally from the shoot and there is also possibly some additional synthesis of auxin in a stimulated root, increasing the amount on the lower side. The difference in reaction of roots and shoots is explained by the very different auxin sensitivities of root and shoot cells (Fig. 9.9, p. 170). The root cells are much more sensitive and concentrations of auxin which are stimulatory to shoot growth are inhibitory to root growth. It is accordingly postulated that the increased auxin concentration in the lower half of a horizontally placed shoot stimulates growth in that half, causing the shoot to curve upwards while, in a horizontal root, the auxin increase on the lower side results in growth inhibition and a downward curvature.

In the light of an increasing amount of observations this basic hypothesis has required modification, especially in the case of roots. For instance, the changes in growth rate are greater than would be expected from the differences in auxin distribution as judged by various bioassays of the 'extractable auxin', so it has been suggested that stimulation could also change the sensitivity to auxin on the two sides of a stimulated organ. The effect of auxin in root geotropism may be indirect, the growth inhibition being brought about by ethylene which is synthesized in response to the increased auxin concentration, and which is a powerful inhibitor of plant cell growth. Moreover in roots, though auxin redistribution occurs, there is evidence for the involvement also of non-auxin growth inhibitors, possibly related to (or even identical with) abscisic acid and the relative importance of auxin and non-auxin hormones is not clear. Recently gibberellins as well as auxins have been found to be asymmetrically distributed in geotropically stimulated roots and shoots. In roots, a higher gibberellin content is found on the upper side but in shoots the gibberellin accumulates on the lower side, i.e. in each case the higher gibberellin content is found on the side which shows the higher growth rate. The overall gibberellin content of the shoots is also considerably increased. The significance of these changes in the amount and distribution of gibberellins in the geotropic growth reaction has not yet been assessed, but the changes are very appreciable; in sunflower shoots, for instance, the lower side acquires a ten-fold higher concentration than the upper, and the total gibberellin content rises three-fold. Hormonal changes of such magnitude can scarcely occur without an effect on growth. As well as acting on growth directly, the gibberellin could influence the cells' sensitivity towards auxin and perhaps also auxin transport. The hormone relations of geotropism are clearly much more complex than envisaged in the original Cholodny–Went theory, but the basic principle holds: geostimulation causes an unequal distribution of growth hormone(s) in the organ.

The root or shoot tip normally plays a double role in the geotropic reaction, being the region of hormone production and the main or exclusive region of perception of the stimulus. Some elegant experiments involving microsurgery to remove caps or to insert minute mica barriers in specified regions of the root have shown that in maize and pea the perceptive cap is itself the source of a hormone that causes growth retardation on the lower side during the geotropic response, i.e. the perception region is a region of hormone synthesis (though the involvement of additional hormone(s) produced in the meristem behind the cap is not ruled out). However, the perception region may not coincide with a region of hormone production in all cases. Decapitation of coleoptiles causes loss of geosensitivity, but the ability to respond may be restored by application of auxin to the cut end, showing that perception can take place behind the tip. Diversion of hormone to the lower side normally takes place within the tip itself on stimulation, but the regions further back reinforce the asymmetry in hormone distribution and in decapitated organs all redistribution must occur in these regions.

The primary perception of gravity must involve the movement of some entity in the sensitive cells; this is the only way in which the physical force of gravity can react on a cell. Molecules of auxin are too small to move appreciably under gravity; one must search for an organelle at least 0·5 μm in diameter. In 1900, Haberlandt and Neměc independently put forward the **statolith theory** of geotropism. This supposes that in certain cells, the **statocytes**, mobile starch grains (the **statoliths**) move under gravity to lie in the lower parts of the cells (Fig. 10.5). Thereby the upper and lower parts of the cells come to differ and the organ acquires an 'up-and-downness', a polarization. Not all starch grains in cells are mobile under gravity and capable of acting as statoliths. On the whole, organs which are geotropically sensitive contain statolith starch, and non-geotropic organs lack it. In root tips, statolith starch is abundant in the root cap; in stems, the endodermis contains movable starch grains, and it has been noted that these statolith starch grains persist even in extreme starvation. Disappearance of the starch grains can be induced by low temperature treatment or by treatment with gibberellins and this leads to loss of geotropic sensitivity; when the cells are allowed to recover their starch, geotropic sensitivity reappears. There is evidence that in some organs bodies such as crystals of calcium oxalate may also function as statoliths. The statolith theory faces the difficulty that some organs known to be sensitive to gravity do not appear to contain statoliths; fungal sporangiophores and the roots of some seedlings are in this category. In these cases, one can postulate that the statoliths have not yet been identified.

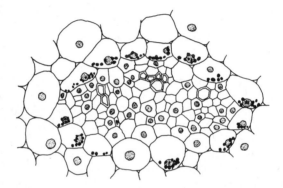

Fig. 10.5 Transverse section of young onion (*Allium cepa*) cotyledon base; the statocytes form a sheath round the vascular bundle and the statolith starch grains (in black) have been made to accumulate on the lower sides of the cells. (From Hawker, 1932, *Ann. Bot.*, **46**, 121–57. By permission of the Clarendon Press, Oxford.)

If the movement of statoliths is the first step in the perception of gravity, the question arises as to how the movement of these structures brings about the observed redistribution of auxin. Provided some upper–lower asymmetry is caused in the statocytes by statolith movement, then there could be a sharp change in cellular physiology at the cell junctions along the line of the gravitational force, resulting in a directed auxin movement along the line of force. The physiological change could be brought about by the statoliths themselves, or the statoliths could have the purely mechanical function of displacing upwards in the cell lighter organelles, these organelles being active in the physiological reactions that lead to auxin movement. In stimulated root tips of broad bean and maize, electron microscopy has revealed a higher concentration of endoplasmic reticulum on the upper sides of statocyte cells, while in *Avena* coleoptiles sedimentation of Golgi

bodies and mitochondria has been noted. For direct action by the statoliths it has been suggested that changes occur in the permeability properties
of cellular membranes as the statoliths impinge on them. The membrane
affected by the statoliths was at first thought to be the plasmalemma. On
the basis of studies on the geoperceptive root cap cells of cress (*Lepidium
sativum*), it has, however, been suggested that changes in pressure on the
endoplasmic reticulum might be important. The sensitive cells contain
near their walls layers of endoplasmic reticulum arranged in a precise way
(Fig. 10.6) and the shape of the cells and the arrangement of the membranes
are such that, with the root in the vertical position, the amyloplasts press
equally against the endoplasmic reticulum in cells on both sides of the root
axis. An actual pressing of the amyloplasts against the endoplasmic reticulum is indicated by visible deformation of the membranes beneath the

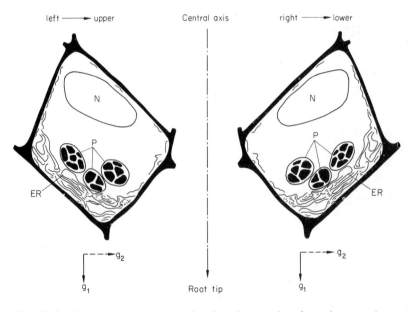

Fig. 10.6 Diagrammatic representation, based on tracings from electron micrographs, of two cells on either side of the root axis of a *Lepidium sativum* root cap.
In the vertical position as here drawn (gravity acting in the direction g_1) the
amyloplasts P press equally on the endoplasmic reticulum, ER, in the two cells.
When the root is placed horizontally (gravity acting in the direction g_2), sedimentation of the amyloplasts will greatly relieve pressure on the ER in the cell
remaining uppermost, the left-hand cell in the drawing, but in the lower (right-
hand) cell, the amyloplasts will move less and still remain largely in contact with
the ER. N = nucleus. (From Sievers and Volkman, 1972, *Planta*, **102**, 160–72.)

plastids. When the root is placed horizontally, the plastids slide off the endoplasmic reticulum and considerably relieve pressure on it, in the *upper* cells only, i.e. the cells above the central axis of the root; in the *lower* cells the pressure scarcely changes (Fig. 10.6). There is not only a change in pressure on the membranes, but the pressure after stimulation is now different in the upper and lower cells, which could account for different amounts of hormones being passed back from the upper and lower halves of the cap. The proponents of this idea point out that the perception time of this tissue (and of some other tissues, too) is much shorter than expected from the speed of movement of amyloplasts to the lower sides of cells but, whereas the plastids take several minutes to reach a new equilibrium position when the root is placed horizontally, pressure relief is instantaneous. In root cap cells of other species, endoplasmic reticulum complexes near cell walls have been observed, though the arrangement of organelles does not appear as regular in all cases as in the cress. How pressure changes on membranes affect the transport and/or synthesis of hormones still remains unexplained. It may be noted that pressure changes of the magnitude that would be produced by the movement of plastids can affect the activity of enzymes. Another difficulty is to visualize how hormone is diverted to the lower side of the organ outside the statocytes, which may be very few in number, whilst the final effect is produced in many thousands of cells in which no visible polarization has yet been detected.

A plant organ placed horizontally develops an electric potential between the upper and lower surfaces, the lower side becoming electropositive with respect to the upper by 5–30 millivolts. This phenomenon, known as the **geoelectric effect**, was at one time evoked as the primary cause of auxin movement; indoleacetic acid ions, being negatively charged, were postulated to move to the more positive, lower, side. However, studies since 1960 have shown that the geoelectric effect does not develop until some 15 minutes after stimulation, whereas the presentation time may be as little as 2 minutes; the geoelectric effect thus appears long after the primary induction processes have taken place, and must be regarded as a result rather than as the cause of the asymmetric auxin distribution. A 'geoelectric effect' can be produced artificially by applying auxin to one side of an organ.

As indicated above, the means by which the lateral hormone transport is achieved remain essentially unexplained, even if one accepts the statolith theory. In addition to a differential hormone distribution, the two sides of the stimulated organ develop differences in pH, in concentration of reducing sugars, in osmotic pressure, in respiration rate and in catalase activity. Stimulation by gravity thus brings about a profound change in the metabolic state of the tissues on the upper and lower sides of the reacting organ.

PHOTOTROPISM

Phototropism has been studied mainly in etiolated grass coleoptiles, particularly in those of oats, wheat and maize, and in the epicotyls and hypocotyls of light-grown dicotyledon seedlings, particularly of pea and sunflower. The direction of curvature may depend on the amount of light received. The threshold of stimulation is 3–25 lux-seconds. As the amount of light is increased, the response of coleoptiles changes as shown in Fig. 10.7, from a first positive to a first negative, to a second positive, to a second negative and finally to a third positive curvature. But not all organs show this sequence; light-grown radish seedlings for example are insensitive to stimulation in the first positive and first negative ranges and begin

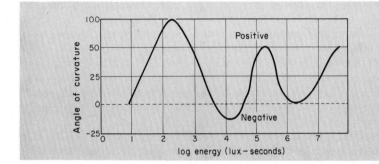

Fig. 10.7 Reversal of phototropic curvature of *Avena* coleoptile with varying light intensity. (From Galston, 1959, based on data of DuBuy and Nuernbergk, 1934, *Encyclopedia of Plant Physiology*, ed. Ruhland, **17**/1, 492–529. Springer-Verlag, Berlin.)

to curve (positively) only in the second positive range. The light intensities encountered in nature are such as to call forth the second positive curvatures; hence all the shoot organs mentioned above are generally stated to be positively phototropic and research has concentrated on their first and second positive curvatures. The third positive reaction is probably a damage manifestation, caused by turgor loss on the intensely illuminated side. Roots are negatively phototropic or indifferent towards light.

The phototropic reaction has a number of features in common with geotropism. There is a presentation time and a reaction time, a threshold for reaction, and the stimulus-quantity law holds for the first positive and first negative curvatures (beyond these, the response is no longer proportional to the amount of light). Intermittent sub-threshold stimulations are additive. At high light intensities, the presentation time may be a fraction of a second, and the reaction time a few seconds. In coleoptiles, the tip is again the most sensitive region of perception, but some sensitivity is shown throughout the length of the organ. Decapitated coleoptiles supplied with auxin from agar blocks show a weak phototropism, and unilaterally illuminated coleoptile stumps and hypocotyl segments divert auxin to the shaded side (Fig. 10.1). Conduction of a hormonal stimulus thus takes place within the organ and the differential growth rates resulting in curvature were originally believed to result from auxin redistribution, the side away from light receiving more auxin than the lighted side (Fig. 10.1). In a shoot this would increase the growth rate on the shaded side and the organ would bend towards the light. In those roots which show phototropism, the growth rate would be retarded on the shaded side and a negative curvature would result. As in the case of geotropism, difficulties arise in explaining the differences in growth rate on the basis of the observed differences in auxin levels on the two sides of the organ, and auxin may not be the only hormone involved. While some workers have obtained good evidence for the redistribution of applied radioactive IAA in phototropically stimulated maize and wheat coleoptiles, others have found identical amounts of endogenous IAA by chemical analysis of shaded and lighted halves of sunflower seedlings. Thus for phototropism, too, we have a two-fold problem to solve: what is the precise nature of the hormones involved in the growth reaction, and how does unilateral illumination bring about the differences in hormone level on the two sides of an organ?

Although a grass coleoptile is a delicate, translucent object, it is hollow and hence light entering it suffers considerable internal reflection. Unilateral illumination of such a coleoptile therefore produces in it a light intensity gradient in the direction of the illumination. This gradient can vary from 1·5:1 to 35:1 depending on factors such as the intensity of the incident light and the region of the coleoptile under illumination. It has been shown that phototropic curvature occurs in a coleoptile provided that there is a 1% intensity difference between the illuminated and shaded sides. In more robust plant organs, there is sufficient light absorption in the lighted side to produce a steep illumination gradient.

The primary step in any light-mediated reaction must be the absorption of the light by, and hence activation of, a photoreceptor chemical. Theoretically one should be able to identify the photoreceptor from the action spectrum of phototropism. The action spectrum of a reaction is obtained by plotting the amount of response obtained at different wavelengths of incident light against the wavelength. Usually the response to the same number of incident quanta at each wavelength is plotted (a quantized action spectrum) but sometimes the response is measured for the same amount of total incident energy (e.g. $erg/cm^2/s$) at each wavelength. The action spectrum so obtained can then be compared with the absorption spectra of known pigments, i.e. the plots of light absorption by these pigments against wavelength. Coincidence of the action spectrum of a reaction with the absorption spectrum of a specific pigment is taken to mean that this pigment absorbs the light utilized for the reaction. The action spectrum situation in the case of phototropism is complicated, because the spectra for the first and second positive curvatures are not quite the same, and the regions of the coleoptiles involved in the two curvatures do not coincide; the first curvature occurs mainly near the tip, the second extends nearer to the base. There may be two distinct phototropic reactions. In general, blue light is the most effective in phototropism and, in the action spectrum of the first positive curvature, there are two peaks in the blue, one at 440 nm, a second at 480 nm, and a third peak in the near ultraviolet (Fig. 10.8A). This action spectrum does not correspond exactly with the absorption spectrum of any known pigment, but two classes of pigments absorb in the blue region of activity, the flavins and the carotenoids. Most workers consider that the action spectrum corresponds more closely to that to be expected if carotenoids rather than flavins are involved. In the visible region the correspondence with carotenoids is very good (Fig. 10.8B, C), but extracted carotenoids show no absorption corresponding to the ultraviolet peak of the action spectrum. Flavins absorb in the ultraviolet, but not in the precise position of the action spectrum peak. The absorption spectra of pigments in the cell may of course be modified by combination of the pigments with other molecules, and it has been suggested that a protein-carotenoid complex could be responsible for the ultraviolet peak in the action spectrum.

Carotenoids are present in organs showing phototropism, and several mutants with a lowered carotenoid content also show a lowered phototropic sensitivity (the flavin content of such mutants being normal). On the other hand, some phototropically reactive mutants have a very low carotenoid content indeed; thus a maize mutant, in which the coleoptile contains not more than 0.1% of the normal carotenoid content, is still 50–80% as reactive as the normal type. From calculations of light absorption and quantum yield (a measure of the number of quanta required for the response), it has been concluded that the effective pigment concentration needs to be only about 10^{-9} M. Since carotenoids are photoreceptors in phototaxis and in animal vision, their involvement in phototropism would not be unexpected. Those who favour flavins as the photoreceptors point to their universal presence in sensitive organs and to their absorption peak in the ultraviolet. Riboflavin, one universally distributed flavin, has recently also been implicated in animal vision. Finally, some authors have attempted to resolve the controversy by suggesting that riboflavin is the photochemically active pigment, but that the carotenoids act as 'light screens', controlling the amount of light received by the riboflavin. It must

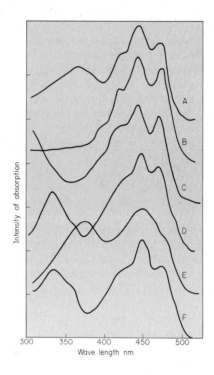

Fig. 10.8   The action spectrum of the phototropism of the *Avena* coleoptile (A), compared with absorption spectra of: α-carotene in hexane (B); hexane extract of 50 coleoptile tips (C); 9-9′ *cis*-β-carotene in hexane (curve of Inhoffen *et al.*, 1950) (D); riboflavin in water (E); 3-methyl-lumiflavin in benzene (curve of Hanbury *et al.*, 1959) (F). (From Thimann and Curry, 1961, in *Light and Life*, ed. McElroy and Glass, 646–72. Johns Hopkins Press, Baltimore.)

be concluded that the identity of the photoreceptor pigment in phototropism is not yet resolved.

Hypotheses as to how light absorbed by a pigment might cause the unequal distribution of auxin have been advanced for both types of pigment. In 1949 Galston discovered that, *in vitro*, riboflavin catalyses the breakdown of auxin by light, and a hypothesis was advanced that the phototropic reaction results from a riboflavin-mediated destruction of auxin on the lighted side. However uniform illumination of an organ, with light of an intensity which would be effective in inducing its phototropic curvature, does not decrease the quantity of auxin in it, and with unilateral illumination, the lower concentration of auxin on the lighted side has been shown fairly conclusively to result from diversion of auxin to the opposite side, rather than from its destruction. Faced with these objections the hypothesis has been modified to the suggestion that the light absorbed by riboflavin causes a temporary inactivation of an enzyme synthesizing auxin on the lighted side and as a result more auxin precursor reaches the shaded side and is there converted to auxin. In support of this view is the fact that riboflavin has been shown to catalyse photo-inactivation of some enzymes. However, this fails to explain the observation that with light treatments producing negative curvatures there is more auxin on the lighted than on the shaded side.

Carotenoids do not catalyse photo-oxidations of auxin or of other compounds, but rather can protect auxin against the photo-oxidations catalysed by riboflavin. Carotenoids are located mainly in plastids, and Thimann and Curry in 1961 suggested that light absorbed by the carotenoids may cause the plastids to move to the cell walls which are at right angles to the direction of illumination, and thus favour auxin transport across these walls, i.e. laterally. It is well known that the chloroplasts in some cells orientate themselves according to the direction and intensity of illumination along certain walls, but it has not yet been demonstrated that the etiolated plastids of organs commonly used in experiments on phototropism move in this way. If the plastids change their direction of movement with changing light intensity congregating at the walls nearest to or furthest from the light source, then more auxin could be transported to the lighted side or to the shaded side. An attraction of this hypothesis is that it proposes a mechanism of phototropic perception similar to that postulated in the statolith theory of geotropism, involving the movement of cell inclusions in response to the unilateral stimulus. Light and gravity stimuli can be made to act additively, or to cancel each other out, although this in itself does not imply a common mechanism of perception of the stimuli.

More recently another reaction mechanism involving carotenoids has been put forward, based on the observation that photolysis of carotenoids (*in vitro*) can give rise to compounds resembling ABA (abscisic acid) in chemical properties and biological activity. It has also been found that ABA can inhibit auxin transport through coleoptiles. If ABA-related compounds are produced from carotenoids on the lighted side of an organ, the inhibition of polar auxin transport down the lighted side could result in an increased movement of auxins to the shaded side.

Plagiotropic and diatropic reactions towards gravity and light

The discussion developed above has been confined to a consideration of mechanisms which might account for the orthotropic reactions to gravity and light. It is clear that the mechanisms underlying these orthotropic reactions are by no means elucidated. We are still less able to explain the plagiotropic reactions which keep the natural direction of growth at a fixed angle to the controlling stimulus rather than parallel to it. In nature, such plagiotropic growth reactions are much more numerous than orthotropic reactions and are more difficult to investigate because the growth angle is usually controlled by an interaction between several factors.

Leaves of many species are stated to be diaphototropic. In some instances (e.g. *Tropaeolum*) the orientation of the leaf blade at right angles to the incident illumination is due to a positive orthotropic response of the petiole, the curvature of the petiole towards light bringing the blade to lie transversely to the incident light. Here the organ of perception is the petiole, although the presence of the blade is necessary, since this is the source of the auxin reaching the petiole. A debladed petiole behaves like a decapitated coleoptile: it is able to react phototropically only when auxin is supplied to its apical cut surface. In other cases of diaphototropic leaves the lamina actively participates in the orientation movement, as in rosette plants such as species of plantain (*Plantago*), species of hawk-weed (*Hieracium*), and the shepherd's purse (*Capsella bursa-pastoris*).

In many instances the natural position of an organ is achieved by the balanced interaction of several influences. The apparent plagiotropic response of side shoots and some leaves has been found to result from a negative geotropism tending to make the organ grow up, balanced by an autonomous **epinasty** (inherent tendency for greater growth on the upper surface, see p. 210) tending to bend it down. The inherent epinasty can be revealed by eliminating the influence of gravity on a klinostat, in which case the continued excess growth on the upper side causes the organ to coil up. The epinasty of side shoots can be eliminated by removal of the main axis growing point (a source of auxin), when the negative geotropism becomes apparent and the shoots grow upwards. Auxin is apparently involved in all plagiotropic reactions, but how it acts is obscure. One notable difference between organs reacting orthotropically and those reacting plagiotropically is that the former are radially symmetrical, while the latter are dorsiventrally symmetrical, with distinct upper (dorsal) and lower (ventral) surfaces. This suggests very strongly that the symmetry of an organ is of basic importance in determining the type of growth movement executed.

Rhizomes of many plants grow horizontally at a more or less fixed level below the soil surface, and if the level is disturbed, they will grow up or down at an angle till they reach the normal depth, and then proceed to grow horizontally once more. The horizontal natural direction is generally regarded as a diageotropic response, but it is not clear how the constant level is maintained. Rhizomes of *Aegopodium podagraria* react to light by a positive geotropism (the response, which is elicited even by weak red light, is not a negative phototropism); this causes the rhizomes to turn down when they chance to come too near the surface. Plagiotropic roots and rhizomes of some other species are also known to react similarly towards illumination. Less is known of the factor(s) preventing such organs from penetrating to excessive depths; in the case of *Aegopodium* rhizomes, the controlling factor may be the increased carbon dioxide concentration at greater depths, since the rhizomes react to high carbon dioxide concentrations by turning upwards. For *Polygonatum multiflorum* rhizomes, the control has been suggested to reside in a balance between negative geotropism and photoepinasty, the rhizomes growing below the surface at a level where the light intensity is just sufficient to induce a nastic reaction balancing the inherent negative geotropism.

Haptotropism (thigmotropism)

Haptotropism, the reaction of plants to the stimulus of touch (described variously as a tactile, mechanical or rubbing stimulus) is shown by many plant organs. The response is mostly positive, but an autotropic counter-reaction in the opposite direction may set in and result finally in a negative curvature away from the side touched. A very strong positive response is shown by the stems of climbers and by tendrils, causing them to twine round supports, a response which may be enhanced by circumnutation. The general principles of threshold stimulation and reaction time also apply to haptotropism. Tendrils are highly sensitive and can be induced to react to a weight as small as 1 mg. Rubbing is essential: uniform static pressure will not produce a haptotropic response. The first reaction, which occurs within seconds, is a contraction of the cells on the side which becomes concave, with simultaneous expansion of cells on the opposite flank. This is a turgor reaction and is reversible. Then the growth rate increases 40–200-fold on the side which becomes convex, while on the other side growth decreases or stops completely. The region of curvature usually coincides with that of perception, but from a stimulated region the stimulus may be conducted over lengths varying from a few mm to many cm, so that the curvature extends beyond the part stimulated. The sensitivity of tendrils decreases from the tip back, and may be confined to a short length of tip. Seedling parts such as coleoptiles and hypocotyls also exhibit positive haptotropism but there is usually no indication of sensitivity being confined to the tips in these organs, and decapitation of seedlings does not abolish their sensitivity to touch. However in the central tentacles of the sundew leaf (*Drosera*), the tips are sensitive to the touch stimulus, but the growth curvature takes place at the base. Where tendrils are differentiated dorsiventrally, sensitivity is greater on the lower side; in some only the lower side is sensitive and, in yet other species, the bending occurs towards the lower side whichever side is rubbed. The stimulus is believed to be perceived in tendrils by special epidermal cells which either bulge out as thin-walled papillae, or have very thin areas in their outer walls. Stimulation of tendrils results in an increase in their auxin content, and application of auxin can replace stimulation, inducing both coiling and morphogenetic effects (see below). Ethylene is also produced in a stimulated tendril and can replace auxin treatment. This indicates that the haptotropic response is controlled by auxin, possibly mediated by auxin-induced ethylene synthesis.

The mechanical stimulation not only causes curvature but acts as a morphogenetic factor. Tendrils which have clasped a support become thickened to a marked degree, and following this there is increased development of mechanical tissue in the whole plant which is dependent on the tactile stimulus, since mere binding up of the plant is ineffective. In *Bignonia* and *Ampelopsis*, suckers or discs are produced on tendrils as a result of stimulation and the haustoria of the dodder (*Cuscuta*) differentiate in response to touch. A touch stimulus *may* be necessary for the outgrowth of root hairs. Mechanical stimulation has also been shown to promote the formation of supporting tissue and to inhibit internode elongation. In a study during which plants were rubbed daily over a 7–10 day period, 11 species out of the 14 tested showed inhibitions of stem elongation ranging from 30 to 70 per cent.

NASTIC MOVEMENTS

Nastic reactions are also movements in response to external stimuli, nastic growth movements involving unequal growth on opposite sides of an organ, nastic variation movements (which will not be discussed here) resulting from turgor changes. They are stimulated by a change in the environmental conditions, and the direction of the response is determined by the organ, not by the stimulus. A higher growth rate on the upper surface of an organ is termed *epinasty*; a higher growth rate on the lower, *hyponasty*. Geonastic, photonastic, thermonastic, haptonastic and chemonastic movements are known. Autonasty also occurs, i.e. unequal growth on two sides of an organ independent of external conditions; such autonastic growth causes for instance young leaves in buds and young inflorescences (e.g. of *Drosera*) to grow rolled up.

Numerous dicotyledonous leaves exhibit *photonasty*: when grown in the dark the leaves curl upwards (hyponasty), but when transferred to the light the laminae flatten out (epinasty). Here the presence or absence of light determines which surface grows faster. The unfolding of young leaves and inflorescences may also require light. The diurnal movements of leaves of some species which take up sleep positions at night may be due to photonasty in the petiole or lamina. (Many diurnal leaf movements are however mediated by turgor changes in leaf or leaflet bases or petioles rather than by differential growth). The nastic leaf movements, once initiated by a light stimulus, may persist for some time in darkness with a roughly 24-hour periodicity; in *Hyoscyamus niger*, for instance, the movements continue in the dark for about two cycles with diminishing vigour. The flowers of tulip (*Tulipa*) and crocus (*Crocus*) show thermonasty, responding to an increase in temperature by increased growth on the upper side of the perianth segments so that the flowers open; cooling accentuates growth on the lower surfaces, making the flowers close (Fig. 10.9). Under natural conditions, this reaction causes the flowers to open by day and to close by night. Strong chemonasty is typical of the long peripheral tentacles on sundew leaves, which respond to the presence of organic nitrogenous compounds by bending towards the middle of the leaf (the inner short tentacles react predominantly chemotropically to the same substances). There is conduction of the stimulus from the tip of the sundew tentacles to their bases, and into adjacent tentacles. In another insectivorous plant, the butterwort (*Pinguicula*), nitrogenous compounds elicit a chemonastic response starting at the leaf margins and causing the leaf to curl inwards on both sides of the midrib.

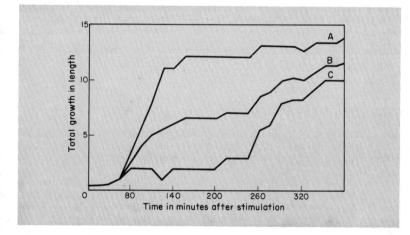

Fig. 10.9 Curves to illustrate the course of growth on the two sides of a perianth segment of *Crocus* as a result of thermonastic stimulation. A: inner side; B: middle zone; C: outer side. (From Wiedersheim, 1904, *Jb. wiss. Bot.*, **40**, 230–78.)

The physiological basis of nastic growth movements is still puzzling, but it is known that nastic growth reactions, like tropisms, are auxin-controlled, and hence the view has been advanced that the only fundamental difference between organs showing a tropic or a nastic reaction to the same type of stimulus is that anatomical or physiological differentiation in the organ showing a nastic reaction determines that the curvature must occur in a fixed direction, irrespective of the direction of the stimulus. There is considerable resemblance between certain nastic and plagiotropic reactions and in some instances, e.g. for numerous leaf orientations, it is disputable whether they should be classed as tropic or nastic responses.

FURTHER READING

ANKER, L. (1962). Ortho-geotropism in shoots and coleoptiles. In *Encyclopedia of Plant Physiology*, ed. RUHLAND, W., **17**/2, 103–99. Springer-Verlag, Berlin.

GALSTON, A. W. (1959). Phototropism of stems, roots and coleoptiles. In *Encyclopedia of Plant Physiology*, ed. RUHLAND, W., **17**/1, 492–529. Springer-Verlag, Berlin.

JAFFE, M. J. and GALSTON, A. W. (1968). The physiology of tendrils. *A. Rev. Pl. Physiol.*, **19**, 417–34.

LARSEN, P. (1962). Geotropism. An Introduction. In *Encyclopedia of Plant Physiology*, ed. RUHLAND, W., **17**/2, 34–73. Springer-Verlag, Berlin.

STILES, W. and COCKING, E. C. (1969). *An Introduction to the Principles of Plant Physiology*, 3rd edition. Methuen, London.

THIMANN, K. V. and CURRY, G. M. (1961). Phototropism. In *Light and Life*, ed. MCELROY, W. D. and GLASS, B., 646–72. Johns Hopkins Press, Baltimore.

WENT, F. W. and THIMANN, K. V. (1937). *The Phytohormones*. Macmillan, New York.

WILKINS, M. B. (ed.) (1969). *Physiology of Plant Growth and Development*. McGraw-Hill, London.

SELECTED REFERENCES

BRIGGS, W. R. (1960). Light dosage and phototropic responses of corn and oat coleoptiles. *Pl. Physiol., Lancaster*, **35**, 951–62.

EVERETT, M. (1974). Dose–response curves for radish seedling phototropism. *Pl. Physiol., Lancaster*, **54**, 222–5.

JUNIPER, B. E. and FRENCH, A. (1973). The distribution and redistribution of endoplasmic reticulum (ER) in geoperceptive cells. *Planta*, **109**, 211–24.

JUNIPER, B. E., GROVES, S., LANDAU-SCHACHAR, B. and AUDUS, L. J. (1966). Root cap and the perception of gravity. *Nature, Lond.*, **209**, 93–4.

KUNDU, K. K. and AUDUS, L. J. (1974). Root growth inhibitors from root cap and root meristem of *Zea mays* L. *J. exp. Bot.*, **25**, 479–89.

PERBAL, G. (1974). L'action des statolithes dans la réponse géotropique des racines de *Lens culinaris*. *Planta*, **116**, 153–71.

SHAW, S. and WILKINS, M. B. (1973). The source and lateral transport of growth inhibitors in geotropically stimulated roots of *Zea mays* and *Pisum sativum*. *Planta*, **109**, 11–26.

VOLKMANN, D. (1974). Amyloplasten und Endomembranen: das Geoperzeptionssytem der Primärwurzel. *Protoplasma*, **79**, 159–83.

11

Vegetative Development

MORPHOGENESIS

Morphogenesis may be defined as the genesis or initiation of form and the study of plant morphogenesis is directed to identifying the physiological events which have their visible manifestation in the appearance of new structures in the plant body. The term development embraces, at the level of the individual organ, all the changes which intervene between the initiation of form and the achievement of the mature morphology and, at the level of the organism, the whole sequence of changes in form and function which intervene between the fertilized ovum and the death of the plant. Morphogenetic events may therefore be regarded as the qualitative changes through which the patterns of development unfold. Further, only if we concentrate our attention on some particular criterion of change do we talk of developmental morphology, anatomy or physiology. Only if we concern ourselves with particular levels of organization do we distinguish between cellular differentiation, organization of tissues, organ development, and the ontogeny of the individual organism. Clearly a vast field of biological enquiry can properly be regarded as directed towards an understanding of development. However this chapter and the following chapter will concentrate upon certain selected facets of plant development considered from the stand-point of physiology with particular reference to their control by natural growth-promoting and growth-inhibiting substances.

INITIATION OF LATERAL ROOTS AND BUDS

Lateral root primordia arise in the pericycle at positions related to the primary xylem poles of the central cylinder. Initiation takes place at a level where cell differentiation is proceeding in the primary root tissues and it may be that the substances inducing localized divisions in the pericycle are released by differentiating vascular elements. There is also evidence that the shoot system influences root branching and it has been postulated that both lateral root and adventitious root development are controlled by substances (*rhizocalines*) synthesized in the shoot. The observations that auxin may greatly enhance lateral root initiation in cultured roots and adventitious roots formed on stem cuttings points to auxin of shoot origin as a rhizocaline.

With cultured roots, an initial application of auxin to roots in their first or second culture passage may greatly enhance lateral development. However, a second application to such roots or an initial application to roots which have already been in culture for some time may completely fail to result in lateral initiation. When auxin is the limiting factor its application results in lateral initiation; at other times absence of other essential factors renders auxin ineffective. In particular instances other factors have been shown to enhance lateral initiation; these include the amino acids arginine, ornithine and lysine, the vitamins thiamine and nicotinic acid, the growth hormones kinetin and gibberellic acid, and certain concentrations of CO_2 in the solution bathing the roots. Hence it is likely that root initiation is determined by the balance between acropetal transport from the shoot or older regions of the root of auxin, vitamins and amino acids and basipetal transport from the root apex of cytokinin(s) and gibberellin(s) which are believed to be synthesized in the root apex.

Various workers have attempted to study the factors involved in bud and leaf initiation in flowering plants and ferns by experiments involving excision, removal and culture of primordia or isolation of segments of the stem apex from adjacent tissues by incisions at right angles to the surface of the apical meristematic dome. Studies of this kind have revealed that the lateral centres of cell division arising at the shoot apex are for a time capable of giving rise to either a bud or a leaf; there is a developmental interval between initiation of the lateral growth centre and its determination as a leaf or bud primordium. Such investigations have also shown that each lateral growth centre is surrounded by a zone in which the immediate origin of further growth centres is inhibited and that such interacting 'spheres of influence' are concerned in the determination of the characteristic leaf and bud arrangement of the growing shoot. It is however from studies with callus cultures that some insight has been gained into the chemical factors which may control bud initiation.

As mentioned in Chapter 9 (p. 160), it was found that the growth in culture of tobacco callus required the presence in the culture medium of both an auxin and a cytokinin. The callus remained parenchymatous when grown in a medium containing 2·0 mg/l IAA and 0·2 mg/l kinetin. However if the ratio of auxin to kinetin was decreased either by raising the concentration of kinetin (to 0·5–1·0 mg/l) or lowering the concentration of auxin (to 0·03 mg/l) the cultures initiated shoot buds which grew into leafy shoots (Fig. 11.1). With a medium containing an auxin:kinetin

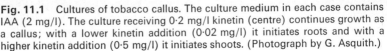

Fig. 11.1 Cultures of tobacco callus. The culture medium in each case contains IAA (2 mg/l). The culture receiving 0·2 mg/l kinetin (centre) continues growth as a callus; with a lower kinetin addition (0·02 mg/l) it initiates roots and with a higher kinetin addition (0·5 mg/l) it initiates shoots. (Photograph by G. Asquith.)

ratio favourable to bud initiation it was further observed that addition of casein hydrolysate or of the single amino acid, tyrosine, enhanced bud initiation and promoted subsequent growth of the buds (Fig. 11.2). Manipulation of the levels of auxin and kinetin to give a high ratio of auxin to kinetin also initiates organogenesis but now roots and not shoot buds are initiated (Fig. 11.1). The auxin:cytokinin balances appear to exert a controlling influence upon morphogenesis in the tobacco callus. Further work on organogenesis in callus cultures points to cytokinins and auxin being generally involved in meristem initiation; some other callus cultures react like tobacco and cases are known where addition of auxin alone or of a cytokinin alone results in bud initiation. Other growth factors than auxin and cytokinin are also clearly involved. Application of the natural plant growth-inhibitor, abscisic acid, but not cytokinin, is essential for bud formation in cultures of potato and sweet potato and

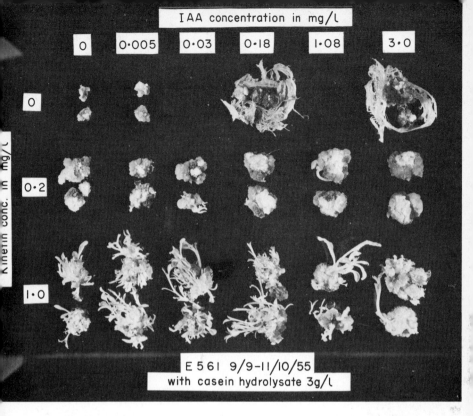

Fig. 11.2 Organogenesis in tobacco callus. Effects of increasing IAA concentration at different levels of kinetin and in the presence of casein hydrolysate (3 g/l) on growth and organ formation. Age of cultures 62 days. Note root formation in absence of kinetin and in the presence of 0·18 and 3·0 mg/l IAA, and shoot formation in the presence of 1·0 mg/l kinetin, particularly with IAA concentrations in the range 0·005–0·18 mg/l IAA. (From Skoog and Miller, 1957, *Symp. Soc. exp. Biol.*, **11**, 118–31.)

gibberellic acid will induce bud formation in *Chrysanthemum* callus. However, the number of callus cultures where it appears that it is just the endogeneous level of known growth factors which prevents spontaneous bud initiation is limited. There are many callus cultures in which organogenesis cannot be induced by application of known growth factors or of natural extracts like coconut milk. In all such cases it may be that meristem initiation is prevented by a depletion or accumulation, during growth in culture, of as yet unknown growth regulating factors.

There is, however, another possible reason why no root or bud initiation has ever been observed in some callus cultures. Callus cultures normally arise by activation of division in partially or completely differentiated tissue cells in the organ explant in response to its excision from the plant (an injury response) and the chemical stimuli in the culture medium. Even when meristematic cells in the explant are involved they may already be committed to the formation of particular tissue cells (e.g. cambial cells to the formation of vascular tissue cells). The cells in the explant are induced to divide but the extent to which they undergo dedifferentiation during callus induction may depend upon the species, the nature of the organ explant and the cultural conditions operating during the induction process. Thus activation of the mechanisms involved in cell division and cell growth may occur without a sufficiently profound change in cellular physiology to permit the cells to express their totipotency via root and shoot initiation (see also Chapter 12, Embryo development, p. 254).

Prior to the formation of root and shoot primordia in a callus tissue there can be distinguished groups of tightly packed meristematic cells characterized by their small size, dense cytoplasm and prominent nuclei (these groups have been termed meristemoids). These groups apparently respond to directional organizing stimuli within the callus to form an organized organ primordium. The formation of these meristemoids may involve the operation of a contagion phenomenon whereby a cell embarking upon division entrains adjacent cells to divide and a 'sink' effect whereby a localized centre of cell division draws upon nutrients and metabolites from adjacent cells thereby inhibiting their division. Once the meristemoid has formed it must develop an axis of polarity (see p. 175) to give rise to a primordium. The nature of the physico–chemical gradients within the callus which determine this polarity are at present not known, nor can the induction of this polarity be recognized in terms of the development of an axis of symmetry in the structure of the initiating cells by either light or electron microscopy.

LEAF INITIATION AND GROWTH

Leaves are arranged on the shoot in a regular manner as a consequence of the spatial regularity with which primordia arise at the shoot apex. This arrangement of the leaf primordia—*phyllotaxis*—depends upon the species and the stage of development and rate of growth of the individual plant (see Chapter 8, p. 147). Changes in the time interval separating the initiation of successive primordia (the *plastochron*) and changes in phyllotaxy occur during development and are correlated with changes in the growth activity of the apical meristem and with the shape of the apical dome of meristematic cells. New primordia arise in succession so that, at any moment in time, there is a free surface area of the apex above the last initiated primordium; it is in this 'next available space' that the next primordium will arise. This space must be able to accommodate the primordium as it develops and it must arise in the correct relationship to existing primordia if the phyllotaxy is to persist. Its point of origin appears to be controlled by the interaction of influences emanating both from the main axis meristem and the adjacent primordia. The chemical (or physical) nature of these influences awaits identification. A physiological interpretation of orderly leaf arrangement has yet to emerge.

The development of leaves involves the functioning in sequence and for a limited time of a number of zones of meristematic activity and an associated programme of cell expansion and differentiation. This developmental anatomy has now been worked out in some detail for the leaves of a very limited number of species. Such studies only serve to emphasize how far we are from understanding what controls such highly integrated developmental programmes. One possible experimental approach to this is to see how far such development is dependent upon the culture medium supplying particular nutrients and growth factors.

This experimental approach has been followed in studies of the growth and development in culture of excised leaf primordia of ferns (species of *Osmunda*, *Leptopteris* and *Dryopteris*). The culture medium solidified with agar has contained sucrose, inorganic ions and various combinations of vitamins and other growth factors. Although the most recently initiated primordia can be successfully cultured such primordia develop into shoots and their growth becomes indeterminate. Primordia, however, show, with passage of time from inception to excision, an increasing tendency to develop into leaves in culture and, in *Osmunda cinnamomea*, primordia which are about 800 μm long (there are 8 to 10 younger primordia at the apex) always give rise to leaves. The cultured primordia follow a pattern of growth essentially similar to that of attached fronds except that their growth is completed precociously and the resulting leaves are smaller than normal due to reduced cell number per leaf (rather than to any reduction in mean cell size) (Fig. 11.3). The cultured leaves remain healthy for many weeks after completing their development. Additions to the basal medium of vitamins, auxin, amino acids or substances such as coconut milk do not profoundly modify development although they may increase final leaf weight. Crozier uncurling does not occur unless the cultures are exposed to light. These observations indicate: (1) that some influence (possibly a leaf-forming substance) moving from the shoot apex programmes the primordium to ensure its subsequent dorsiventral and determinate growth into a leaf; (2) that once the primordium is so determined it can complete its development to give a miniature leaf similar in form to the naturally developed frond without needing special metabolites or growth factors; (3) that leaf size is controlled by some influence of the shoot which either prevents cell expansion occurring precociously or ensures that cell divisions proceed in the leaf meristems at a sufficient rate and for an appropriate time.

APICAL DOMINANCE

Apical dominance is the phenomenon of suppression of lateral root emergence or lateral bud outgrowth by an actively growing main root or main shoot apex. Evidence has been obtained in work with roots that this suppression of lateral development is due to the release of inhibitor(s) (not however yet isolated in pure form) whose action cannot be reproduced by

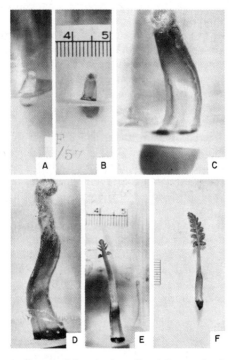

Fig. 11.3 Culture of excised frond primordia of *Osmunda cinnamomea*.
(A) Primordium at time of excision (9·7 mm long).
(B) After 2 weeks' culture—crozier formation stage.
(C) After 5 weeks' culture—full crozier stage.
(D) After 7 weeks' culture—completion of crozier elevation.
(E) Crozier uncoiling.
(F) After 11 weeks' culture—development complete (average length 46 mm, average number of pairs of pinnae 9·7). (From Caponettio and Steeves, 1963, *Can. J. Bot.*, **41**, 545–56.)

auxin applied at a growth-inhibitory concentration. The natural inhibitor, abscisic acid, known to occur in roots, is an inhibitor of root growth but not a specific inhibitor of lateral initiation and extension. A number of workers, using cultured excised roots, have reported that light can suppress lateral root initiation, that in this respect red light is much more active than light from other regions of the visible spectrum and that this action of red light is reversed by immediate subsequent exposure of the roots to far-red light. As discussed later in this chapter—Photomorphogenesis (p. 230)—red light is now known to have a number of morphogenic effects which are reversible by far-red light.

Apical dominance in shoots is usually quoted as the most clear-cut example of a growth correlation in plants. An actively growing main shoot apex inhibits the growth of lateral buds nearest to the apex and the distance over which the suppression operates is a measure of the intensity of the apical dominance. If the apex is excised, punctured or arrested in its growth the lateral buds begin to develop and elongate and in many instances this growth can be arrested by applying a lanoline paste containing an auxin like IAA at the site of the removed apex. Apical dominance has therefore been explained on the basis that the growing shoot apex is a centre of auxin synthesis, that this auxin is transported basipetally from the meristem and that it accumulates at the loci of the axillary buds to a concentration which inhibits their growth. In some instances spraying intact shoots with gibberellin has increased their apical dominance and in other cases simultaneous application of IAA and gibberellin to decapitated shoots has been more effective than IAA alone in maintaining lateral bud inhibition. The observation that, when ^{14}C-labelled IAA has been applied to decapitated shoots of certain species, the accumulation of ^{14}C at the level of the inhibited buds has been enhanced by the simultaneous application of unlabelled gibberellic acid, has led to the view that gibberellin may act by promoting endogenous auxin synthesis or release or by enhancing its basipetal transport.

The concept that apical dominance results from a direct suppression of lateral bud outgrowth must be now modified in the light of additional experimental work. The actual level of auxin in lateral buds is often too low to be inhibitory and in certain instances lateral buds can be induced to grow by direct application of auxin to them. Although lanoline paste containing a high level of IAA does in many instances suppress lateral bud growth when applied to the decapitated shoot apex, this suppression usually persists for only a limited period and in some species (e.g. *Coleus* sp.) IAA application is quite ineffective in suppressing lateral bud growth. Apical dominance in the intact shoot or in decapitated shoots supplied with auxin can in some species be broken by the application of the cytokinin kinetin to the lateral buds (Fig. 11.4). With intact shoots this release is usually transient but if auxin is also applied to the buds their growth continues.

Clearly an actively growing apical meristem is a 'sink' for the metabolites needed for the synthesis of protein and other cell constituents and some authors have attempted to explain apical dominance in terms of competition for such food materials; the operational 'sink' diverts food material from potential 'sinks'. This concept is supported by the observation that apical dominance in the shoot is intensified under conditions of nutrient deficiency. Evidence for 'auxin-directed' transport of nutrients

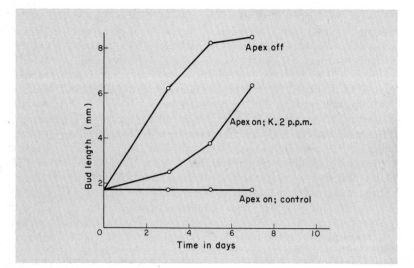

Fig. 11.4   Promotion of lateral bud growth of intact pea shoots resulting from application to the buds of kinetin (K. 2 p.p.m.). (From Wickson and Thimann, 1958, *Physiologia Pl.*, **11**, 62–74.)

has come from experiments where it has been demonstrated that the application of auxin to decapitated shoots causes rapid accumulation at the cut surface of radioactive ^{32}P-phosphate applied to the base of the shoot or of ^{14}C-sucrose applied to the leaves. No such accumulation occurs in the absence of applied auxin. Such 'auxin-directed' transport could result in nutrient competition between the main shoot meristem as a site of auxin release and the quiescent lateral buds which do not release auxin. The mechanism of the 'auxin-directed' transport is not fully understood but one effect of the auxin application to decapitated shoots in certain species has been inhibition of the development of vascular connections between the lateral buds and the main vascular supplies of the shoot. Cytokinin, apparently essential to bud growth, is synthesized in the root and transported to the shoot; 'auxin-directed' transport of this cytokinin to the main apex may starve the lateral buds of an essential growth factor.

Apical dominance is expressed not only in the inhibition of lateral roots and axillary buds but controls the orientation of the lateral roots and branches (affects their geotropic sensitivity, see Chapter 10). In the potato the stolons which arise from a basal node of the stem normally grow horizontally at or below the soil surface and show elongated internodes, and rudimentary leaves. If the aerial shoot is decapitated the stolons turn upwards and become typical leafy shoots. If lanoline paste containing auxin and gibberellin is applied to the decapitated shoot apex the stolons retain their characteristic morphology and direction of growth; if kinetin is applied directly to the stolons this antagonizes the action of the auxin + gibberellin and a leafy shoot develops.

These studies of apical dominance, still obviously far from revealing the complete story, indicate that growth correlations are probably determined by the distribution patterns of growth regulators and nutrients and that growth regulators may play a critical role in determining these distribution patterns.

BUD DORMANCY

Cessation of growth can occur in response to unfavourable external conditions such as low temperature or lack of water (then usually referred to as quiescence or enforced dormancy). However dormancy can result from conditions developed within the plant tissues when no obviously unfavourable environmental factor is operative (innate dormancy or rest).

Resting buds of most temperate trees and shrubs are formed by a correlative inhibition under the influence of the mature leaves in summer and then enter a state of innate dormancy, often termed winter dormancy, in response to the shortening daylengths of autumn. The phenomenon of physiological change occurring in response to appropriate daylength is termed *photoperiodism*. Photoperiodism is also involved in flowering (see Chapter 12, p. 235), control of vegetative habit (rosette versus bolting), tuberization in plants like potato and Jerusalem artichoke, bulb formation, 'simultaneous' leaf fall in deciduous trees and in the dark carbon dioxide fixation activity of many succulent plants.

The photoperiodic stimulus is perceived by the leaves—expanded leaves or, in some species, by young leaves in the bud. The short-day induction not only induces the buds to become dormant but enhances their cold resistance (though for maximum cold hardening, lowered temperatures are also necessary). In many species, the buds must then be chilled (by normal winter temperatures) before they will resume growth (bud burst) in response to the rising temperatures of the spring. Some species have no cold requirement but will break dormancy in response to the warmer temperatures and increasing daylengths of spring. Artificially bud dormancy can be broken by immersing the shoots in warm water (30–35°C) for 9–12 hours or by treatment with chemicals (ethylene chlorohydrin, thiourea).

Following the introduction of paper chromatography as a technique permitting the separation of auxins in plant extracts it became clear that such extracts contained not only substances promotive of growth in auxin bio-assays like the Went coleoptile test (see p. 168) but growth inhibitors. The activity of an inhibitory zone (β-complex) of the chromatograms was usually observed to be high in extracts from dormant potato tubers and resting buds of ash. When the dormancy of potato tubers was broken by ethylene chlorohydrin the activity of this inhibitor zone fell to a low level. Later work showed that the inhibitor activity of an extract of sycamore leaves increased when these leaves were exposed to short days (the condition which sends the buds into winter dormancy). From this extract a natural inhibitor was isolated and crystallized which at low concentration could induce bud dormancy in mature sycamore and black currant bushes and in seedlings of birch. This substance (then termed dormin) seems to be the primary agent in inducing winter dormancy. At almost the same time the same compound (then termed abscisin II) was isolated from the fruit stalk of cotton and shown to be involved in the abscission (shedding) of the cotton bolls. This compound is the d(+) isomer of **abscisic acid** (usually abbreviated to ABA) (chemical structure shown in Fig. 9.3, p. 161) and probably is a universal constituent of higher plants.

Winter dormancy of the buds of a number of trees can be broken by application of gibberellic acid and it is now known that there occurs a significant increase in the natural gibberellin content of winter buds during the chilling treatment normally involved in the breaking of their dormancy. Winter dormancy of buds therefore seems to be induced by abscisic acid accumulation and broken by a rise in gibberellin level (the activation of growth thereby induced also being associated with a fall in abscisic acid content).

LEAF SENESCENCE AND LEAF ABSCISSION

Although plant development is a continuous process there can occur sharp qualitative changes such as the transition from vegetative to reproductive development. Similarly in some plants there occurs a rapid transition from a juvenile to an adult form as reflected by leaf form and growth habit. This transition and the phenomena of heteroblastic leaf development are discussed in Chapter 8 (p. 150).

Maturity is sooner or later followed by ageing (senescence) and death. Senescence can be defined as the complex of catabolic events which, if not reversed, lead to death of the cell, organ or organism. Many plants (and particularly annuals and biennials) flower once during their life history (are monocarpic) and senescence leading to death of the whole plant follows their flowering and fruiting. In such plants the onset of senescence is clearly part of an inherited programme of development. The situation is less clear in perennial plants, particularly in woody perennials, where death due to disease or catastrophes (such as flooding, drought, wind damage, mineral deficiency) makes it difficult to establish a clear onset of senescence in the whole organism. However it is clear that as such plants increase in stature they show a fall in relative growth rate and that their leaf area to plant weight index falls. Such plants may therefore reach a stage when they are increasingly susceptible to un-favourable environmental influences. Such loss of vigour may be related to an increasing failure of the organism to nurture its regions of growth, to establish any steady state relationship between its meristems and its mature tissues.

At the level of individual plant organs it is difficult to distinguish between an inherited programme leading to senescence and an ageing of the organ imposed by the whole plant of which it is a part. If different organs enter into competition with one another for food materials the growth and development of one organ may result in the senescence and death of another. Thus developing leaves, flowers and fruits may initiate the onset of senescence in mature leaves.

There is evidence that under certain circumstances there can occur a progressive accumulation of damage to the genetic information of cells. This can apparently occur during the storage of dry seeds. The signifi-cance of this phenomenon in the growing plant is, however, very doubtful since the chances are that such impaired cells are eliminated at the growing points of the plant. It seems more pertinent to enquire whether the individual differentiated cells are programmed to senesce and die. Clearly certain lines of differentiation rapidly and without interruption lead to cell death (as for instance in the development of vessels, tracheids and fibres). In other cases however the differentiated cell reaches a metabolic 'plateau' which can persist (the pith cells of perennials can remain alive for many years). Are such cells intrinsically limited in life span? We refer to differentiation as involving sequential activation and repression of genes but we do not understand the timing mechanism in this sequence; perhaps when this is understood it will be possible to answer whether the timed sequence involves a determination of senescence and ensuing death.

As indicated above, senescence in annual plants follows more or less rapidly upon fruit development and the index of this senescence is the yellowing and withering of the foliage leaves. In herbaceous perennials we observe a similar senescence of the aerial shoot. In deciduous perennials there is an annual senescence and abscission of leaves and an associated induction of bud dormancy. Active abscission (falling) is not confined to leaves; a similar phenomenon is seen in flower and fruit fall. Leaf senescence is characterized by yellowing, export of amino acids from the leaf blade, decline in leaf protein content and drying out. Since these changes in annual plants are associated with fruit development it has been suggested that senescence is a consequence of leaf starvation. However in dioecious species senescence follows flowering in both male and female plants so that it is not apparently dependent upon competition between the leaves and the 'food sinks' represented by developing fruits. However senescence in leaves is affected by other parts of the shoot system and reversals of senescence following removal of the younger leaves and apical buds and supplying a source of nitrogen such as ammonium sulphate have been reported from experiments with barley and tobacco.

It has long been known that leaf excision promotes leaf yellowing. When leaves are excised and their petioles placed in water, amino acids move out of the blade and protein breakdown occurs well in advance of decay of the protein synthesis potential of the leaf cells as judged by incorporation of amino acids into protein by leaf discs and by subcellular fractions. If roots are initiated at the base of the petiole, yellowing of the leaves is immediately reversed and as long ago as 1939 it was suggested by A. C. Chibnall that some hormone of root origin might exert a controlling influence on protein metabolism in the leaf. This hormone may be a natural cytokinin for we know that cytokinins are synthesized in roots and transported from the root to the shoot; also that application of kinetin to detached leaves either via the petiole or directly to the leaf blade has been found in some species to arrest their senescence (Fig. 11.5). Where kinetin is applied to the blade its effect is often strictly localized, regions painted with the kinetin remaining green while adjacent areas show yellowing. The areas receiving kinetin do not lose amino acids and amino acids migrate to these regions from the untreated areas (Fig. 11.6). The treated areas show enhanced protein and RNA synthesis compared with the untreated areas. The induction of senescence by fruit development and the promotion of senescence in older leaves by the presence of growing leaves and buds may on this basis be explained either by diversion of the root hormone to these regions or, and this would apply particularly to flowers and developing fruits, by these regions being themselves centres of cytokinin synthesis.

The above hypothesis is however clearly an over-simplification for senescence in some leaves cannot be arrested by kinetin application and in some of these cases senescence is prevented by auxin application (as in

Fig. 11.5 Detached leaves of *Xanthium* 10 days after detachment and culture with petioles in water (top row) and in 5 mg kinetin per litre (bottom row). Note retention of green colour in kinetin-treated leaves and yellowing in leaves cultured in water. (From Richmond and Lang, 1957, *Science, N.Y.*, **125**, 650–1.)

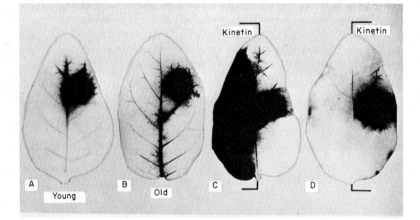

Fig. 11.6   Radioautographs of leaves of *Nicotiana rustica* treated with a spot of a radioactive amino acid (DL-aminoisobutyric acid-^{14}C). A: A young leaf revealing the position on the leaf where the amino acid solution was applied; it has spread very little from the point of application; B: an adult leaf similarly treated—the radioactivity has spread into the vein system and moved from the leaf lamina into the petiole (not shown); C: adult leaf, the left hand side of which has been painted with kinetin solution—note the spread of amino acid applied to the other half only into this kinetin-treated half; D: adult leaf, the right half of which has been painted with kinetin and amino acid—the amino acid has spread very little so that its autoradiograph resembles that of the young leaf. (From Mothes, in *Régulateurs Naturels de la Croissance Végétale*, 1964, 131–40. Centre National de la Recherche Scientifique, Paris.)

the leaves of *Prunus serrulata*). The complexity of the hormonal regulation of leaf metabolism is illustrated by experiments with *Euonymus japonicus*. In this plant auxin application promotes leaf senescence. However, if the auxin (2,4-D) is applied to discrete areas of the leaf blade the treated areas of the leaf blade do not senesce (they retain their colour, show active respiration and protein synthesis and accumulation of ^{14}C-labelled photosynthate and amino acids) but the surrounding areas show accelerated senescence and the leaves absciss prematurely.

Leaf fall and flower and fruit drop are the consequence of the development in the petiole or peduncle of an abscission zone and there is a correlation between senescence in leaves and fruits and cytolysis of the cells of the separation layer located at the distal face (face adjacent to the leaf blade or fruit) of this zone. Cytolysis in the separation layer may involve dissolution of the middle lamella or breakdown of both middle lamella and cell walls. Prior to cytolysis, conducting elements crossing the abscission zone become blocked and a protective layer of suberized or lignified cells may form proximal to the separation layer (i.e. adjacent to the main axis).

As senescence develops the output of auxin to the petiole or peduncle falls and this fall in auxin output has been considered to be a critical factor in abscission. In many experiments IAA applied to petiole stumps has retarded abscission, and IAA application to the adjacent stem tissue has speeded it up. On the basis of such observations the hypothesis was advanced that it is the auxin gradient across the separation layer which suppresses or initiates cytolysis, i.e. if the gradient is steep from high on the distal side to lower on the proximal side abscission is suppressed; if the gradient becomes less steep or is reversed, by fall in auxin output of the leaf blade or fruit or by rise in the stem auxin level, then abscission occurs.

A number of observations have proved difficult to accommodate in this auxin-gradient hypothesis. The response to auxin of explants (stem segment-petiole stump units) depends upon the time interval between excision and auxin application. Auxin applied immediately acts as expected from the gradient hypothesis. If however auxin application is delayed then auxin applied either to the petiole stump or the stem tissue promotes abscission. This has led to a two-stage hypothesis; that auxin reaching the separation layer by diffusion from the leaf inhibits abscission but that once abscission has been triggered then auxin applied either distal or proximal to the layer promotes abscission. Attempts to determine directly the levels of auxin and other growth-regulators proximal and distal to the abscission zone face great technical problems; such extractions and assays as have been performed in general support the concept that auxin distal to the zone is important in preventing abscission but have revealed also the presence of natural growth-inhibiting substances. In 1955 Dr. D. J. Osborne reported that diffusates from yellowing leaves of deciduous plants and from certain evergreen leaves in their last year of life contained an abscission-accelerator which antagonized the abscission-retarding influence of distally applied auxin. This was followed by the demonstration that two abscission-promoting substances are released from the peduncle of the cotton fruit. One of these, at first termed abscisin II, is abscisic acid (see p. 224 and Fig. 9.3, p. 161).

Abscisic acid may accelerate abscission by antagonism of the action of the auxin moving from the leaf or fruit, but this is not proven. The promotion of abscission by the gas ethylene has been known for a long time but its activity cannot be readily fitted in the concept that auxin is the primary controlling factor in abscission. There is some evidence that ethylene can enhance the enzymic destruction of auxin, but other workers take the opposite view that ethylene acts like auxin (may promote auxin synthesis and release) to promote the postulated second stage of the abscission process (see two-stage hypothesis above).

PHOTOMORPHOGENESIS

Light controls plant growth, differentiation and morphological development independently of its involvement in photosynthesis. The study of this aspect of light as an environmental factor—often referred to as photomorphogenesis—has become a very active field of research following upon the discovery and implication in the control of a great number of photoresponses of the very widely distributed photoreceptor—*phytochrome*.

The seeds of certain varieties of lettuce have a light requirement for germination. Between 1934 and 1937 it was shown that red light (500–700 nm) stimulated and far-red light (700–800 nm) inhibited germination of imbibed lettuce seeds. Then in 1952 Hendricks and Borthwick and their associates at the U.S. Department of Agriculture at Beltsville, Maryland, showed that the induction of lettuce seed germination by red light (peak activity 660 nm) could be reversed by immediately following treatment with far-red (peak activity 730 nm). By repeatedly alternating the red and far-red exposures they found that the light applied last determined whether the seeds germinated or not.

This suggested the occurrence of a photoreceptor existing in two reversible forms: one absorbing red light (Pr) and being thereby converted to the second form (Pfr) with peak absorption in the far-red (and in the presence of far-red being converted back to Pr) thus:

$$Pr \underset{730\,nm}{\overset{660\,nm}{\rightleftharpoons}} Pfr.$$

Incidentally when both wavelengths strike the pigment simultaneously, as in sunlight, an equilibrium mixture of the two forms occurs with a preponderance of Pfr (owing to the higher absorption constant of and quantum yield from Pr). White light acts therefore primarily as a red source which is of significance since Pfr appears to be the active form in most of the physiological responses mediated by the pigment. Pfr decays to Pr in darkness.

The direct detection of the pigment proved difficult because of its low concentration and the simultaneous presence of other interfering pigments (particularly chlorophyll) in many plant tissues. However this was achieved by using etiolated tissues and a specially designed differential spectrophotometer and measuring the absorption of low intensity monochromatic beams of light (one red and one far-red) alternating with one another several times a second. Extracts and subsequently very pure preparations of the pigment were obtained; in 1959 it was named phytochrome and shown to be a protein associated with a tetrapyrrole chromophore unit.

Phytochrome is now known to be involved in a number of aspects of vegetative development; red light is necessary for the normal growth of dicotyledonous leaves (primarily due to prolongation of the cell division phase), unfolding of the plumular hook in dicotyledonous seedlings (after the passage of the seedling plumule through the soil), inhibition of excessive internode and particularly mesocotyl elongation (i.e. prevention of etiolation) and formation of anthocyanins and other flavonoid compounds in apple fruit and seedlings of turnips and varieties of cabbage. Red–far-red reversible biochemical changes include changes in respiration rate and in rates of synthesis of RNA, of total cellular protein and of particular enzymes.

Phytochrome is also implicated in the photoperiodic control of flowering and therefore its discussion forms a natural link between this chapter and Chapter 12 devoted to Reproductive Development.

Typical phytochrome responses are achieved by low radiation intensities (1×10^5 ergs/cm^2) acting for short periods. The growth of etiolated stems of some species is inhibited by such low intensities of red light. However in some species this is quite ineffective but inhibition can be achieved with higher intensities (1×10^7 ergs/cm^2 or higher) of far-red or blue light. The system involved in such responses has been termed by Mohr the high energy reaction (HER). The anthocyanin synthesis (mentioned above) is in all cases stimulated by high intensity blue and in some cases also by high intensity far-red. In the case of anthocyanin synthesis in seedlings of *Sorghum vulgare* red light is quite ineffective. However in all these cases the involvement of phytochrome can also be demonstrated. If *Sorghum* seedlings are exposed to high intensity blue radiation anthocyanin synthesis is initiated and continues on return to darkness. However if immediately prior to darkness the seedlings are exposed to low intensity far-red the synthesis of anthocyanin is markedly repressed and this repression is reversible by an immediately following exposure to low intensity red light. The nature of the HER has not been satisfactorily elucidated but present evidence suggests that phytochrome may also be involved in the high intensity far-red effect but that a riboflavin-containing pigment mediates the blue light effect.

FURTHER READING

MOHR, H. (1972). *Lectures on Photomorphogenesis*. Springer-Verlag, Berlin.
SALISBURY, F. B. and ROSS, C. (1969). *Plant Physiology*. Wadsworth Publ. Co., California.

STREET, H. E. (1966). Growth, differentiation and organogenesis in plant tissue and organ cultures. *Cells and Tissues in Culture*, ed. WILLMER, E. N., Vol. 3, Chap. 10, 631–89. Academic Press, New York.

STREET, H. E. (1969). Growth in organized and unorganized systems: knowledge gained by culture of organs and tissue explants. In *Plant Physiology*, ed. STEWARD, F. C., Vol. 5B, Chap. 6, 3–224. Academic Press, New York and London.

WAREING, P. F. (1969). Germination and dormancy. In *Physiology of Plant Growth and Development*, ed. WILKINS, M. B., 605–46. McGraw-Hill, London.

WOOLHOUSE, H. W. (ed.) (1967). *Aspects of the Biology of Ageing*. Symp. Soc. exp. Biol., 21. Cambridge University Press, London.

WOOLHOUSE, H. W. (1972). *Ageing Processes in Higher Plants*. Oxford Biology Readers, 30. Oxford University Press, London.

SELECTED REFERENCES

ADDICOTT, F. T. (1965). Physiology of abscission. In *Encyclopedia of Plant Physiology*, ed. RUHLAND, W., sub-ed. LANG, A., 15 (2), 1094–126. Springer-Verlag, Berlin.

CARNS, H. R. (1966). Abscission and its control. *A. Rev. Pl. Physiol.*, 17, 295–314.

DOORENBOS, J. (1965). Juvenile and adult phases in woody plants. In *Encyclopedia of Plant Physiology*, ed. RUHLAND, W., sub-ed. LANG, A., 15 (1), 1222–35. Springer-Verlag, Berlin.

HILLMAN, W. S. (1967). The physiology of phytochrome. *A. Rev. Pl. Physiol.*, 18, 301–24.

PHILLIPS, I. D. J. (1969). Apical dominance. In *Physiology of Plant Growth and Development*, ed. WILKINS, M. B., 165–202. McGraw-Hill, London.

SIEGELMAN, H. W. (1969). Phytochrome. In *Physiology of Plant Growth and Development*, ed. WILKINS, M. B., 489–507. McGraw-Hill, London.

SMITH, H. (1970). Phytochrome and photomorphogenesis in plants. *Nature, Lond.*, 227, 665–8.

12

Reproductive Development

INTRODUCTION

Vegetative growth sooner or later leads to a transition to reproductive development signalled by the initiation of flower primordia. Plants will not flower, nor in many cases respond to the environmental stimuli which ensure subsequent flowering, until they have completed a part of their vegetative development—until they have reached a 'ripeness to flower'. The sharpness of this transition and the extent to which the reproductive phase occurs along with continuing vegetative development or is marked by a virtual cessation of further vegetative growth vary very widely between species. The shoot meristems usually undergo a major shift in morphology associated with the switch from initiating leaves and vegetative axillary buds to. the formation of flowers and their subtending bracts. This morphological change is the basis for early detection of flower induction.

Reproductive development will here be interpreted to encompass not only flower initiation but flower development, the formation of the haploid sex cells, fertilization and the growth and ripening of the fruit including development of the embryo and seed structures from the fertilized ovule. We are therefore here concerned to survey the physiological aspects of all the changes which intervene from the initiation of reproductive development to the formation of viable seed capable by its germination of giving rise to the next generation of plants.

FLOWERING

Our knowledge of flowering derives from studies with a selected number of species from amongst those cases where appropriate conditions of temperature and/or daylength are essential to flowering or can greatly hasten or delay the onset and abundance of this process. It should however be emphasized that many species are not exacting and will flower under almost any conditions compatible with continuing growth. Any general theory must therefore be able to explain flowering in plants differing profoundly in the sensitivity of this process to environmental stimuli.

Vernalization

Some plants require a cold treatment (**vernalization**) before they will flower and in certain of these cases it has been shown that it is the stem apex which is the sensitive region and that this has to reach the required maturity before the cold treatment is effective (biennial *Hyoscyamus niger*, and *Beta vulgaris*). In photoperiodic plants (those whose flowering depends upon exposure to an appropriate daylength) it is the leaves which must reach the appropriate maturity; photoperiodic induction is effective only after a particular number of nodes have been formed. Winter cereals have a cold requirement and a long-day requirement; the cold requirement can be achieved by the embryo of the immature seed or in the moistened mature seed but the daylength requirement can be met only when the young plant has grown to the appropriate stature.

Vernalization may be essential to flowering or merely hasten the onset of flowering. Winter rye has no absolute cold requirement but when vernalized the winter varieties flower as rapidly as the spring varieties. By contrast the biennial variety of *Hyoscyamus niger* (henbane) has an absolute cold requirement and if over-wintered at too high a temperature will remain vegetative indefinitely. Both the above species are long-day plants (see discussion of photoperiodism below) but cold requirements for flowering are also found in a short-day variety of chrysanthemum and in a number of day-neutral species (various spp. of *Geum, Lychnis* and *Erysimum*, and in *Senecio jacobaea, Pyrethrum cinerariaefolium, Saxifraga rotundifolia*).

The temperature most effective in vernalization is at or near to 6°C, and the duration of treatment for maximum acceleration of flowering can range according to species from 4 days to 3 months. Vernalization can be reversed by an immediately following period of high temperature. This suggests that there is a neutral temperature, below which vernalization occurs and above which vernalization tends to be reversed. It has been shown that in *Hyoscyamus* this neutral temperature is at about 20°C.

The German botanist G. Melchers first demonstrated that vernalization could be transmitted from a vernalized to an unvernalized *Hyoscyamus* plant through a graft union. To explain this he postulated the formation during vernalization of an effector substance and named this ***vernalin***. To explain the accumulation of such a substance at low temperature it has been postulated that some destroying system is preferentially reduced in activity at low temperature compared with a system controlling the synthesis or partial synthesis of vernalin. The reversibility of vernalization by high temperature applied immediately would then be by activation of the destroying system and stabilization of vernalization, unless high temperature immediately follows the cold treatment, would imply that the unstable substance accumulating at low temperature is subsequently converted to the stable vernalin. These relationships can be expressed diagrammatically thus:

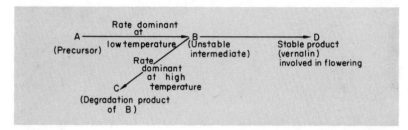

Following the availability of gibberellins isolated from culture filtrates of *Gibberella* and from higher plants (Fig. 9.3, p. 161) it was shown, particularly by Anton Lang and his collaborators at Pasadena, that application of these substances can substitute for the cold treatment for vernalization (Fig. 12.1). Further it was shown that the vernalized plants have enhanced endogenous levels of substances with gibberellin activity as compared with unvernalized control plants of the same species. Although vernalin has not been identified with certainty, it now seems possible that it is a particular gibberellin or mixture of gibberellins. The only objection to this view is that in some instances the pattern of growth and flowering following gibberellin treatment is not exactly that which follows cold treatment.

Photoperiodism

Experimental study of the role of light in controlling flowering dates from the work by W. W. Garner and H. A. Allard first published in 1920. These workers noticed that although the Maryland Mammoth variety of tobacco, despite its vigorous vegetative growth, failed to flower and set seed during the summer, nevertheless root stocks transferred to the greenhouse gave rise readily during winter to small flowering plants. They also found that successive spring sowings of a variety of soybean (*Glycine max (soja)*) all came into flower at the same time and that flowering

Fig. 12.1 Carrot plants (var. Early French Forcing). *Left*: control; *centre*: maintained at 17°C but supplied 10 mg of gibberellin daily for 4 weeks; *right*: plant given vernalizing cold treatment (six weeks). All photographed 8 weeks after completion of cold treatment. (From Lang, 1957, *Proc. natn. Acad. Sci. U.S.A.*, **43**, 709–17.)

occurred quickly and in quite small plants grown in the greenhouse in winter. No significant promotive effect on the flowering of these plants could be traced to the moisture conditions, temperature and light intensities within the greenhouses. Garner and Allard therefore examined the effect of daylength by extending the natural day with artificial light and shortening the day by placing the plants in light-proof cabinets at the appropriate time. The consequence of these studies was to show that these varieties of tobacco and soybean required a period of exposure to short days in order to flower and that after an appropriate period of short days (*photoperiodic induction*) they would flower irrespective of the subsequent daylength. Garner and Allard then examined further plants for their response to daylength and concluded that some plants had no special daylength requirements (day-neutral plants), others were short-day plants (SDP) and still others long-day plants (LDP). The phenomenon of flower induction by appropriate daylength treatment is therefore a further instance of photoperiodism (see Bud dormancy, Chapter 11, p. 223).

The situation exposed by the pioneer studies of Garner and Allard has proved, on further study, to be much more complex. There are, for example, plants with an absolute requirement for short-day induction, but others whose flowering is only hastened by short days. Some plants require a combination of daylengths, e.g. short days followed by long days. There are complex interactions between temperature and daylength, e.g. an absolute daylength requirement at one temperature and no daylength requirement at another. These are examples of the many response types which will one day have to be fitted into a comprehensive theory of flowering. We shall however confine our attention mainly to a consideration of a plant with an absolute requirement for short-day induction like *Xanthium pennsylvanicum* (syn. *X. strumarium*) and an obligate long-day plant such as the annual strain of *Hyoscyamus niger*.

When grown under normal conditions all plants have a light requirement for flowering since they need photosynthetic products to grow and develop. However plants with no daylength requirement can be brought to flowering in darkness if supplied with sugar. The need for a 'high intensity' light reaction for flowering is therefore a photosynthetic requirement not specifically related to flower induction. With this background it is possible now to discuss an important discovery regarding photoperiodism, the discovery that it is the length of the *dark* period that is normally determinative in both short- and long-day plants. A SDP is induced by a dark period or succession of dark periods *exceeding* a critical length (in *Xanthium* the dark period must be 8·5 hours or longer), a LDP flowers provided the dark periods are *less than* a critical length (in *Hyoscyamus* the dark period must not exceed 13 hours). Recognition of the importance of the dark period followed from the demonstration that a SDP like *Xanthium* placed under inductive conditions will flower if the light period is interrupted by a short dark period but will not flower if the dark period is interrupted by a short light period. Similarly a LDP will flower in short days provided the dark period is appropriately interrupted.

Photoperiodic induction occurs in the leaves and the flowering stimulus moves out from the leaves to the meristems where flowers are to be initiated. Not only can a partially defoliated *Xanthium* plant be caused to flower by appropriate induction of the remaining single leaf but a single induced leaf can cause flowering when the other leaves on the same plant are maintained under non-inductive conditions. These observations

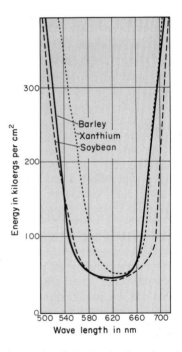

Fig. 12.2 Action spectrum for light breaks in otherwise inductive or non-inductive dark periods. The light breaks in the inductive dark periods of the short-day plants (*Xanthium* and Biloxi soybean) suppress flower initiation; the light breaks in the non-inductive dark periods of the long-day barley plants promote spike formation and stem elongation (after Borthwick, Hendricks and Parker, 1948, *Bot. Gaz.*, **110**, 103–18). The wavelength region where the energy requirement is lowest indicates the most effective wavelength for respectively the suppression or promotion of flowering.

together with the failure of applied metabolites (such as sugars and amino acids) to cause flower initiation indicate that it is not the general synthetic output of the leaves which is involved but their production under inductive conditions of a hormonal stimulus to flower initiation (a flowering hormone or *florigen*). The concept of a flowering hormone, probably identical in all photoperiodic plants, is supported by the observation that the flowering stimulus can be transmitted from an induced to a non-induced plant of the same species across a graft union and by several demonstrations that this can also be achieved between different species with different photoperiodic requirements, e.g. the induction of flowering in a SDP (non-induced) by transmission from a LDP (induced), and between day-neutral and day-sensitive plants.

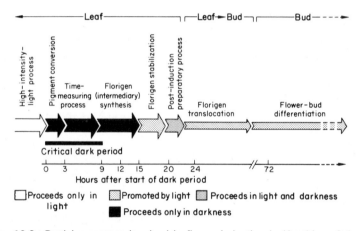

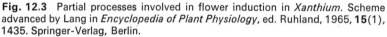

Fig. 12.3 Partial processes involved in flower induction in *Xanthium*. Scheme advanced by Lang in *Encyclopedia of Plant Physiology*, ed. Ruhland, 1965, **15**(1), 1435. Springer-Verlag, Berlin.

Contemporary with their study of the light stimulation of lettuce seed germination, the Beltsville group (see Photomorphogenesis, Chapter 11, p. 230) also examined the action spectrum of the suppression of flowering in *Xanthium* by a short break (5 min.) of low intensity light given during the effective dark period of not less than 8.5 hours. These studies, first published in 1954, showed that red light (peak activity between 640–680 nm) was most effective (Fig. 12.2) and that the effect of red light could be nullified by a succeeding exposure to far-red (710–740 nm). This implicated phytochrome in photoperiodic induction.

The discovery of phytochrome raised the whole question of the processes which proceed in the critical dark period. These are not understood although there is experimental evidence strongly suggesting that a sequence of events is involved and that one of these is a timing reaction (Fig. 12.3). If red light suppresses flowering in SDP it must be assumed that phytochrome in the dark period is normally in the Pr form and when all the phytochrome is in this form the dose of red light required for maximum inhibition should reach a fixed value (before that less red light would be required to reverse the existing Pr to Pfr). Experimental studies based on this reasoning show that early in the critical dark period all the phytochrome is in the Pr form (in less than the first 4 hours of the critical 8·5 hours in *Xanthium*). Further points for consideration here are (i) that plants can measure the duration of the dark period accurately (± 15 minutes in *Xanthium*), (ii) that irradiation with far-red (thereby completing rapidly the Pfr–Pr change which occurs more slowly in darkness) early in the dark period does not in general reduce the length of the dark period required for induction and (iii) that cobalt ions, which do not delay Pr formation, nevertheless increase the critical dark period. Thus the time-measuring process is not the conversion of Pfr to Pr nor apparently is this process triggered off by a critical level of Pr relative to Pfr. The release of flowering stimulus from the leaves does not immediately follow the critical dark period and its release once initiated continues subsequently for many hours in *Xanthium*, and as discussed below for very long periods in some plants. Synthesis of the flowering stimulus therefore may be regarded as the terminal step in a multistage induction process. Although the biochemical nature of the processes involved is still very incompletely understood it is possible to express this multistage induction process by tentative schemes such as that shown in Fig. 12.3.

Although *Xanthium* is exceptional in that it can be induced to flower by a single critical night (often referred to as a single inductive cycle), it is found when using a population of plants that about 3 inductive cycles are needed to cause 100% of the plants to flower. Further inductive cycles increase the number of flowers formed and the speed with which flowering takes place. A similar situation appears where, as is usually the case, a number of inductive cycles are essential to flowering.

The change that takes place during photoperiodic induction can be very stable or decay very rapidly. Although in *Xanthium* export of the flowering stimulus from induced leaves does not persist, nevertheless, once the plant is induced, leafy shoots formed subsequently can transmit the flowering stimulus to non-induced plants by grafting and the induced plant will go on flowering for a long time in non-inductive conditions. In the flowering *Xanthium* plant the flowering hormone pervades the plant and is not diluted out; persistent production of hormones seems to be localized in the stem apices. A rather different situation is seen in the SDP, *Perilla ocymoides*. Here also there is persistence of the induced state but it remains localized in the leaves submitted to the inductive cycles. As these particular leaves age and die the plant becomes vegetative again. Biloxi soybean plants require continuous inductive conditions for flowering and formation of flowers ceases very rapidly when the plants are transferred to non-inductive conditions.

The discussion developed above has been in terms of the formation of a specific positive stimulus to flowering, of a floral hormone (florigen). The most telling evidence for this hypothesis is the transmission of the flowering stimulus through grafts (Fig. 12.4). If a dark period in excess of some critical value is needed to produce such a morphogenetic factor or its precursor in SDP, we might conclude that in LDP a dark period in excess of the critical value acts in the reverse sense and suppresses the formation of the same agent. Such a paradox suggested that the critical dark period may not be directly concerned in the synthesis of the flowering hormone. LDP will flower in continuous light, i.e. they have no need of a dark period to develop the flowering stimulus. Again there are a number of plants which are photoperiodic at one temperature and day-neutral at another temperature. Further, if the influence of dark periods in photoperiodic plants was to alter the level of other cell constituents which in turn controlled florigen synthesis then darkness could act in the same sense in both SDP or LDP. The dark reaction could tend to raise the level of such a factor—a night in excess of the critical length being needed to achieve the appropriate concentration in SDP whereas in LDP the factor could reach an inhibitory level if the critical period of darkness was exceeded. Alternatively the dark period could be one in which the level of some factor decreased, a dark period in excess of the critical length being needed in SDP to lower a previously inhibitory concentration.

Do other growth regulating substances exert an influence on flowering? First there is the observation that in *Chenopodium* inductive photo-periods lead to marked increases in the growth rate of the leaves and that photoperiodic induction of *Xanthium* is associated with a marked stimulation of cell division in the apical meristems. We have already referred to the possible identity of vernalin with gibberellins and there are many recorded instances of the promotion of flowering in LDP from application of gibberellins. Auxin applications are used commercially to induce flowering in the pineapple (*Ananas comosus*) and in the litchi tree (*Litchi chinensis*). In pineapple the auxin seems to act by inducing ethylene synthesis. More recently auxin-induced flowering in two LDP, winter barley and *Hyoscyamus niger*, has been reported. There are many instances of the inhibition of flowering from auxin application. The present weakness in the hypothesis that critical dark periods are concerned with regulating levels of auxins or gibberellins or possibly of other regulators to levels compatible with florigen synthesis is that significant changes in the endogenous levels of auxins, gibberellins or cytokinins following photoperiodic induction have not been demonstrated. However in view of the limited specificity of bioassays for such growth regulators and uncertainty about the quantitative nature of extraction techniques this evidence does not warrant rejection of the above hypothesis. Here again as in the other morphogenetic phenomena in plants we may have complex interactions between growth regulating

Fig. 12.4 Transmission of the flowering stimulus from a short-day plant (*Nicotiana tabacum* 'Maryland Mammoth') to a non-induced long-day plant (*Hyoscyamus niger*, annual variety). In each case the *Hyoscyamus* graft is on the left. A: entire graft on short days; short-day partner induced, long-day partner flowering (flowers on donor removed). B: short-day partner on long days, long-day partner on short days—no flower formation. (From Khudairi and Lang, via Lang, *Encyclopedia of Plant Physiology*, ed. Ruhland, 1965, **15**(1), 1406. Springer-Verlag, Berlin.)

substances leading to certain cells being programmed to synthesize a flowering stimulus.

The timing reaction in phototropism

Reference was made earlier (Chapter 8, p. 145) to diurnal rhythms of growth and to their endogenous control by a 'biological clock'. Such rhythms are often referred to as ***circadian rhythms*** (from circa, about, and diem, day) because their period approximates to 24 hours. Such rhythms are involved in leaf movements such as can be observed in the runner bean, in the opening and closing of flowers (e.g. in *Kalanchoë blossfeldiana*), in root pressure (see Chapter 4, Fig. 4.4, p. 55) and in aspects of metabolism (such as the dark-fixation of CO_2 in succulents like *Bryophyllum fedtschenkoi*). The hypothesis that such rhythms are implicated in photoperiodism was first advanced by Erwin Bünning in the early 1930s and defended by him in subsequent publications. He postulated the continuous alternation of two phases, a photophile (light-loving) phase and a scotophile (dark-loving) phase (also called photophobe—light-fearing) and that light received during the former was promotive of flowering, while in the latter light inhibited (darkness promoted) flowering. A precisely regulated circadian rhythm of such a kind involving quantitative and qualitative changes in responsiveness to light could form the basis of the timing mechanism in photoperiodism. Evidence in support of the involvement of the 'biological clock' in photoperiodism comes mainly from studies where SDP have been submitted to very long dark periods (thereby involving cycles in excess of 24 hours). For instance when soybean plants received 8 hours of light followed by dark periods ranging from 8 to 62 hours, flowering was obtained when the light + dark period was approximately 24 hours or a *multiple* of 24 hours. Plants remained vegetative when the 'artificial days' had intermediate values (e.g. 36 hours). When plants of the SDP *Chenopodium rubrum* (inducible by a single photoperiod) were submitted to 72 hour dark periods interrupted at various times by 2 minute 'light-breaks' of red light, the light-breaks effectively inhibited flowering when given 6, 33 or 60 hours from the beginning of the dark period, i.e. at the times when the plant, on an approximately 24-hour inductive cycle, would have been in the dark. Light-breaks were quite ineffective at or near 18 and 46 hours into the dark period (Fig. 12.5), when the plant would normally have been in the light. Such results are consistent with the operation of a rhythm with a period of 27–30 hours divided into two phases of reversed light sensitivity. The elusiveness of florigen, now possibly linked in its synthesis to a 'biological clock' of unknown nature, emphasizes the incompleteness of our knowledge of the control of flowering.

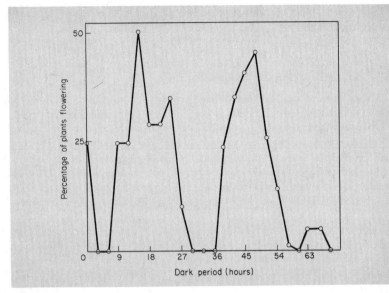

Fig. 12.5 The effect on the flowering of *Chenopodium rubrum* of red 'light-breaks' of 2 minutes' duration when applied at random times (O) during a period of continuous darkness of 72 hours. After the single dark period the plants were kept in continuous light and scored for flowering. (Modified from Cumming, Hendricks and Borthwick, 1965, *Can. J. Bot.*, **43**, 825–53.)

Flower development

The above discussion has concentrated upon the events which determine that flowering will occur in photoperiodic plants. It has not considered flowering in 'day-neutral' plants where no specific environmental control of flowering operates, nor factors affecting the profusion of flowering nor the processes involved in the transformation of a vegetative apex into a reproductive apex and the factors controlling the development of functional flowers. Considerations of heteroblastic development and the transition from the juvenile to the adult vegetative form (Chapter 8, p. 150) are aspects of an endogenously controlled development (sometimes referred to as phasic development). In day-neutral plants transition to flowering is similarly endogenously controlled. It may nevertheless involve a similar sequence of changes (leading to synthesis and release of florigen) as those which operate in photoperiodic plants. This is supported by the existence of quantitative or facultative SDP and LDP which will flower ultimately under any daylength but flower more rapidly under appropriate photoperiods. Furthermore flowering has been induced in a long-day tobacco variety by grafting onto a flowering day-neutral variety.

The abundance of flowering can be controlled by nutritional factors and, in photoperiodic plants, by the number of successive photoperiodic cycles. Often the speed of flowering (interval between induction and flower appearance) and the number of flowers formed increase as the number of consecutive inductive photoperiods increases. However the photoperiodic conditions essential for flower induction may not be optimal for flower development. A high nitrogen status in some cases promotes vigorous vegetative growth but reduces the profusion of flowering and fruiting (this is the case in some fruit trees); in other cases (e.g. *Xanthium*) high nitrogen promotes vigorous vegetative growth under non-flowering conditions and increases the abundance of flowers under inductive conditions. A number of synthetic growth-retarding substances are now widely used in ornamental horticulture to produce 'dwarf' plants; some of these, applied to particular species, also speed up flowering and increase flower number. Some of these retardants are considered to act by inhibiting the synthesis of endogenous gibberellins (high levels of gibberellins are inhibitory to flowering in some species) and are therefore termed anti-gibberellins (e.g. AMO 1618, CCC, phosphon D). A number of these observations point to an antagonism between vegetative growth and reproductive development; examples of reproductive development as the trigger for senescence of vegetative structures have already been considered (see Chapter 11, p. 225).

Most studies on flower development have been in terms of morphology and developmental anatomy (for an excellent account of such work the reader is referred to *Plant Anatomy. Part 2. Organs* by Elizabeth G. Cutter, Edward Arnold, London, 1971). The science-based bulb industry of the Netherlands has however made very detailed studies of the influence of conditions of storage, particularly temperature, upon flower development. The development of flowers in *Tulipa gesneriana* involves three main stages, each with a different temperature requirement: (i) differentiation of the embryonic flower bud, a stage involving active cell division and requiring high temperature (20°C); (ii) an apparent rest which needs about 13 weeks at an optimum temperature of 8–9°C; (iii) a period of rapid growth of the floral organs and elongation of the flower stalk which takes about 9 weeks at an optimum of 13–15°C.

The role of growth-regulating substances in the growth of floral organs is very incompletely understood. The apparently controlling role of auxin in the growth and orientation of the flower stalk of *Fritillaria meleagris* has however been demonstrated (Fig. 12.6). The level of diffusible auxin in the stalk closely follows its pattern of growth. By careful excision experiments evidence was obtained that the source of this auxin moving into the flower stalk was the ovules. The drooping stage (b in Fig. 12.6), which corresponds with the first auxin peak, occurred at a time when there was intense cell division in the ovules and formation of the embryo sac. The subsequent fall in 'auxin activity' was shown in part to be due to the release of an inhibitor from the young anthers, the output of this inhibitor falling sharply as the stage of anthesis approached. Other examples of growth regulators from one floral organ affecting the growth of another part of the flower are known. Thus removal of young stamens from the flower of *Glechoma hederacea* causes a marked reduction in growth of the corolla. This growth can be restored by gibberellin application but not by auxin.

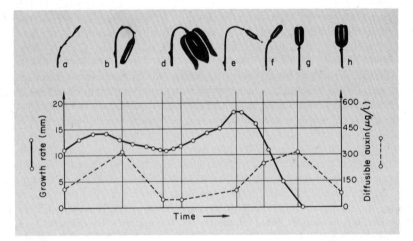

Fig. 12.6 Stages (a–h) in the development of the flower of *Fritillaria meleagris* showing the reversal of the geotropic response of the flower stalk during the development of the flower and fruit. Graphs: top curve, growth rate of the flower stalk in mm per day; lower curve, amount of auxin diffusing from the flower and through the flower stalk. (From Kaldewey, 1957, *Planta*, **49**, 300–44.)

Some evidence has been obtained of the role of growth regulators in sex expression in species which produce unisexual flowers. In a number of species auxin application has promoted development of female as against male flowers, and gibberellic acid of male as against female flowers. An interesting series of experiments with excised cultured flower primordia of cucumber (*Cucumis sativus*) confirmed this 'triggering' of development towards female or male flowers in monoecious strains by IAA and gibberellic acid. However with primordia excised from hermaphrodite plants (producing bisexual flowers) these hormones failed to produce unisexual flowers.

FERTILIZATION

The physiological processes involved in the production of the male (germinated pollen grains) and female (8-nucleate embryo sac) gametophytes and within these of the male nuclei and egg cell are very incompletely understood. Central to this aspect of reproductive development is the induction of meiosis in the pollen (microspore) mother cells and in the megaspore mother cell. Attempts to study the development of the microspores by culturing excised anthers have emphasized that further development can be achieved in culture only after meiosis has been initiated in the spore mother cells and that successful completion of meiosis is normally achieved only when the spore mother cells at the time of anther excision are already advanced in meiosis to the pachytene stage. Work with anthers of onion excised at or near this stage of meiosis has demonstrated the beneficial effect on tetrad formation and the later stage of uninucleate microspore development of supplementation of the sugar–mineral salt medium with cytokinin, gibberellin and RNA or RNA nucleotides. These studies however shed no light on what factors programme cells to embark upon meiosis—the critical step in the alternation of generations and in genetic segregation.

Studies on pollen grain development in attached anthers have shown that the spore mother cells lose most of their cytoplasmic RNA and protein at the time of microspore formation. This may be an essential preparation for the change in cell metabolism associated with the switch to the gametophytic pathway which leads to the formation of the mature pollen grains. The production of such grains involves new synthesis of RNA and protein (the precursors for which are probably transported to the newly formed tetrad from the tapetal layer of the anther wall), temporary isolation of the tetrad of spores by enclosure within an impermeable polysaccharide (callose) wall, and synthesis of the several-layered pollen grain wall. The latter includes the ektexine layer which becomes impregnated with the highly resistant sporopollenin, probably derived from material released by the breakdown of the callose wall of the tetrad and the walls of the tapetal cells. Finally the microspore undergoes an asymmetric mitosis to give rise to a smaller generative cell with a condensed usually lens-shaped nucleus (from which by a further mitosis arise the two male nuclei) and a vegetative cell with a larger and more diffusely staining spherical nucleus (tube nucleus).

If the anthers of a number of Solanaceous plants (*Nicotiana* spp. including tobacco, *N. tabacum*, *Datura* spp., and *Atropa belladonna*) are excised immediately prior to or at the time of this pollen grain mitosis and cultured in a simple sugar-mineral salt medium a large proportion of the microspores become non-viable, a proportion mature into pollen grains

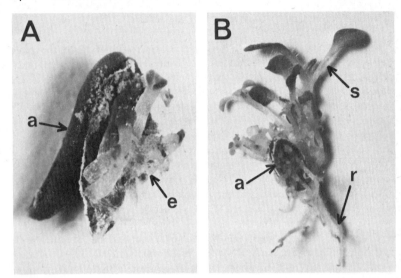

Fig. 12.7 Excised anther cultures of *Nicotiana tabacum* showing embryogenesis from microspores. A: stage of dehiscence of the cultured anthers showing embryoids (e) within the anthers (a).   B: seedlings developing from the embryoids. s, Shoot with leaves; r, roots. (Photographs by M. Horner, Botanical Laboratories, University of Leicester.)

and a proportion are directed from the gametophytic pathway and embark upon a continuing sequence of cell divisions to give rise to haploid plantlets (pollen embryoids) (Fig. 12.7). The proportion of microspores which embark upon this sporophytic pathway can be increased by submitting the anthers to a low temperature shock (4°C) for 48 hours before transferring them to the culture medium. This phenomenon, particularly if it can be induced in anthers of a wider range of species, will be of considerable practical importance as a source of haploid plants which spontaneously or following colchicine treatment can give rise to homozygous fertile diploid lines. It shows that sporophyte versus gametophyte development is not controlled by ploidy level and that isolated cells can spontaneously develop the necessary polarity required for the early emergence in embryology of a shoot and a root pole. To achieve this switch to sporophyte development it is necessary to remove, by anther excision, an influence arising from attachment of the stamen to the parent sporophyte and to do this while the microspores are still uninucleate or have only just embarked upon the microspore mitosis—before they are fully committed to the gametophytic pathway. A similar increasing determination to a fixed pathway of development was noted in relation to the culture of excised leaf primordia (see Chapter 11, p. 219).

The act of fertilization requires the pollen grains released from the mature anther to reach the stigma and to germinate there to give rise to a pollen tube which will grow into the stigma, down the style into the ovary and usually ultimately to the micropyle of the ovule. Pollen grains can however in most cases be germinated *in vitro*. The pollen of some species will show some germination in water but the percentage germination is low, pollen tube growth slow and restricted, and pollen tube bursting common. The percentage germination and the extent of pollen tube growth can usually be increased by using a sugar solution (sucrose often being the most effective sugar). The sugar acts both as a nutrient and to make the osmotic potential of the solution more favourable. Further improvement in pollen tube growth can often be achieved by including, in the culture solution, calcium and other cations and boric acid (within the concentration range 0·001–0·01%). In a culture solution supplying these constituents at appropriate concentrations percentage germination and pollen tube growth similar in rate and extent respectively to those occurring during normal fertilization can be achieved with some species. Further there is evidence that all these factors are supplied naturally to the pollen tubes by the stigma and style tissues. In other cases additional factors are required in culture (gibberellin, particular amino acids) and in still other cases it is not possible to achieve fully effective germination and pollen tube growth *in vitro*. Pollen tubes growing on the stigma and within the style secrete enzymes which soften the cutin of the stigma and the middle lamella of the cell walls (thereby facilitating pollen tube penetration) and also produce auxin (or a factor promoting auxin synthesis) involved in the initiation of fruit development. The initial penetration of the pollen tube into the stigma involves its positive hydrotropic and negative aerotropic responses. In the final stages of its growth the pollen tube shows a positive chemotropism to a substance released at the micropyle of the ovule. Effective pollination requires the pollen to land on a compatible stigma. Successful pollination normally occurs only with pollen of the same species and where self-incompatibility occurs only with pollen from a different plant of the same species. Incompatibility occurs because of failure of the pollen tube to penetrate the stigma (e.g. failure to receive an appropriate stimulus to synthesize and release the necessary cutinase) or owing to inhibition of pollen tube growth within the stigma and style as a result of a genetically determined interaction between a pollen tube and a stigma–style product. The chemical nature of the interacting molecules (S-factors) and how their reaction product inhibits pollen tube growth remain unresolved.

The generative nucleus in the pollen grain undergoes mitosis to form the two male nuclei; this may occur before the pollen grains are shed or during pollen tube growth. The pollen tube entering the ovule via the micropyle comes into contact with the embryo sac at the site of the synergids. Often one of the synergids breaks down and the tip of the pollen tube enters this degenerating cell; the male nuclei are released through a sub-apical pore in the pollen tube. The two male nuclei migrate into the embryo sac (it is not clear how this movement is effected) and one fuses with the egg nucleus to give the diploid zygote from which the embryo develops and the other fuses with the diploid nucleus of the central cell to give the triploid endosperm nucleus.

FRUIT DEVELOPMENT

The development of fruit is normally a consequence of pollination; unpollinated flowers fall, pollinated flowers show fruit set. Germinating pollen is a rich source of auxin and there is evidence that pollen tube growth not only supplies auxin but that pollination may activate auxin synthesis by the tissues of the gynaecium, particularly by stylar and/or locular tissue. Recognition of the importance of this auxin for fruit set followed from the demonstration by Gustafson in 1936 that in some species application of auxin to unpollinated flowers led to the development of seedless (parthenocarpic) fruit. However about 80% of horticultural species cannot be set by auxin application. Applications of gibberellins can similarly induce parthenocarpic fruit development in some species, some of which will not set fruit by auxin application. Singly or in combination, applications of these growth regulators however succeed only with a very few species, and these are plants in which some degree of natural parthenocarpic fruit development occurs. Where natural parthenocarpy occurs or is induced by growth regulator application it seems that for a time ovule development including growth of the seed coat and nucellus proceeds and that the seedless nature of the mature fruit follows from abortion of the pseudo-seeds. In most species it is the double fertilization which leads to active growth of the nucellus and seed coat and to an associated rapid increase in fruit growth. The importance of seed development to fruit growth is well illustrated by studies in the strawberry where fruit size and form are determined by the number of fertile achenes (Figs. 12.8 and 12.9). In this case the promotion of receptacle growth can be achieved, following removal of all achenes, by an appropriate application of the synthetic auxin, 2-naphthoxyacetic acid (2-NOA) (Fig. 12.10), and it can be shown that the developing achenes are a rich source of diffusible auxin. Many other developing seeds have been shown to be centres of auxin synthesis. Young seeds are also rich sources of natural gibberellins and the first successful isolation (in 1958) of a gibberellin from a higher plant was the isolation of gibberellin A_8 from *immature* seeds of *Phaseolus multiflorus* (Fig. 9.3, p. 161). Endosperm in the free nuclear stage (the outstanding example being

Fig. 12.8 Effects of developing achenes on the growth of the strawberry receptacle. 1 : Unpollinated flower: no development of receptacle. 2 : One pollinated achene: growth of the receptacle around it. 3 : Several pollinated achenes: several areas of receptacle growth. 4 : Many pollinated achenes. (From Nitsch, 1965, *Encyclopedia of Plant Physiology*, ed. Ruhland, **15**(1), 1601. Springer-Verlag, Berlin.)

coconut milk) and immature seeds and fruitlets are rich sources of cyto-kinin activity; the first natural cytokinin to be isolated (1964) was from immature maize kernels and was hence termed zeatin (Fig. 9.3, p. 161).

Fruit development following pollination involves growth of the seeds to maturity and enlargement of the ovary or receptacle. Cell division, cell expansion and accumulation of food reserves are involved in seed development (see Chapter 8). Growth of the fruit may, subsequent to pollination, involve only cell expansion but in many cases there is also a short phase of cell division. The development of fleshy fruits involves considerable accumulation of organic metabolites (organic acids, sugars) into the succulent pericarp and associated tissues. The importance of seeds to fruit development suggests a controlling influence of auxins,

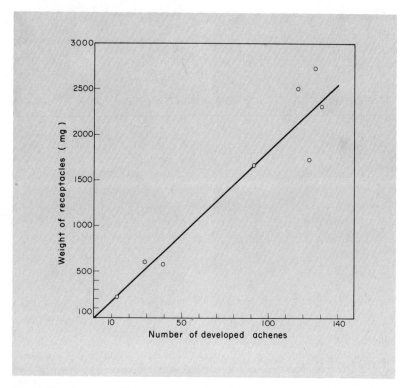

Fig. 12.9 Proportionality between number of developed achenes and weight of the receptacle in strawberry. (From Nitsch, 1950, *Am. J. Bot.*, **37**, 211–15.)

gibberellins and cytokinins liberated by the seeds. These growth regulators thus make the developing fruit a 'sink' for food materials synthesized in the leaves and fruit development is normally associated with a marked check to vegetative growth and in annuals with senescence of the whole plant. Removal of fruits immediately halts leaf senescence. In *Phaseolus vulgaris* a similar diversion of ^{32}P and of the carbon of $^{14}CO_2$ from the leaves to the peduncles can be achieved either by leaving the pods attached or applying a mixture of IAA, GA and kinetin in lanoline paste to the decapitated peduncles.

The concept that the growth-regulating substances essential to fruit development are synthesized in the fertilized ovules is supported by experiments involving the culture of excised flowers. Fruit development to maturity has been demonstrated in a number of species using a simple medium containing only inorganic salts and sucrose always provided that the flowers had been pollinated two or more days before they were

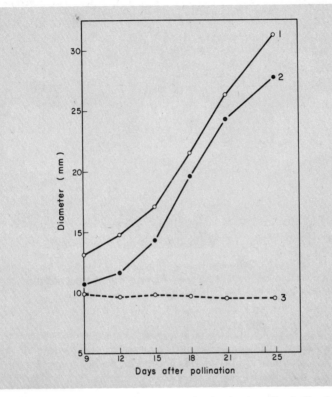

Fig. 12.10 Growth curves of three strawberries (variety Marshall) which were pollinated on the same day. 1 : Control. 2 : Fruit which had all its achenes removed on the ninth day and replaced with a lanoline paste containing 100 mg/l of the synthetic auxin, 2-naphthoxyacetic acid. 3 : Fruit which had all its achenes removed on the ninth day and replaced with plain lanoline. (From Nitsch, 1950, *Am. J. Bot.*, **37**, 211–15.)

separated from the mother plant (Fig. 12.11). Studies with unpollinated tomato flowers showed that parthenocarpic fruit development could be obtained by incorporating 2-NOA into the culture medium. Addition into the medium of tomato juice (which contains a cytokinin) gave larger fruits. Similar cultures of pollinated flowers of a number of species have shown the importance of the sepals in nitrate assimilation, and indicated that the sepals (and sometimes also the petals) synthesize auxin, gibberellin and cytokinin and export these hormones to the developing fruit.

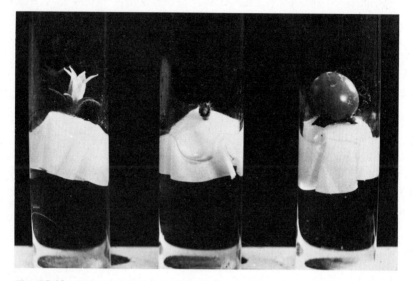

Fig. 12.11 Culture of a tomato fruit from a pollinated excised flower. Flower trimmed down to ovary (middle picture). *Right*: small fruit developed in culture (photograph supplied by Dr. J. P. Nitsch).

EMBRYO DEVELOPMENT

The fertilized ovum develops into the embryo plant within the seed and in the immediate vicinity of the endosperm. To begin with the zygote is to begin at the beginning of morphogenesis. The first division of the zygote leads to a predictable cleavage; the plane of division and the extent to which the two daughter cells are unequal are the first features of an embryology characteristic of the species. Thus for instance in some pteridophytes the daughter cell adjacent to the neck of the archegonium is the first cell of the embryonic shoot, whereas in others the shoot axis is directed away from the neck. Polarity is early recognizable in the zygote of flowering plants often due to the location of the large vacuole towards the micropylar end. The first division of the zygote is transverse and often unequal to give a smaller terminal cell rich in mitochondria and plastids and a large vacuolated basal cell (at the micropylar pole). The basal cell by further divisions gives rise to the suspensor, the terminal cell to the proembryo proper. The globular stages of the proembryo include quadrant,

octant, 16- and 32-celled stages. In dicotyledonous embryos the transition
from the globular to the heart-shaped stage (resulting from the formation
of the primordia of the cotyledons) clearly identifies the axis of the embryo
with the incipient plumular meristem directed away from the micropyle
and a provascular strand directed to the root pole where the root meristem
and root cap will be organized (this often involving cells arising from the
adjacent cell (hypophysis) of the suspensor).

In certain instances it has been possible to show gradients in the zygote
cytoplasm with respect to the density of membranes of the endoplasmic
reticulum, ribosomes, mitochondria and other cytoplasmic structures.
However this protoplasmic pattern can be disturbed by centrifuging and
yet the normal polarity can persist or be rapidly re-established. It has
therefore been suggested that the polarity lies in the plasmalemma or in an
outer immobile (gelled) cytoplasmic layer which is not displaced during
centrifugation. Thus aspects of the heterogeneous distribution associated
with polarity can be described (albeit imperfectly) but the determining
forces in polarity are as yet quite unknown.

Zygotes in which the influence of environmental factors on polarity
has been studied are the fertilized ova of brown algae, and particularly
of *Fucus* spp. The fertilized ovum, originally spherical, becomes pear-
shaped as a rhizoid begins to grow out from the basal pole and a wall is
formed cutting off the first rhizoidal cell from an apical cell. Further
divisions take place in both the rhizoidal and apical cell to give a filament
with a distinct apex and base. If zygotes are kept in the dark and as free
as possible from external gradients of environmental factors polarity is
nevertheless manifested by rhizoid development. If the zygotes are
submitted to various environmental gradients these can however determine the axis of polarity. Unilateral illumination results in rhizoid
development on the shaded side, an electrical field in its development
towards the positive pole, a pH gradient (6·0–8·0) in its development
on the acid side, an auxin gradient in its development towards the higher
concentration and a gentle temperature gradient in its development
towards the warmer side. If zygotes are allowed to cluster, rhizoids
develop towards the centre of the cluster. Stratification of *Fucus* or
Sargassum ova by centrifuging does not determine the point of origin of
the rhizoidal outgrowth. These ova appear to have an incipient polarity
either endogenously initiated or developed during oogenesis which is labile
and can in consequence be orientated by certain environmental gradients.
Such observations however do not indicate what physico-chemical
processes are involved in the initiation and fixation of the polarity.

The maintenance of polarity in an embryo appears to depend upon the
association of its cells and it seems that both physical forces developing
as the embryo enlarges and polarization of its biochemical activities

together determine the growth and associated segmentation pattern. Physical forces, such as those of surface tension, will tend towards maximum reductions in the extent of the surfaces created by cell divisions. Cells will thus tend to divide by walls of minimal area, so that the new walls are perpendicular to the previous direction of growth and at right angles to those already present. Modifying this basic pattern of segmentation will be the chemical gradients and physical restraints imposed upon the embryo as it develops within the ovule.

Significant progress has recently been made in our understanding of the factors which induce cells to embark upon embryogenesis and of the nutritive requirements of such cells. This progress arises from studies on natural polyembryony and on the formation of 'adventive embryos' or embryoids from cultured callus tissues and cell suspension cultures.

Polyembryony (presence of more than one embryo within each seed) can arise in several ways. For instance it may involve the young embryo splitting into two and each fragment then generating an embryo. This phenomenon shows the plasticity of the young embryo; it also shows that the earlier concept of the role of the daughter cells of the zygote being strictly determined (prescribed as to their contribution to the separate regions of the embryo) right from the first few divisions of the zygote is untenable. Polyembryony can also arise by the development of embryos from cells of the nucellus of the ovule. This shows that the act of fertilization is not essential to embryogenesis, and that cells of the sporophyte can be embryogenic. Further the segmentations observed during the early development of such nucellar embryos rarely correspond closely with those during embryo development from the zygote. This again shows that a strict (and genetically controlled) pattern in the early divisions is not essential for the formation of a perfect embryo (an embryo which achieves the characteristic morphology of the species as it matures). One of the species showing natural polyembryony from cells of the nucellus is *Citrus macrocarpa*. A callus developed in culture from the nucellus of this species or from *Citrus reticulata* will give rise on its upper surface to numerous plantlets and it is these that have been named 'adventive embryos' or embryoids. Similar embryoids arise profusely from the surface of a callus culture derived from young flower buds of *Ranunculus sceleratus* (Fig. 12.12) and seedlings derived from these embryoids spontaneously initiate new embryos all along their stem surfaces starting at the base of the hypocotyl. These new embryos arise from single epidermal cells of the stem and pass through the 4-celled, 8-celled, globular, cordate and torpedo stages typical of the embryology of the species (Fig. 12.13). Callus or cell suspension cultures derived from carrot embryos and embryos of *Cichorium endivia* also show a prolific spontaneous capacity to give rise to embryos apparently by segmentation in single cells.

Perhaps even more striking than the cases quoted above are the instances when embryogenesis has been induced in callus or cell cultures derived from the organs of mature plants. The classical instance is the development of embryo-like structures from cell suspension cultures initiated from the young phloem of the storage root and from the living tissues of other vegetative parts of the carrot plant (Fig. 12.14). Suspension cultures of carrot can be grown in an undifferentiated state in a defined culture medium containing auxin. Such suspensions consist of small

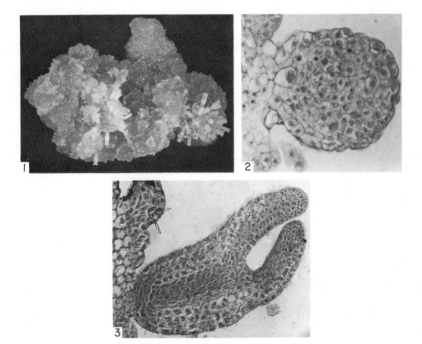

Fig. 12.12 Origin of embryoids from callus cultures derived from a flower bud of *Ranunculus sceleratus*. 1: Embryoids growing out of the surface of the callus culture. 2: Late globular embryoid on the surface of the callus. 3: Mature embryoid. (Photographs supplied by R. N. Konar and K. Nataraja.)

aggregates of highly cytoplasmic dividing cells and larger vacuolated free-floating cells released as the enlarging aggregates fragment in the moving culture solution (Fig. 12.14, 3ii, **a**). When such suspensions are transferred to a medium from which the auxin has been omitted many of the superficial cells of the cell aggregates give rise to embryoids which remain attached to the aggregates up to the late globular stage (Fig. 12.14, 4ii, **b**). These

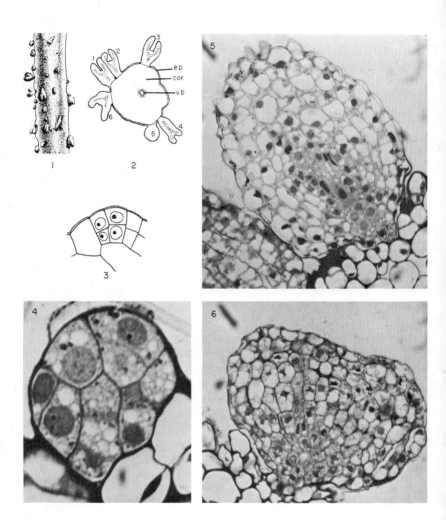

Fig. 12.13 Embryo development from the epidermis of the hypocotyl of embryoid-derived seedlings of *Ranunculus sceleratus*. 1: Portion of the hypocotyl bearing accessory embryos. 2: Transverse section of the hypocotyl showing six developing embryos; ep, epidermis; cor, cortex; vb, vascular bundle. 3: 4-celled stage of epidermal embryo. 4: More advanced stage. 5: Full globular stage. 6: Heart-shaped stage. (1, 2. 3 from Konar and Nataraya, 1965, *Phytomorphology*, **15**, 132–7; 4, 5, 6 from Konar, Thomas and Street, 1972, *J. Cell Sci.*, **11**, 77–93.)

embryoids then break away and continue their development as free-floating structures until they show typical seedling morphology (Fig. 12.14, 5, 6). At this stage they can be transferred to filter paper bridges (Fig. 12.14, 7) and grown to the stage where they can be planted out to give rise to normal carrot plants. The superficial cells of the aggregates which give rise to the embryoids undergo regular segmentations forming the pro-embryo and suspensor and produce normal globular embryos of single cell origin (Fig. 12.14, **c, d, e**). The segmentations however do not correspond to those described as typical of zygotic embryology in carrot. Similar embryogenesis has now been described in suspension culture of *Atropa belladonna* and embryogenesis from superficial cells of callus cultures has been reported for a considerable number of different species. These studies fully justify the statement made in 1961 by F. C. Steward and H. Y. Mohan Ram that 'the capacity to produce the plant body does not, however, reside in the zygote alone—indeed in the light of recent work it may well persist, even though suppressed, in almost any living cell of the plant body . . . cells which have passed through many cell generations in culture, may still retain a degree of totipotency which is comparable with that of the zygote'. *Totipotency* in the sense used in this quotation is the potentiality to embark upon any of the differentiation sequences observed in tissue development or to recapitulate the sequence of development which separates the zygote from the mature embryo of the species. The evidence that, under the appropriate conditions, somatic (body tissue) cells can initiate embryos also indicates that plant cells can undergo differentiation without loss of the initial genetic potentialities of the zygote from which they were ultimately derived (see also Chapter 9, p. 178).

How far can we define the conditions which permit somatic cells to function like the zygote? These certainly include release of the cells from the limitations (physical and biochemical) imposed upon them by the plant body ('cells are as they are because of where they are'). This release is effected by their *in vitro* culture. The conditions of culture also provide the nutritional factors and growth factor stimuli to induce rapid division in previously non-dividing cells. Further this meristematic activity is expressed in the absence of a morphogenetic field imposing a pattern of tissue differentiation such as operates upon dividing cells within a plant organ. These two conditions alone, however, do not necessarily lead to expression of embryogenic potential. Many actively growing callus and cell suspension cultures cannot at present be induced to generate embryoids. We do not know why this is but a clue to this is probably contained in the observation that in species where embryogenesis can occur in culture whether or not this actually occurs can depend upon the nutritive and environmental conditions during the stage of the original callus induction from the organ explant and even on the nature and age of the organ explant

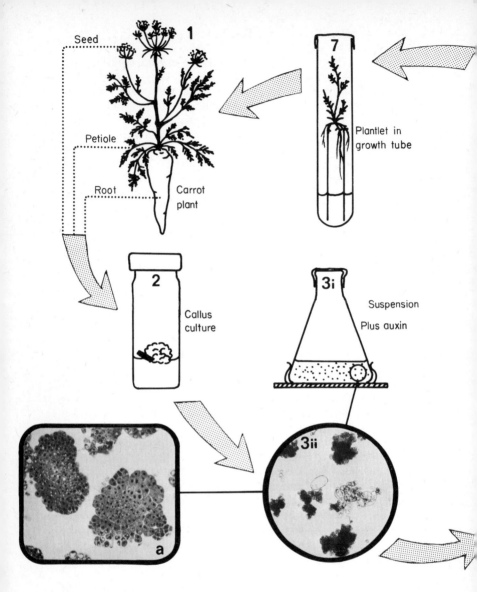

Fig. 12.14 Propagation of carrot via somatic embryogenesis induced in suspension cultures. Sequence of steps involved indicated by broad arrows. 2: Callus culture derived from petiole and growing on medium solidified with agar. 3i and 4i show flasks containing the suspension cultures mounted on a platform shaker which imparts a rotary motion to the cultures. 3ii: Low power microscope view of the suspension cultured in presence of auxin showing the small-celled aggregates which will give rise to embryoids ; **a**, section of such aggregates at higher magnification. 4ii: Low power microscope view of suspension after culture in medium lacking auxin shows the embryoids developing attached to the cell

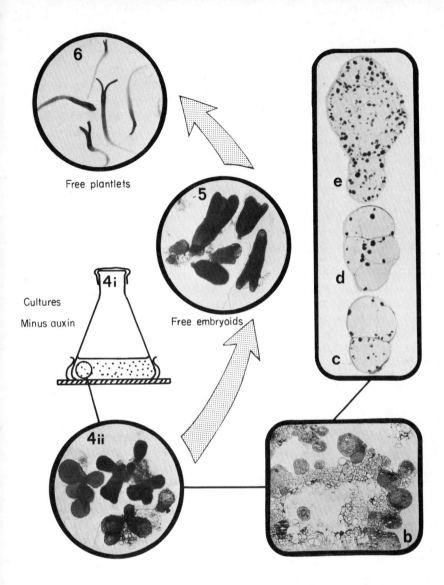

6 Free plantlets

5 Free embryoids

4i Cultures Minus auxin

4ii

e

d

c

b

aggregates; **b**, section of such an aggregate with well developed globular embryoids; **c, d, e**, a sequence showing stages in the development of a globular embryoid at higher magnification. 7: Plantlet growing on a filter paper bridge which conducts culture solution to the root system. The plantlet developed in such a tube can be transplanted to a medium such as vermiculite. All stages conducted under aseptic conditions from sterilization of organ explant from the carrot plant to transplantation of plantlet from growth tube to vermiculite. For full description see text. (Figure prepared from research material by Dr. Lyndsey A. Withers, Botanical Laboratories, University of Leicester.)

used. Some change in physiology (gene expression) over and above that necessary to render the cell actively dividing may be needed to induce the embryogenic state (see also Chapter 11 where this problem is discussed in relation to the capacity of cultured tissues to initiate organ primordia, p. 217). The facts that embryoids readily give rise to further embryoids from their surface cells (Fig. 12.13) and that cultures derived from immature or even mature zygotic embryos are sometimes more embryogenic than those derived from organ explants of more mature plants also point in this direction.

The pioneer detection of embryogenesis in carrot cultures by Steward and his coworkers during the early 1960s involved the use of a culture medium containing 10–20% of coconut milk (the liquid endosperm of the coconut) and it was argued that the use of this complex nutrient fluid, designed to nurture an immature embryo, was critical to the induction of somatic embryogenesis. Subsequently however it was shown, with cultures of carrot and of several other species, that prolific embryoid yield can be obtained by culture on a defined medium supplying sugar (sucrose), a mixture of inorganic ions (relatively rich in potassium and nitrogen and in which part of the nitrogen is as ammonium ions or glutamine), a mixture of B vitamins, the sugar alcohol *meso*-inositol and a cytokinin. For active proliferation without embryogenesis an auxin is also added (0·5–2.0 mg/l 2,4-dichlorophenoxyacetic acid—2,4-D) and this medium is used to propagate the culture serially. Embryogenesis is then induced by transfer to the same synthetic medium with the auxin omitted (Fig. 12.14). Such a medium defines the nutritional requirements of the cultures but, as discussed below, the embryogenic cells of the cellular aggregates in suspension, or at the surface of a callus culture, may have more exacting requirements. Clearly, however, in suspension cultures, embryoids released as free-floating structures at the late globular or early heart-shaped stage can continue their further development in isolation from the meristematic cell aggregates in such a medium.

The evidence that the embryoids are normally of single-cell origin rests primarily on the observation of all stages of development down to the two-celled stage and the recognition of the earliest pro-embryo stages at the surface of the aggregates in suspension (Fig. 12.14, **a**, **b**, **c**) and at the surface of embryogenic callus. It is also clear that the embryoids show a consistent polarity—the root pole and suspensor developing towards the centre of the aggregate or callus tissue and the plumular pole outwards from it. The polarity is induced by the associated cells. There is still some uncertainty as to whether cytoplasmic discontinuity (breakage of plasmo-desmata) is established between the cellular aggregate and the embryogenic cell before the segmentations of embryogenesis occur. The balance of evidence is however that this is not so although at a very early stage (in

Ranunculus sceleratus and carrot at least by the 4-cell stage) discontinuity is clearly visible and the pro-embryo appears to have a continuous external delimiting cuticle.

These studies of somatic embryogenesis indicate that the segmentations giving rise to the globular embryoids are more uniform between species than is the case for their zygotic embryos. The apparently specific (and often regarded as phylogenetically significant) early segmentation patterns of zygotic embryos probably reflect the influence on segmentation pattern of chemical gradients and physical forces imposed on the embryo by the ovule in which it is developing.

A rather different approach to the experimental study of embryo nutrition is that of the aseptic culture of immature embryos dissected out from fertilized ovules. Such studies have shown that the growth requirements of the embryo become less exacting as embryology progresses. Successful completion of embryology can be achieved only with embryos which have at least completed the globular stage before isolation though this limitation may be due to the difficulty of removing younger embryos without injury and the susceptibility of very young embryos to osmotic shock. Successful culture of young embryos has required the use of culture media containing not only sucrose, salts and a form of reduced nitrogen but also an appropriate mixture of growth-regulating substances. Thus globular embryos (50–80 μm in length) of *Capsella bursa-pastoris* were successfully cultured by using a medium containing IAA, kinetin and adenine. Culture of small embryos of *Hordeum sativum* was achieved in a medium containing glutamine (or a complex mixture of amino acids) and coconut milk. Coconut milk and liquid endosperms obtained from several species, yeast extracts and protein hydrolysates have proved to be effective supplements to basal media for the culture of immature embryos of a number of species, particularly of *Datura* spp., *Cucurbita maxima* and *Cocos nucifera*. Liquid endosperms are the natural nutritive environment of immature embryos and their activity appears to be due to their content of organic nitrogen compounds, of sugar alcohols and of growth-regulating substances. A particular balance of growth-regulating substances seems to be of great importance in early embryology and to prevent premature expansion of the embryonic cells. Some experiments have pointed to the importance of a high osmotic value of the bathing medium in early embryology and later of a lower osmotic value to permit germination of more mature embryos. The significance of the osmotic value in regulating embryo development is however uncertain. Thus in experiments with immature *Capsella* embryos a high osmotic value (achieved by 12–18% sucrose) was only promotive of development in the absence of an effective addition of growth-regulating substances and was less effective than the latter.

Since no one has achieved successful culture of the isolated zygote it is possible that the really exacting nutritional requirements for embryogenesis have already been met by the stage at which embryos can be successfully excised and cultured. This view is supported by the great difficulty which is encountered when attempts are made to raise in culture a callus tissue from a single cell. The development of such single-cell clones at present requires the nurturing of the single cell by placing it in direct contact with or very close to an actively growing multicellular colony (Fig. 12.15). Some progress has been made towards replacing the 'nurse' colony by using more complex culture media and carefully regulating the carbon dioxide concentration of the culture atmosphere but not to the point of inducing completely isolated single cells to divide. The reasons for the origin of embryoids at or in the surface of cultured cell aggregates may not only be that this location promotes the establishment of polarity but that it is one where the initiating cell is nurtured by the associated growing multicellular mass. Further, the ability of defined media to support the growth of the released embryoids may be due to its having been conditioned ('enriched') by the growing culture as a whole.

The endosperm nucleus divides very soon after the double fertilization, often well in advance of division in the zygote. When both begin division at about the same time the rate of mitosis in the developing endosperm is much more rapid. The growth of the endosperm is at the expense of the nucellus and it normally does not slow down until the nucellus has almost disappeared. Throughout endosperm development embryo growth is slow and there is usually during this period no visible disorganization of the endosperm cells adjacent to the embryo. It may well be therefore that the embryo, at least during its early stages of development, absorbs nutrients directly from the nucellus via the suspensor and this is supported by the existence of well developed plasmodesmata throughout the suspensor and pro-embryo and by the presence of internal wall projections in the basal cells of the suspensor closely resembling those that occur in transfer cells (see Chapter 6, p. 105). The endosperm however may function as a nutritive tissue during the latter stage of embryo development even in those cases where the ripe seed is endospermic; clearly there is a massive transfer of material from the endosperm to the cotyledons in non-endospermic seeds. During the development of the embryo and endosperm, the integuments of the ovule become the testa of the seed.

SEED DORMANCY

The next generation of sporophytes is established by germination of the seed. When shed many seeds are immediately capable of germination if provided with water and oxygen at an appropriate temperature. For

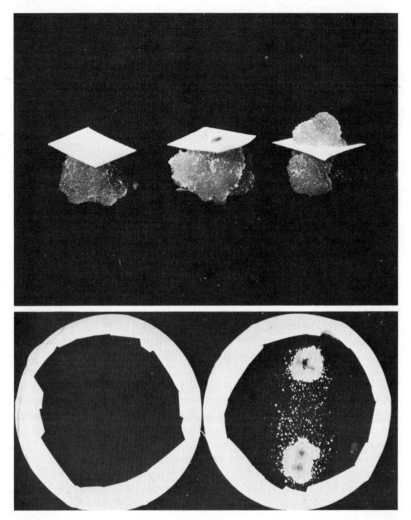

Fig. 12.15 (a) Growth of single isolated cells on the upper surface of a piece of filter paper in contact with a 'nurse' piece of callus. (*Left*: at time of placing the single cell in position; *right*: when a callus has developed from the single cell. (From Muir, 1953, Ph.D. thesis, University of Wisconsin.) (b) Colony formation on an agar plate seeded with a suspension of cultured cells derived from *Acer pseudoplatanus* and incubated for 28 days. Both dishes were seeded with the cell suspension but the dish on the right was also seeded with two pieces of callus of the same culture. Note cells have divided and given rise to visible colonies adjacent to and in particular between the two pieces of callus whereas no colonies have developed on the other petri dish not seeded with growing callus.

various reasons however the seeds of many species show dormancy. Sometimes the seed coat is hard and impermeable to water and must undergo a measure of microbial decay before germination can occur (this is the case in a number of leguminous seeds). In other plants the embryo, at the time of seed dispersal, is still immature and must complete its development before germination; this often requires a period at an appropriate temperature after imbibition. In the discussion of photomorphogenesis (Chapter 11, p. 230) reference was made to the necessity for the seeds of certain lettuce varieties to imbibe water and then be exposed to light before germination could occur. Light-requiring seeds occur in many genera (e.g. *Nicotiana, Digitalis, Epilobium*, and *Rumex*). The germination of other seeds is inhibited by light (e.g. *Nigella, Phlox drummondii*).

Still other seeds, although not enclosed in a hard seed coat and although the embryo is fully developed, require an *after-ripening* period before they will germinate. For instance many cereal grains gradually increase in germination capacity during storage in the dry state. This dormancy protects them from germination in the ear or immediately after ripening in the autumn. Seeds of other plants of temperature zones are even better protected from too early germination by requiring, after imbibition, a period of *chilling* before they will germinate. This normally means that they will over-winter and then germinate in the spring. The seeds of many herbaceous and woody plants show this behaviour.

In some cases where the seed has an after-ripening or chilling requirement, the embryo itself is dormant but in other cases dormancy is broken by breaking or removing the seed coat. The dormancy induced by the seed coat is due to one or both of the following: impeding of oxygen uptake; presence in the seed coat of germination inhibitor(s). Germination inhibitor(s) present in the embryo or endosperm can also be responsible for embryo dormancy. In some cases the inhibitor can be leached out by running water. With seeds having a light or chilling requirement it has been shown in several instances that the appropriate treatment to break dormancy causes a rise in the endogenous level of gibberellins. Direct application of gibberellic acid will in some cases substitute for a light or chilling requirement. The very high oxygen demand of some seeds may be related to the presence of a germination inhibitor and when its action is antagonized by gibberellin growth can readily proceed at a lower oxygen tension. Although in many cases the chemical nature of the natural inhibitor(s) of germination has not been established, in others the principal inhibitor has been shown to be abscisic acid. Where abscisic acid is the inhibitor and release from dormancy is associated with a rise in gibberellins, seed dormancy is controlled in a similar manner to winter dormancy in buds (see Chapter 11, p. 223).

FURTHER READING

HILLMAN, W. S. (1969). Photoperiodism and vernalization. In *Physiology of Plant Growth and Development*, ed. WILKINS, M. B., 559–604. McGraw-Hill, London.

SALISBURY, F. B. (1963). *The Flowering Process*. Pergamon, London.

STREET, H. E. (1969). Growth in organized and unorganized systems: knowledge gained by culture of organs and tissue explants. In *Plant Physiology*, ed. STEWARD, F. C., Vol. 5B, Chap. 6, 3–224. Academic Press, New York and London.

STREET, H. E. (1975). Experimental embryogenesis—the totipotency of cultured cells. In *Textbook of Developmental Biology*, ed. GRAHAM, C. F. and WAREING, P. F. (in press). Blackwell Scientific Publications, Oxford.

SELECTED REFERENCES

BÜNNING, E. (1973). *The Physiological Clock*. Academic Press, New York.

NITSCH, J. P. (1965). Physiology of flower and fruit development. In *Encyclopedia of Plant Physiology*, ed. RUHLAND, W., 15 (1), 1537–1647. Springer-Verlag, Berlin.

SUNDERLAND, N. (1973). Pollen and anther culture. In *Plant Tissue and Cell Culture*, ed. STREET, H. E., 205–39. Blackwell Scientific Publications, Oxford.

WAREING, P. F. (1963). The germination of seeds. *Vistas in Botany*, 3, 197–227.

Units of Measurement—Conversion Table

Since 1960, a modified system of measurement, the SI units (Système International d'Unités), has been gradually gaining acceptance. In this system, the basic units of mass, length and time are the kilogramme (kg), metre (m) and second (s); a number of common units, e.g. litre, hour, are abandoned. In the present text some previously employed units are retained but a conversion table for these to SI units is given below.

Previously employed units	Corresponding SI units
Length	
Basic unit metre, m	Basic unit metre, m
1 μ, micron $=10^{-6}$ m	1 μm, micrometre $=10^{-6}$ m
1 mμ, millimicron $=10^{-9}$ m	1 nm, nanometre $=10^{-9}$ m
Volume	
Basic unit litre, l	Basic unit cubic metre, m³ (l$=10^{-3}$ m³ $=$dm³)
1 ml, millilitre $=10^{-3}$ l	10^{-6} m³
1 μl, microlitre $=10^{-6}$ l	10^{-9} m³
Energy	
Basic unit erg	Basic unit joule, J$=1$ kg m² s^{-2}
1 J, joule $=10^7$ ergs	1 J, joule
1 cal, calorie $=4 \cdot 18 \times 10^7$ erg	4·18 J
Temperature	
Measured in degrees centigrade (Celsius), °C	Measured in degrees Kelvin, K 1 °C$=1°$ K, but the Kelvin scale starts at absolute zero, so that 0° K $\simeq -273$°C, and 0°C $\simeq 273$°K
Pressure	
Various units, e.g. atmosphere (atm), bar	Basic unit Newton per square metre, the Pascal (Pa), N m^{-2} (1 N$=1$ kg m s^{-2}, and 1 atm$=101\ 325$ N m^{-2})
Amount of substance and concentration	
Gram molecule	Mole (symbol mol), amount of substance of a system which contains as many elementary units as there are carbon atoms in 0·012 kg of ^{12}carbon
Molar (M)	A solution which has a concentration of 10^3 mol m^{-3}
Time	
Days, hours (h), minutes (min), seconds (sec)	Basic unit$=$second, symbol$=$s
Planck's constant (h)	$6 \cdot 6256 \times 10^{-34}$ J s
Avogadro number (N)	$6 \cdot 02252 \times 10^{23}$ mol^{-1}

Further information on SI Units and Symbols may be obtained from:

PENNYCUICK, C. J. (1974). *Handy Matrices.* Edward Arnold, London.

Symbols, Signs and Abbreviations. Symbols Committee of the Royal Society, Royal Society, London 1969.

The Use of SI Units. British Standards Institution Publication, PD 5686, London 1972.

Index